Palgrave Stud
   in a Global Perspective

Aim of the series
The transformation of China into a global super-power is often attributed to the country's robust education system, and this series seeks to provide a comprehensive, in-depth understanding of the development of Chinese education on a global scale. The books in this series will analyze and problematize the revolutions, reforms, innovations and transformations of Chinese education which are often misunderstood or misrepresented beyond its own borders, and they will examine the changes in Chinese education over the past 30 years and the issues as well as challenges that the future of Chinese education faces.

More information about this series at
http://www.springer.com/series/14568

Jiani Zhu

Chinese Overseas Students and Intercultural Learning Environments

Academic Adjustment, Adaptation and Experience

Jiani Zhu
Shanghai Jiao Tong University
Shanghai, China

Palgrave Studies on Chinese Education in a Global Perspective
ISBN 978-1-137-53392-0   ISBN 978-1-137-53393-7   (eBook)
DOI 10.1057/978-1-137-53393-7

Library of Congress Control Number: 2016938709

© The Editor(s) (if applicable) and The Author(s) 2016
The author(s) has/have asserted their right(s) to be identified as the author(s) of this work in accordance with the Copyright, Designs and Patents Act 1988.
This work is subject to copyright. All rights are solely and exclusively licensed by the Publisher, whether the whole or part of the material is concerned, specifically the rights of translation, reprinting, reuse of illustrations, recitation, broadcasting, reproduction on microfilms or in any other physical way, and transmission or information storage and retrieval, electronic adaptation, computer software, or by similar or dissimilar methodology now known or hereafter developed.
The use of general descriptive names, registered names, trademarks, service marks, etc. in this publication does not imply, even in the absence of a specific statement, that such names are exempt from the relevant protective laws and regulations and therefore free for general use.
The publisher, the authors and the editors are safe to assume that the advice and information in this book are believed to be true and accurate at the date of publication. Neither the publisher nor the authors or the editors give a warranty, express or implied, with respect to the material contained herein or for any errors or omissions that may have been made.

Cover illustration: Cover image © Old Images / Alamy

Printed on acid-free paper

This Palgrave Macmillan imprint is published by Springer Nature
The registered company is Macmillan Publishers Ltd. London

Foreword

Over the last two decades the world has become increasingly interested in China's social and economic development, mainly as a result of China's integration in the worldwide processes of globalization and internationlization. As far as education is concerned, China has moved from being a peripheral point of reference for the world's educational attention to a more central position, dramatically attracting the world's research interest. This is mainly due to economic and (geo)political considerations and a dramatic expansion and reorganization of the education system, especially in higher education. As a result, there have been far-reaching consequences for the international flow of Chinese students and scholars. Several factors have led to an increase in the international interest in China's education: the global craze for institutional rankings in higher education, the new status of Chinese universities in the world higher education community, and the Shanghai results in large-scale international student assessment (PISA). Not surprisingly, a number of research clusters on the subject of international Chinese student/s have emerged, in China as well as outside, some of which are listed below:

(i) Challenges for international Chinese students and scholars caused by processes of adaptation and integration in host countries (as well as reverse processes on their return).
(ii) Recognition and interpretation of culture-based learning style(s) and their effect on host countries' higher education.
(iii) Challenges for returned academics who are seeking jobs.

(iv) The impact of returning scholars on Chinese institutional settings/culture and society.
(v) Regional developments in Chinese higher education and the growing educational inequality.
(vi) The tension between globalization, glocalization and regional autonomy, and the question of (cultural) belonging.

The first three out of these six research clusters have been treated in Jiani Zhu's contribution in an amazingly analytical, well-documented, and highly original interdisciplinary approach. Given the fact that international Chinese student/s currently (and for some time to come) represent the world's largest floating intellectual capital, Zhu's publication will be welcomed as a timely contribution to increase our awareness and understanding of the importance of this group and its complex positioning in the academic world system.

Perhaps the greatest value of Zhu's work comes from her ability to deconstruct and reconstruct the Western imagination of a fairly homogenous body of international Chinese student/s and their assumed mode of identity formation and adaption and adjustment in host countries' environments. But this also applies to her critical analysis of what is internationally labeled as Chinese learner or Chinese/Asian learning style.

What makes this publication different from a wide range of similar research work is the meticulous and rigorous attempt to reread international research publications on international Chinese student/s and to map these students' highly diverse experiences and strategies of adaptation and adjustment from various perspectives in order to come up with a more differentiated picture than previous research had to offer. As a former doctoral student in Germany, the author uses Chinese students' experiences in Germany as a case study for further explorations of their complex modes adaptation, adjustment, and configuration of Self. A strong point of the research is the longitudinal approach to follow Chinese students' development, using an affective, cognitive, and behavioral model of adaption and adjustment.

Zhu's interpretation of international Chinese student/s as 'constructed entities' serves as some kind of eye-opener, placing her research in a multifaceted perspective where Chinese students are foremost received (i) as customers, (ii) as a source of revenue in higher education, (iii) as a source of irritation, initiating or inducing change in the respective host country institution, (iv) as a challenge and option for collective learning and enrichment in theory building, (v) as floating academic potential in a highly competitive world education market, and (vi) as a new and permanent object of research on culture shock, adaptation/adjustment, and learning (styles).

The result of this complex approach of research is a book that will be appropriate for a broad range of audiences. *Chinese Overseas Students and Intercultural Learning Environments* will enrich the international discourse on Chinese (international) students as a group with assumed special, culturally transmitted characteristics. This can be applied to current lines of discussion about the creation of the Self and identity, culture shock, adaptation, and adjustment as well as about the existence of culture-specific learning styles, something that has become a hot topic recently. It is a particular strength of Zhu's analysis to avoid any tendency to stereotype and essentialist thinking about culture, something that the reader will greatly acknowledge.

Jürgen Henze
Humboldt-Universität zu Berlin, Germany

Acknowledgments

First and foremost, I am beyond grateful to all of my participants who joined in this research study. This book could never have been developed without their support and trust. Only through their cooperation was I able to make my research idea a reality. I sincerely appreciate all the time and effort they contributed to this project.

I am also profoundly grateful to my supervisor, Professor Jürgen Henze, at the Humboldt-Universität zu Berlin, who is a brilliant, honest, insightful, and true embodiment of a mentor. Without his guidance and expertise in the field of intercultural communication, this book would not have been possible. My time at the Humboldt-Universität was deeply enriched by his research team and colleagues.

I am grateful to Professor Andrä Wolter too for being my reviewer. I was greatly inspired by his colloquia and lectures, and how they introduced me to research on higher education in Germany.

I would like to thank Professor Detlef Müller-Böling for his time and insightful questions. Thank you for providing this former Chinese intern with a year of research experience at the Centrum für Hochschulentwicklung in 2006. This meaningful internship is ultimately what encouraged me to pursue doctoral research later in Berlin.

I also appreciate Professor Nian Cai Liu and Professor Shaoxue Liu and my colleagues in the Graduate School of Education, Shanghai Jiao Tong University, for the encouragement and support for the publication of this book.

Next, I would like to extend my heartfelt thanks to Elizabeth Anne Wesner at the University of Virginia for proofreading the manuscript, and providing suggestions from both an American and a Chinese perspective to make my thoughts understood by people from many cultures. Separated by time and space, we were still united in our passion to explore cross-cultural 'miscommunication'.

Many thanks go to my host families in Germany—Family Petersen in Lüneburg, and Families Schröder and Brinker in Berlin. Because of their hospitality and kindness, I never felt lonely during my time in Germany. I cherish every Christmas, Easter, and other holidays that I celebrated with them.

Finally, I would like to thank the special loved ones in my life—my parents for all their love, encouragement, and support throughout all my pursuits, and my husband, Huijun Wang, for his understanding, patience, and love for me on this journey. Without you in my life, I would not be the person I am today.

Jiani Zhu
Shanghai, August 2015

Contents

1 An Introduction to International Chinese Students   1

2 Review of Literature on International Chinese Students   41

3 An Unprepared Academic Journey: Pre-departure Adjustment   103

4 A Hard Landing: Beginning the Study Abroad   131

5 The Battle Continues: Negotiating with the Differences   157

6 Approaching the End: Appreciating the German Learning Environment   175

7 Key Factors Influencing Chinese Students' Academic Adjustment   187

8 Reflections and Implications   211

Appendix 1: Profile of Participants 235

Appendix 2: Interview Framework/Outline 241

Appendix 3: Questionnaire in Study 3 243

Index 251

Abbreviations

CHC	Confucian Heritage Culture
DAAD	Deutscher Akademischer Austauschdienst (in English: German Academic Exchange Service)
DZHW	Deutsches Zentrum für Hochschul- und Wissenschaftsforschung (in English: German Centre for Research on Higher Education and Science Studies)
MoE	Ministry of Education of the People's Republic of China (in Chinese 中华人民共和国教育部 *zhonghua renmin gongheguo jiaoyubu*)
NBS	National Bureau of Statistics of the People's Republic of China (in Chinese 中华人民共和国国家统计局 zhonghua renmin gongheguo guojia tongjiju)
OECD	Organisation for Economic Co-operation and Development

List of Figures

Figure 1.1	Total international and Chinese students in OECD countries (2002–2012)	3
Figure 1.2	The number of Chinese students studying abroad (1978–2014)	7
Figure 1.3	Distribution of Chinese students studying in the OECD countries in 2012	7
Figure 1.4	Structure of the education system in China	9
Figure 1.5	Chinese students as various 'constructed' entities	17
Figure 1.6	Affective, cognitive, and behavioral model	23
Figure 1.7	Methods conducted in this research	28
Figure 2.1	Structure of literature review on Chinese students abroad	42
Figure 2.2	Landscape of current research on Chinese students	43
Figure 2.3	Number of Chinese going abroad and returning (1978–2014)	72
Figure 2.4	Framework of Chinese students' academic adjustment in Germany	83
Figure 3.1	Decision-making process of new Chinese graduates	104
Figure 3.2	Self-rated academic German language level according to Study 3	117
Figure 3.3	Self-rated academic English language level according to Study 3	118
Figure 3.4	Result of the standardized German tests according to Study 3	119
Figure 3.5	Self-rated daily German language level according to Study 3	120
Figure 3.6	Knowledge of Germany as a country according to Study 3	121

Figure 3.7	Knowledge of German universities according to Study 3	122
Figure 4.1	Frequency of attending further German language training in Germany	152
Figure 5.1	Satisfaction toward the progress according to Study 3	171
Figure 6.1	Satisfaction with the learning experience at German universities according to Study 3	182
Figure 7.1	The use of academic German language at university	188
Figure 7.2	Composition of friend circles in Germany according to Study 3	199
Figure 7.3	Frequency of contact with friends from different national groups according to Study 3	200
Figure 7.4	Frequency of attending local activities/events in Germany according to Study 3	203
Figure 7.5	Situation of accommodation according to Study 3	206
Figure A.1	Current academic degrees pursued at German universities in Study 3 (Round 1)	238

List of Tables

Table 1.1	Possible combinations of the terms of cross-cultural adaptation	19
Table 2.1	Duration of difficulty based on daily life and academic situations	49
Table 3.1	Reasons for going abroad in general according to respondents in Study 3	105
Table 3.2	Reasons for studying in Germany according to respondents in Study 3	106
Table 3.3	Academic degree achieved in China by participants in all three studies	112
Table 3.4	Consistency between previous major in China and current major in Germany	113
Table 3.5	Correlation of self-rated German language level according to Study 3 ($n=24$)	117
Table 3.6	Sources of obtaining knowledge about Germany and German universities according to Study 3	123
Table 5.1	Progress of academic German language skill according to Study 3	158
Table 5.2	Progress of daily German language skill according to Study 3	159
Table 5.3	Progress of knowledge about German universities according to Study 3	159
Table 5.4	Hesitation to voice opinions in class	162
Table 5.5	Unquestioning respect for authority	163
Table 5.6	To ask questions or not?	163
Table 5.7	Correlation of items of achievement according to Study 3 ($n=30$)	171

Table 7.1	Academic support at German universities	192
Table 8.1	Summary of challenges mapped to an 'affective, cognitive, and behavioral dimensions' model	212
Table A.1	Demographic profiles of the participants of Study 1	236
Table A.2	Demographic profiles of the participants of Study 2	237

CHAPTER 1

An Introduction to International Chinese Students

The pursuit of knowledge is superior to all other walks of life.
万般皆下品,唯有读书高

– *WANG Zhu (汪洙)*

The purpose of this book is to introduce how Chinese students adjust to an intercultural learning environment. Previous research has covered a broad spectrum of topics regarding Chinese students, including their psychological and sociocultural adjustment (Spencer-Oatey and Xiong 2006; Wang 2009; Zhao 2007; Zheng and Berry 1991), acculturation (Zheng et al. 2004), and satisfaction with their sociocultural and educational experience (Zhang and Brunton 2007). In spite of that, research particularly focusing on their academic adjustment still deserves more attention than it has received so far. Even though some research does use the term *academic adjustment*, it lacks a clear or scientific definition of the term and its domain (Gong and Chang 2007). Not much research has concretely probed the daily academic experience of Chinese students living in host universities, especially their classroom participation, academic performance, and learning strategies. Considering the fact that only limited research on academic-based problems of academic challenges facing international students has been conducted (Samuelowicz 1987), it is necessary to shed light on their situations and identities as international students. Thus, this book explores how Chinese students adjust academically when studying abroad at foreign universities. Moreover, how do they understand the different learning forms in their new environment and adapt to them in order to better meet academic expectations and demands?

THE GROWING DISCUSSION ON CHINESE STUDENTS

Attention to the broad term 'Chinese students' has grown in the last few decades, especially with regard to investigating Chinese student characteristics. Three proposed reasons for this are: (1) excellent performance of East Asian students in international studies of achievement, (2) the increasing number of Chinese students studying overseas, and (3) the influence of China's economic growth (Rao and Chan 2010).

Indeed, Chinese students demonstrate strong mathematical and scientific aptitude in many cross-national studies. International mathematics tests and competitions, such as the International Assessment of Educational Progress and the Trends in International Mathematics and Science Study (Xu, B. 2010), show that Chinese students score very competitively against their Western counterparts. Results from both the 2009 and 2012 Programme for International Student Assessment (PISA) also indicated that students from Shanghai successively outscored their counterparts in dozens of other countries in all PISA sections of reading, mathematics, and science (OECD 2014a).

Students from China also represent the largest student group in the world to study in foreign countries. Over ten years, the number of Chinese students studying abroad has increased sharply from 181,684 in 2002 to 761,992 in 2012 (Waldmeir 2013, December 29). In 2012, 16.8 per cent of all international students enrolled for study in OECD (The Organisation for Economic Co-operation and Development) areas came from China (OECD 2014b). According to a report from the Chinese Academy of Social Sciences, the rise has been particularly dramatic among middle-class families. With strong economic growth fueling a growing middle class, many Chinese families seek an alternative to the rigorous rote-based learning methods of the domestic system in China. At present, over 90 per cent of the Chinese students going abroad are self-funded (Fig. 1.1).

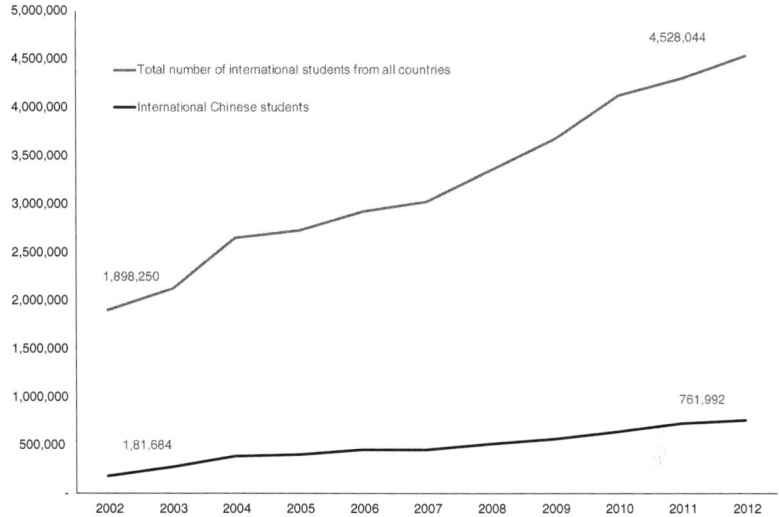

Fig. 1.1 Total international and Chinese students in OECD countries (2002–2012) (Source: Education at a Glance 2004–2014, OECD 2004; OECD 2005; OECD 2006; OECD 2007; OECD 2008; OECD 2009; OECD 2010; OECD 2011; OECD 2012a; OECD 2013; OECD 2014)

Internationalization of Higher Education and Increased Mobility of International Chinese Students

History of International Education: A Brief Retrospective View

Student mobility is not a new phenomenon. In fact, a large number of medieval universities in Europe were essentially international in nature (Altbach et al. 1985). The first universities founded in Paris and Bologna in the thirteenth century housed students and professors from many countries, and used Latin as a common language (Altbach and Teichler 2001, p. 6). Thus, in the beginnings of Western higher education, foreign students were the norm, not the exception (Altbach et al. 1985). It was not until the influence of the Protestant Reformation in the sixteenth century that universities began to teach in their own national languages, and internationalism became less central to university education. Still, many universities maintained international cooperation and exchanges with each other (Altbach and Teichler 2001).

In the eighteenth century, internationalization of education shifted toward what is now considered a more negative direction, as European powers began to expand their empires through colonialization. During this phase, internationalization manifested through the concerted export of education systems from European colonial powers (particularly the UK and France) to their colonies (Knight and de Wit 1995). Meanwhile, universities in the metropole served to train students from their colonies (Altbach and Teichler 2001).

After World War II, a new era of international educational exchange began, with a shift toward international relations. To achieve 'a better understanding of the rest of the world and to maintain and even expand their sphere of influence' (Knight and de Wit 1995, p. 8), the USA and the Soviet Union, the two superpowers that emerged from WWII, began promoting international exchange. Countries that did initiate agreements for student exchange or research cooperation did so on a relatively small scale with a diplomacy-oriented objective (Knight and de Wit 1995). These goals are still visible today in many state-sponsored exchange programs, although, in general, universities have expanded their goals to include various activities (e.g. participating in traditional study abroad programs, upgrading students' international perspectives and skills, etc.) that raise their international profile in volume, scope, and complexity (Altbach and Knight 2007).

The First Overseas Chinese Students
China has a long history of sending students abroad for advanced knowledge. Yung Wing (容闳 or *Rong Hong*[1]), together with Wong Foon (黄宽 or *Huang Kuan*) and Wong Shing (黄胜 or *Huang Sheng*) were the first recorded group of Chinese students in history to study overseas, setting foot in America in 1847.[2] In his book *My Life in China and America*, Yung Wing described his journey to America, and the experience of studying at Yale College (1850–1854). Yung Wing was the first Chinese student to graduate from a US university. Benefiting from his own experience in America, he managed to persuade the Qing Dynasty government to send more young Chinese students abroad (known as the 'Chinese Educational

---

[1] Yung Wing is the pronunciation of his name in Cantonese, which in Mandarin is *Rong Hong*; also, Wong Foon (in Mandarin: *Huang Kuan*) and Wong Shing (in Mandarin: *Huang Sheng*).
[2] Wong Shing later returned to China due to poor health, and Wong Foon entered the University of Edinburgh in Scotland, after graduating from Monson Academy with Yung Wing (1909).

Mission') when he returned. Between 1872 and 1875, the Qing Dynasty sent 120 students to the USA. These young boys were respectively placed with local families in about forty towns in the Connecticut River Valley (Hamilton 2009). By the time the program ended, more than sixty of them had attended colleges, universities, or standard technical schools. There were twenty students at Yale, eight at MIT, one at Harvard, and three at Columbia (Jin 2004, April 22). Although this plan was later abandoned in 1881, many of the students made significant contributions to China's civil services, engineering, and sciences,[3] and effectively established the now long-standing 'modern' tradition of Chinese students studying abroad (Levin 2004).

The 'Reform and Opening Up' of Study Abroad
The late Chinese leader Deng Xiaoping supported the expansion of study-abroad programs for Chinese students to travel overseas. It is worth noting that in the late 1970s and early 1980s, following the Cultural Revolution, study abroad was primarily restricted for those directly sponsored by the Chinese government. As the Chinese economic reform period progressed, the government began to relax restrictions. In 1984, the State Council (国务院 *guowuyuan*) issued Temporary Provisions of Going Abroad for Self-Funded Students (国务院关于自费出国留学的暂行规定 *guowuyuan guanyu zifei chuguo liuxue de zanxing guiding*), which required the provincial and local government to promote self-funded students to apply for overseas study and treat them as equal to government-funded students. One year later, China abolished the policy of Verifying the Qualification of Self-Funded Students Applying for Overseas Study (自费出国留学资格审核 *zifei chuguo liuxue zige shenhe*), signaling that China would now allow self-funded students to study abroad, with the same status and privileges as government-funded students.

Policies shifted from simply relaxing restrictions, to taking a more pro-exchange approach, beginning in the 1990s. In 1993, The Third Plenum of the Fourteenth Central Committee of the Communist Party of China (中共十四届三中全会 *zhonggong shisijie sanzhong quanhui*) stipulated new goals for studying abroad. Namely, the document was meant 'to support students and scholars studying abroad, to encourage them to return to

---

[3] For instance, Tianyou Zhan (詹天佑), a Yale graduate among the 120 students, returned to China and became the first Chinese to undertake a railroad building project using only Chinese funds and Chinese supervisors.

China after the completion of studies, and to guarantee them the freedom of coming and going' (支持留学,鼓励回国,来去自由 *zhichi liuxue, guli huiguo, laiqu ziyou*). Ten years later, in 2003, the process of application itself was simplified immensely when the Ministry of Education issued the Notification of Simplifying the Examination and Approval Procedures of Studying Abroad for Self-Funded Students with Junior-Bachelor Degree or Above (简化大专以上学历人员自费出国留学审批手续的通知 *jianhua dazhuan yishang xueli renyuan zifei chuguo liuxue shenpi shouxu de tongzhi*). This removed many of the challenges facing students wishing to go abroad, and actively encouraged increasing numbers from the growing middle class to apply.

Following these reforms in policy, more self-funded Chinese students had the opportunity to go abroad. In the last thirty-seven years, the number of Chinese students studying abroad has increased from only 860 in 1978 to 459,800 in 2014, at a dramatic growth rate of 533.7 per cent (Fig. 1.2). At present, Chinese students have become the largest international student group in many popular international host countries, such as the USA, UK, Australia, Germany, France, Japan, and Korea.

In terms of distribution, English-speaking countries are the most popular study destinations for Chinese students. According to the OECD, the number of Chinese students studying in the USA, Australia, the UK, Canada, and New Zealand account for 57.3 per cent of all Chinese students studying abroad (Fig. 1.3). The USA is the favored host country, with over 210,000 Chinese students studying there in 2012 constituting 27.6 per cent of the total number of Chinese students abroad.

Apart from English-speaking countries, neighboring countries like Japan and Korea are also favorable, as they are fellow Confucian Heritage Culture (CHC) countries that share similar educational systems. In 2012, about 18.4 per cent of international Chinese students studied in these countries. Especially in light of historical, geographical, and cultural backgrounds, Chinese students are the predominant foreign student group in Japan (at 64.1 per cent) and Korea (at 73.5 per cent) (OECD 2014).

Teaching and Learning in China

Research on Chinese students should—but often fails to—take their psychological attributes, cultural values, and context into consideration (Rao and Chan 2010). Many of the topics related to Chinese students in the news and media often present them from a more statistical standpoint,

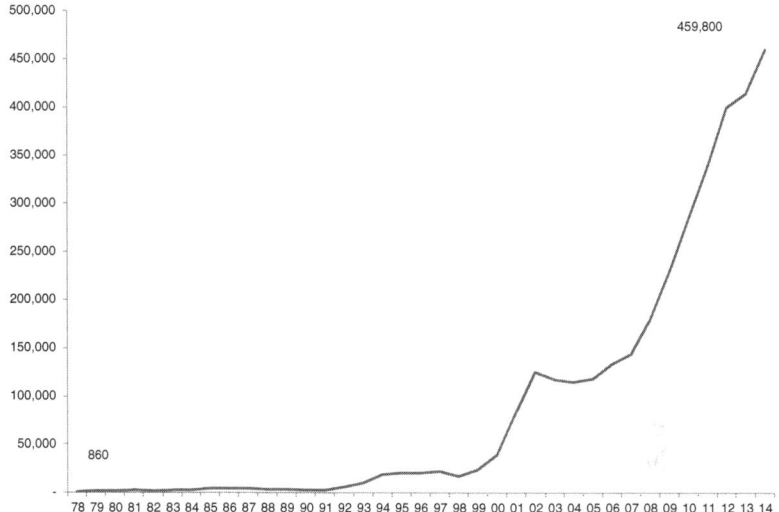

Fig. 1.2 The number of Chinese students studying abroad (1978–2014) (Source: NBS 2014)

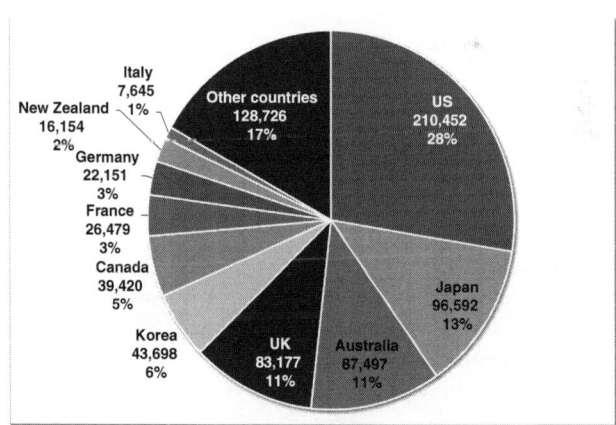

Fig. 1.3 Distribution of Chinese students studying in the OECD countries in 2012 (Source: Education at a Glance. OECD 2014a)

breaking the largest group of students in the world into more easily understood numbers. However, it's very important to understand what these numbers mean, how they come into existence, and what is happening behind them. Thus, it is very important to have at least a basic understanding of the learning traditions and educational backgrounds of Chinese students, when trying to understand their position and academic challenges abroad.

A Highly Competitive Education System
According to the Education Law of the People's Republic of China (中华人民共和国教育法 *zhonghua renmin gongheguo jiaoyufa*), China's educational system has four levels: preschool education (i.e. kindergarten), primary education (i.e. primary or elementary school), secondary education (i.e. junior middle school, senior middle school, and/or specialized secondary school), and higher education (i.e. college, university, and trade school) (Fig. 1.4). The six-year primary education and three-year junior secondary education compose nine years of compulsory education (九年义务教育 *jiunian yiwu jiaoyu*).

Primary education in China normally lasts six years, and begins when children enter school at the age of six.[4] As China used to differentiate between more prestigious key schools (重点学校 *zhongdian xuexiao*) and non-key schools (非重点学校 *fei zhongdian xuexiao*) in secondary education, students would take the Junior Secondary Education Entrance Examinations (小学升初中考试 *xiaoxue sheng chuzhong kaoshi*) at the age of eleven and compete for a seat at better resourced key junior middle schools. However, in the interests of expanding educational access across the country, this examination was abolished successively in various provinces and cities in 1999. Now, primary school graduates enter junior middle school without any selective examinations, and are allocated to schools close to their homes.

Secondary education in China is composed of junior and senior middle school. At the end of their nine-year compulsory education, students take the Senior Secondary Education Entrance Examination, or *Zhongkao* (中考). The results of the *Zhongkao* decide whether students will advance

---

[4] The length of studying in primary education varies. In some provinces (e.g. Shanghai), primary education lasts six years, which is followed by a three-year junior middle school education, instead of a five-year primary education plus four-year junior middle school education in other cities.

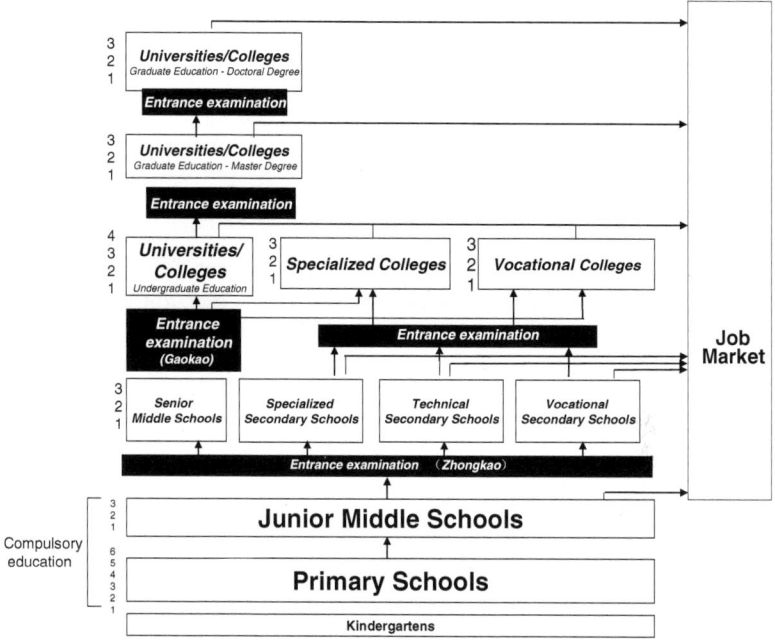

Fig. 1.4 Structure of the education system in China (Source: inspired by Finnish National Board of Education 2007, p. 7; Brandenburg and Zhu 2007, p. 6)

to a standard senior high school, a specialized studies school, a technical or vocational training school, or enter the job market. Of these routes, s*enior high school education* (高中教育 *gaozhong jiaoyu*) and s*enior vocational education* (职业教育 *zhiye jiaoyu*) are the most common. The former enrolls students with higher *Zhongkao* scores than the latter, and is more academics oriented. Students who attend schools in this category typically go on to university. The latter provides specialized and practical education for students who plan to enter the job market immediately after graduating. Once the dominant track, practical and technical training has lost popularity over time as the Chinese economy expanded throughout the 1990s and 2000s. With the expansion of colleges and universities in the education system and the growth of the average income, more students in China have the resources and opportunities to pursue a college-tracked education. In 2013, about 86 per cent of students between the ages of 15 and 17 were enrolled in senior high schools (MoE 2014).

After finishing all three years of high school, students will take what they consider their most vital examination—the *Gaokao* (高考). *Gaokao* is the abbreviation for the National Higher Education Entrance Examination (全国普通高等学校招生统一考试 *quanguo putong gaodeng xuexiao zhaosheng tongyi kaoshi*). This is the test that ultimately decides whether or not students will advance to a university or college or would enter the job market. The *Gaokao* plays an important role in the Chinese education system for two reasons.

First, the number of available spots in higher education is limited; thus, the test is the 'gatekeeper' to universities—and to many, a better life. In the early 1990s, the gross university enrolment of all high school graduates was only 3.5 per cent. In response, China launched nation-wide initiatives of university expansion in 1999. Though university enrolment has increased to 34.5 per cent of high school graduates as of 2013 (MoE 2014), there is still furious competition when advancing to higher education. Compared with their counterparts in North America and Western Europe, Chinese students encounter notoriously more difficult university admission tests and criteria (UNESCO Institute for Statistics 2010).

Second, the *Gaokao* determines not only if a student will advance to higher education, but also at what level. Higher education institutions (HEIs) in China are hierarchically ranked and diversified. National universities are ranked at the top, striving for global excellence (Zha 2011), often receiving extra government funding compared to provincial universities. Provincial universities are ranked in the middle, acting as major higher education providers for increased provincial and local enrolment. Higher vocational colleges and private institutions are at the bottom, providing vocation programs. Depending on the rank of their *Gaokao* test scores, students will receive offers of enrolment from correspondingly ranked schools, as well as suggested majors to study. This has a significant impact on students' future career opportunities, and students may test multiple times over several years to improve their scores so they can get better enrolment offers and more desirable majors of study.

China has a long tradition of stratifying higher education schools. In 1954, six universities were nominated as the first 'key HEIs' (重点大学 *zhongdian daxue*) which would form the starting base of the present-day elite universities. This number increased in 1959 (20 HEIs),[5] in 1963 (68

---

[5] In March 1959, sixteen universities were nominated as 'key universities'. The list of these sixteen universities can be found in the document Notice of Ten Documents on Education

HEIs), and in 1978 (88 HEIs), before ceasing in 1981 when it finally reached ninety-six (Wang et al. 2008). In the early 1990s, 'key universities' were expanded to and replaced by Project 211 in 1995 and Project 985 in 1998. The aim of Project 211 was to strengthen a select number of higher education institutions and key disciplinary areas, while Project 985 focused on building 'World-Class' universities and internationally renowned high-level research universities. Given that only thirty-nine universities have been selected for Project 985, and 112 universities have been selected for Project 211 among 2542 colleges and universities in China, students must work exceedingly hard to be admitted to the leading Project 985 or Project 211 universities.

Education in Chinese Culture
Chinese culture has always placed great emphasis on education. According to one Chinese proverb, 'The pursuit of knowledge is superior to all other walks of life' (万般皆下品,惟有读书高 *wan ban jie xia pin, wei you dushu gao*). Parents and students in China hold that a promising future depends on receiving an education from a renowned university. In the context of the furious competition mentioned above, education in China focuses largely on exam-oriented and teacher-centered methods of instruction (应试教育 *yingshi jiaoyu*). Although many consider these methods to be bad for in-depth student learning, they are still heavily used due to their efficiency. According to the OECD, China has the largest class sizes in terms of both primary and junior middle schools, with the average number of students per class at around fifty students (OECD 2012b). These numbers can vary widely according to district and province resources, with some areas averaging as low as thirty students a class and others with over eighty. Before advancing to each successive level of education, students in China first have to fight each other in 'test wars'. Though many strongly criticize the *Gakao* mechanism, claiming it kills students' creativity and imagination, the *Gaokao* is still considered the most fair and objective form of assessing and selecting qualified university candidates from among the large number of applicants. Young Chinese students learn to endure great academic and psychological pressure to fulfill the requirements and pass through this exam-oriented educational system.

Work Issued by the Central Committee of the Communist Party of China (中共中央关于印发教育工作的十个文件通知), issued on May 17, 1959. Another four universities were later added to the list in the same year.

Teachers as the Center of Education
From their very first class in primary school, Chinese students learn the importance of respecting the role of teachers in their education (尊师重教 *zun shi zhong jiao*). Teachers dominate classrooms in the Chinese educational system, and are viewed as 'someone who can provide advice through all stages of learning' (Chan and Drover 1977, p. 56). Accordingly, teachers are regarded as an authority not to be questioned openly. Students ask them questions very seldom during class, out of fear that frequent questions will break the instructor's rhythm and cause 'ineffective teaching' (Chan 1999, p. 301).

Recently, critics have pushed back against teacher-centeredness in the classrooms, and educational reforms in China have increasingly emphasized developing the competence of 'learning how to learn' (Marton & EDB Chinese Language Research Team 2010). In 2010, China announced the 'Outline for Medium and Long-term Development and Reform of Education' (国家中长期教育改革和发展规划纲要 *guojia zhongchangqi jiaoyu gaige he fazhan guihua gangyao*) to highlight the need to overcome educational disparity and the importance of respect for diversity and individual needs among students. Education in China has experienced substantial changes in the last few decades, as globalization has brought new teaching methodologies and pedagogies into the classroom. Through frequent educational exchange and academic communication with other countries, China has continued to open its doors wider, experimenting with these imported ideas. Moreover, the effects of long-standing policies—most notably the 'One Child' policy—have resulted in age demographic shifts that allow for other educational changes. The total enrolment of students in primary schools decreased from 128.2 million in 1994 to 94.5 million in 2014 (NBS 2015a), making current class sizes smaller than those of twenty years ago. In smaller classes, teachers are able to give more time and attention to individual students in the early stages of their education.

Structure of the Chinese Class
In China, from primary school through college, students are divided into cohort-style classes (班级 *banji*). The 'class' concept is composed of not only the students (学生 *xuesheng*), but also a 'class teacher' (班主任 *banzhuren*), and a 'class overseer' (班长 *banzhang*). While he or she often also teaches one subject (e.g. Chinese, mathematics, English, etc.), the role of the 'class teacher' should not be confused with regular instructors.

The 'class teacher' is in charge of organizing the majority of student study activities and daily life. The 'class overseer' is a student who assists the class teacher in classroom organization, by managing smaller study tasks for peer students in the same class, such as reminding students of upcoming deadlines and collecting student homework and tests for instructors. This kind of close organization leads to close relationships between students.

Depending on the number of students admitted by schools each year, each grade level (年级 *nianji*) has several classes, with an average range of thirty to fifty students in each class. Each class then receives an assigned syllabus from the school in the first week of the new semester. Those who are in the same classes subsequently have the same schedule of courses together. Before university, this means each class is designated one classroom. Students remain in their classrooms for the entire school day, while teachers enter and leave to teach each course. This practice is quite different from that used in some western countries, where students may choose and arrange their own class schedules as early as in middle school.

Once they enter university, Chinese students who belong to the same 'class' also often live together in the same student dormitories on campus. One dormitory room accommodates four to eight students, depending on the university. Thus, Chinese students may be both 'classmates' and 'roommates' at the same time. Some develop very strong bonds of friendship, as a result.

'Little Emperors': The Family's Only Hope

The education of a child is the top priority for a Chinese family. Most of the Chinese students currently studying abroad are the only children in their families (独生子女 *dusheng zinü*), due to the one child policy adopted nationally in 1979. Within this social context, children receive more attention and care from their parents and, in many cases, from both pairs of grandparents as well, than previous generations. Children growing up in families that give lots of attention are often called 'little emperors' (小皇帝 *xiao huangdi*). Compared with their parents, the 'little emperor' generation has grown up with much better material resources. The parent generation (i.e. those who were born in 1950s–1960s) experienced a tough time during their youth, due to numerous political disturbances.[6]

---

[6] For instance, the 'Great Proletariat Cultural Revolution' (无产阶级文化大革命 *wuchan jieji wenhua dageming*) or the 'Down to the Countryside Movement' (上山下乡运动 *shangshan xiaxiang yundong*).

In order to compensate for the difficulties they faced in their own childhoods, parents try every means possible to create a good learning environment for their children, and set high expectations for their only child's talents (望子成龙, 望女成凤 *wang zi cheng long, wang nü cheng feng*) and academic achievement. One survey indicated that Chinese families in urban areas invest approximately 30.1 per cent of their annual income in their children's education (Li and Pan 2012, March 16). Additionally, children may also be regarded as the 'only hope' (Fong 2004) for a family to move to a higher social class. Under such circumstances, it is a big challenge for many students to learn how to take care of themselves, with many young Chinese living with their parents until they get married.

Shifting from Rote Learners to 'Paradox Learners'

Traditional Perceptions of Chinese Students

A typical conception of Chinese students from a western perspective is:

> '[…] respectful of the lecturer's authority; diligent note-takers; preoccupied with fulfilling the expectations of the lecturers; uncritical of information presented in the textbook and by the lecturers; seldom asking questions or volunteering to contribute to tutorial discussions; and unaware of the conventions regarding acknowledging quotes and referencing sources and therefore unwittingly guilty of plagiarism'. (Volet and Renshaw 1996, pp. 205–206)

Another similar perception about Chinese students is they learn 'studiously and respectfully from great master teachers […] [and are] considered to rely heavily on rote memorization using a surface learning strategy, outperform[ing] their counterparts in international tests' (Law et al. 2010, pp. 91–95). Therefore, Chinese students often have been labeled as *rote learners, silent learners, reticent learners,* or *unquestioning learners* (Biggs 1996; Liu 2002). Compared with their counterparts in western countries, Chinese students give the impression of being incredibly passive, often leaving western educators confused as to how Chinese learners construe the purpose of memory and understanding (Marton & EDB Chinese Language Research Team 2010).

Furthermore, contemporary literature on Chinese students tends to dichotomize western and Chinese students into two opposite extremes. Turner (2006) made a comparison between 'model' British students as almost directly the opposite of 'model' Chinese students, while Cortazzi and Jin (1997) differentiated the expectations of British university staff as the reverse of their overseas students. Such comparisons do describe some characteristics of Chinese students at home and abroad. Nevertheless, these descriptions of Chinese learners are oversimplified, and some conclusions have been reached from a purely western perspective without properly considering the rationales behind the Chinese perspective. For example, a diligent Chinese student, who is regarded as a good student in China, might be negatively viewed as a *rote learner* in other learning cultures, where independent thinking and active participation are not only expected, but also defined differently.

Considering this, many researchers have disputed the practice of judging Chinese students using western standards. Volet and Renshaw (1996) pointed out that previous literature failed to fully consider 'students' cognitions and behaviours in interaction with the context in which they are embedded' (p. 206). Many assumptions by western researchers about Chinese learning are commonly based on a western cultural context (Kim 2002), which is obviously not the same context of a Chinese class. Constantly portraying Chinese learning as the classic opposition between the 'West vs. the Chinese' or 'the individualistic vs. collectivistic' visions can cause problems for Chinese students studying abroad, as such 'polarisation [...] will yield inappropriate responses on the part of instructional designers and teachers' (Smith and Smith 1999, p. 77). As such, there is a growing need to reevaluate the modern, diverse, and constantly evolving image of Chinese students.

A New Paradigm of Paradox Learners
In contrast to the above 'classic' Western image of Chinese learners, there is a growing body of literature building a 'new image' of Chinese learners from both western and Chinese perspectives. Of particular interest, especially with regard to the topic of this book, is the idea of Chinese students as 'paradoxical learners'.

John Biggs first proposed *the paradox of the Chinese learner* in 1992. This concept refers to students who typically use rote study methods and display low performance on tasks requiring high-level cognitive engagement, yet are still able to achieve a high cognitive level and better overall academic performance than their western counterparts (Biggs 1996). He regarded the 'classic' image of Chinese learners as a western misperception, and suggested that the 'good educational practice' held by westerners could have flaws. Although Chinese students demonstrate different learning qualities than expected by teachers in western countries, they are not passive learners. Rather, they are active 'independent thinkers' (Cortazzi and Jin 1996) who are reflective, 'deep learners' (Biggs 1996). Chinese students seek to understand, reflect, and question knowledge just like their western counterparts, but in different ways. Rote-learning methods only work on the premise that the student understands the information, indicating a deeper learning than previously assumed (Kingston and Forland 2008).

A New Generation of Students
In addition to re-imagining Chinese students in terms of learning characteristics, it is also necessary to reexamine the new generation of Chinese learners in light of changing global and educational contexts. Students who were born in the 1980s, 1990s, and 2000s (often called the 'post-80s', 'post-90s', and 'post-00s' generations, respectively) grew up in a period of time when China saw dramatic economic and technological development. Immersed in mass media and the internet, these generations are fast learning about many different cultures around the world, especially when compared to their parents' generation. As such, they process and engage with new information differently. Many more have the opportunity to travel abroad or participate in exchange programs more than ever before, all of which has contributed to increased self-confidence. Over time, teachers have reported that students nowadays are much more critical of the knowledge delivered to them in class, compared with students from ten or twenty years ago. Chinese students are increasingly active or even aggressive in class (Cheng 2000), and '[ask] deeper and more high-order questions over time' (Chan 2010, p. 199). If lecturers are wrong, younger students are less and less hesitant to raise their hands and point out the mistakes.

International Chinese Students: Definitions and Current Research Focus

Defining 'Chinese'
This book uses the term *international Chinese students*, defined as students who were born, raised, and initially educated in mainland China. They either are pursuing or have pursued study programs at the college or university level (bachelor's, master's, doctoral, or short-term exchange) abroad. In this case, Chinese students who are studying abroad at the elementary, middle, or high school level, are second generation immigrants (e.g. Chinese-Australian or Chinese-American adolescents who were born

to immigrant parents and grew up abroad), or are Chinese from other CHC countries (e.g. Singaporean-Chinese or Malaysian-Chinese) will not be included in this book.

International Chinese Students: A Variety of 'Constructed' Entities
Current research on international Chinese students has mainly been conducted by countries hosting a large number of Chinese students (e.g. the USA, UK, Australia, etc.), touching upon a diverse range of topics about international Chinese students: academic experience, language, adjustment/adaptation, intercultural communication, and so on. Much of this research conceptualizes international Chinese students as a variety of 'constructed' entities: 'customers', a source of 'irritation', a challenge and option for mutual learning and mutual enrichment, the world's largest mobile group with academic potential, and even a special reference group for general research (Henze and Zhu 2012). Drawing from their contributions, this book further examines the idea of 'Chinese students' according to the following aspects (Fig. 1.5).

Chinese students as 'CHC-learners' From a cultural and historical perspective, there is a dearth of literature looking at international Chinese students as 'CHC learners'. The term *Chinese learners* applies to CHC classrooms that are influenced by traditional Chinese belief systems, particularly Confucian values (Watkins and Biggs 1996). This term is a 'trade-off

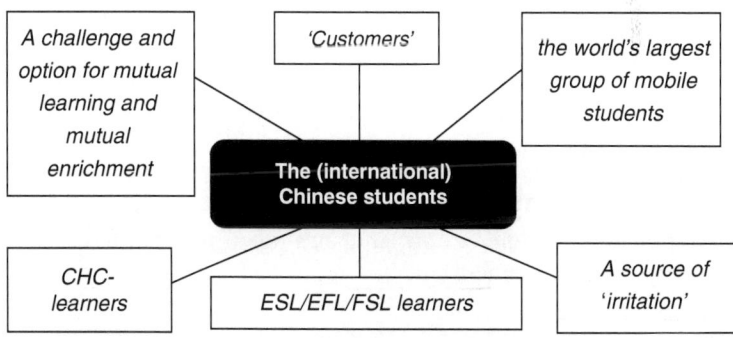

Source: inspired by Henze & Zhu, 2012

Fig. 1.5 Chinese students as various 'constructed' entities (Source: inspired by Henze and Zhu 2012)

between generalization and diversity' (Cortazzi and Jin 2011, p. 314), as it generalizes Chinese students as a whole, but also acknowledges differences and diversity within the group. Likewise, the following chapters in this book will not only look at international Chinese students as CHC learners as a whole in a study abroad context, but also at the individual ways in which they adapt to it.

Chinese students as a 'source of irritation' More international students are appearing on campuses and in classrooms in countries all around the world. However, despite the economic value they represent as customers, international students have also often been regarded as somewhat 'problematic' (Harris 1995). The presence of Chinese students—as well as other international students—in class brings a new set of challenges that lecturers and native classmates would not otherwise have to face. For instance, instructors might have difficulties organizing effective lessons to meet the needs of both native and Chinese students, as they may lack knowledge of their students' previous teaching and learning contexts or linguistic needs.

Chinese students as foreign language learners Research on second language learning (e.g., English as a Second Language, ESL; English as a Foreign Language EFL; French as a Second Language, FSL) also constitutes a large portion of the literature on international Chinese students, as Chinese students who study abroad often face challenges in their English language learning. While this research topic primarily focuses on English language learning, it can also include Chinese students learning foreign languages in non-English-speaking countries. However, research on challenges in foreign language learning often focuses on one specific language skill, such as academic listening (Huang 2005, 2006), reading (Liu 2015), academic writing (Arkoudis and Tran 2007; Lan 2015; Zhang 2011), or vocabulary learning (Wang 2015). In contrast, this book takes a more holistic approach, examining how language affects many different aspects of how international Chinese students adjust to foreign contexts.

International Chinese students as 'customers' Driven by economic, political, and intellectual motives, recent research conclusions have shifted from blaming problems in school on students to probing the relationship between the needs of overseas students and the resources provided by universities to satisfy them (Harris 1995). As the largest international student

can be cited
population across the world, Chinese students have become very important 'customers' in the international education market. In US colleges and universities alone, they contributed $8.04 billion to the US economy in the 2013–2014 academic year (IIE 2014). Thus, host countries are taking much greater care to ensure 'customer satisfaction' and the export market of education (Campbell and Li 2007). The end of this book will endeavor to provide suggestions for universities and researchers alike to better meet the needs of one of their most important 'clients'.

What Is 'Academic Adjustment?'

In the past few decades, research on cross-cultural adaptation has been generally characterized by theoretical diversity and has received substantial attention worldwide. However, when discussing the process that sojourners go through in a new culture, the inconsistent use of terminology is one of the biggest problems challenging the research on intercultural adjustment, as the terms *adaptation, acculturation, adjustment,* and *accommodation* have been used interchangeably (Kim 1988; Searle and Ward 1990). Readers are easily confused by the creative and flexible combination of the terms. To illustrate this problem, Table 1.1 demonstrates an example of the inconsistent usage of the terminologies. In the left column (Term 1) are adjectives (*intercultural, cross-cultural,* and *sociocultural*) and in the right (Term 2) are the terms *adjustment* and *adaptation*. Thus far, scholars have adopted combinations between the Term 1 and Term 2 columns, such as *intercultural adjustment* (Gundykunst 1998), *intercultural adaptation* (Zhao 2007; Zhao and Bourne 2011), *cross-cultural adjustment* (Black and Gregersen 1991), *cross-cultural adaptation* (Anderson 1994; Lewthwaite 1996; Kim 1988, 2007), *sociocultural adjustment* (Delgado-Gaitan 1988; Spencer-Oatey and Xiong 2006), *sociocultural adaptation* (Ward and Kennedy 1999), and *cultural*

Table 1.1 Possible combinations of the terms of cross-cultural adaptation

Term 1	Term 2
A. Intercultural	a. Adjustment
B. Cross-cultural	b. Adaptation
C. Sociocultural	
D. Cultural	

adjustment (Kagan and Cohen 1990). Anderson (1994) suggested the term cross-cultural adaptation could be compared to a 'grab-bag term[s], camouflaging a heterogeneous and complex reality' (Anderson 1994, p. 307). Thus, it is crucial to clarify the concepts of *adjustment, adaptation,* and *acculturation,* before further exploring the academic adjustment of Chinese students.

The difference between the terms *adjustment, adaptation,* and *acculturation* can be described from the perspectives of different academic disciplines. The term *adaptation* is more frequently referred to in biology literature than in other disciplines (Ogburn and Nimkoff 1964). In psychology, researchers and scholars often employ the term *adjustment,* while the term *acculturation* is often applied in anthropology. The term *acculturation,* according to anthropology, concerns groups of individuals contacting another group of people from a different culture background, and making subsequent changes in the original cultural patterns. Meanwhile, the terms *adaptation* and *adjustment* concern changes made at the individual level. The difference between these two concepts is that the former often refers to long-term residents or the endpoint of survival status, while the latter describes short-term sojourners. Accordingly, this book uses the base term *adjustment* to describe the individual learning experiences of and changes made by Chinese students who only intend to spend a temporary period abroad.

Moreover, the following chapters will focus specifically on *academic adjustment,* as international Chinese students' academic status is an important factor that differentiates them from other sojourners.

Academic adjustment is more than simply academic achievement. Often, the definition of *academic adjustment* is closely related to the assessment of international students. However, successful academic performance does not necessarily promise the ideal academic adjustment, and a seemingly excellent student might lead a lonely life, concentrating only on his studies, in isolation from the host culture (Klein et al. 1971). Moreover, adjustment in the host country does not mean that international students should be expected to abandon their original values or beliefs for learning. Rather, the significance of academic adjustment lies in the comprehension of the rules that govern social interpersonal relationships in the host country. Thus, international students learn to 'play the game' with native students according to these rules (Bochner 1972). Criteria for defining international students' adjustment should also include various aspects of adaptation in a study's research design itself, including analysis of 'completion of educational and professional goals, development of positive, friendly contacts with [foreigners], successful career placement, a continued sense of confidence, health, and well-being, and the emergence of differentiated and detailed perspectives on [foreign] life' (Klein et al. 1971, p. 79). Similarly, 'a complex set of shifting associations between language mastery, social interaction, personal development and academic outcomes' (Schweisfurth and Day 2010, p. 20) should also be included.

Following these criteria regarding international students' academic adjustment, this book defines *academic adjustment* for Chinese students as: (1) awareness of the different academic expectations between their home universities and host universities, and subsequent adoption of the necessary strategies to cope with difficulties caused by these differences in order to fulfill academic tasks and requirements; (2) efforts to improve foreign language proficiency (both spoken and written foreign language) that demonstrate campus-wide intercultural communication through participation in different academic activities, and good communication and relationships with host students and academic staff; and (3) the development of self-confidence and personal growth in their educational development as a result of overcoming difficulties in the intercultural learning milieu.

Chinese Sojourners and Their Adjustment

> 'The colonist, the foreign trader, the diplomat, the foreign student, the international journalist, the foreign missionary, the research anthropologist abroad, and all sorts of migrant group in different areas on the globe, in various degree, may be considered sojourners in the sociological sense'. (Siu 1952, p. 34)

In discussing the definition of adjustment, it is also important to look at the subject undergoing the adjustment: the *sojourner*. In order to differentiate the adjustment of international students from other sojourner identities, some scholars use the term *student sojourner* (Hechanova-Alampay et al. 2002; Kinginger 2015; Martin 1986, 1987; Pitts 2009; Rohrlich and Martin 1991). Most international Chinese students fall into the category of sojourners, who differentiate themselves from other settlers (e.g. immigrants, refugees, tourists, etc.) in three points. First, concerning the purpose of going abroad, sojourners often voluntarily leave their countries in order to obtain an education, fulfill employment responsibilities, or engage in humanitarian reasons (Church 1982; Ward 2001). Second, in terms of duration abroad, a sojourner has no intention of permanent settlement in the host country. Some sojourners may choose to work or live in that host country beyond the time of their original purpose, while others are expected to leave the host country upon completion of their task. A commonly cited parameter for sojourners abroad is anywhere from six months to five years (Ward et al. 2006). Third, a sojourner typically does not try to integrate into the host country, but rather '[cling] to the culture of his own ethnic group as in contrast to the bicultural complex of the marginal man' (Siu 1952, p. 34).

Conceptual Framework

Different Chinese sojourners can be expected to experience different adjustment processes, depending on the host of individual, cultural, and external factors (Brown and Holloway 2008). For instance, the frequency of difficulties that international Chinese students encounter in general life, social life, and study life changed over time and the pattern of changes differed (Zhou and Todman 2009). Indeed, 'no two individuals' characteristics and no two host culture contexts are exactly the same, with the result that adjustment processes and outcomes are highly individual and subjective' (Pearson-Evans 2006, p. 53). Given that, many of the current models on adaptation have not taken the dynamic profile of individual's adjustment into full consideration, as Chinese sojourners will experience adjustment differently across host countries and demonstrate different processes of adjustment accordingly.

Affective, Cognitive and Behavioral Model

Regarding the dynamic character of adjustment, this research analyzes the intercultural academic journey of Chinese students' initial experiences at foreign universities through the lens of Anderson's 'affective, cognitive and behavioral' model, which advocates cross-cultural adjustment as 'a dialectical process' (Fig. 1.6). This model characterizes adjustment as a cyclical and recursive process of overcoming obstacles and solving problems that can be compared to 'a ferris wheel or roller-coaster ride, with depression and elation, successes and failures in overcoming obstacles providing the hills and valleys' (p. 307). The three dimensions of Anderson's model are affective/emotional, cognitive/perceptual, and (overt) behavioral, where 'different obstacles will produce different sets of cognitive, affective, and behavior events and responses' (p. 309).

CULTURAL ENCOUNTER

AFFECTIVE
- excitement, fascination with new/exotic
- surprise
- resentment, uneasiness discomfort
- etc.

COGNITIVE
- spectator set: alertness to bizarre, stereotyping, see more differences
- deny differences, selective perception
- disorientation, perceptual chaos, cogn. dissonance, etc.

BEHAVIORAL
- start to meet survival needs, attend lang. classes, seek out co-nationals, superficial relationships with hosts
- etc.

OBSTACLE

AFFECTIVE
- crisis: loss of social ties, homesickness, psychosomatic problems, hopelessness, apathy
- lowering self-confidence/esteem
- increasing prof./academic satisfaction, dissatisfaction with superficial relationships
- self-centered/conscious
- etc.

COGNITIVE
- perceptual filter being overwhelmed, bewilderment, underbelly now glimpsed
- defence vs rejection of differences
- awareness of inadequacies, self-esteem dropping
- home fading, overidealized, host reference groups clearer
- etc.

BEHAVIORAL
- develop job role
- tackle complexities, start role relationships
- try out behaviors, violent swings between active/outward and inward/retreat activity
- continue information-gathering
- step up social interaction
- etc.

RESPONSE GENERATION

AFFECTIVE
- regression, intense ingroup solidarity, insecurity
- grief, homesickness, clinging to old identity
- shame, guilt, embarrassment at inadequacy, depression, frustration at relationships, feeling trapped, between two worlds, bitterness, tension rising
- apathy, hopelessness
- learn from hosts (less impulsiveness, patience), attitudes more realistic
- detachedness, doing one's best
- etc.

COGNITIVE
- rejection, regression, superciliousness
- blame self
- crisis: old identity/ reference groups fading, new ego incomplete, inner world disintegrating
- perceptions more complex, differentiated
- start to accept situation: fatalism, resignation
- etc.

BEHAVIORAL
- no solution/ obstacle persists–exhaustion
- do nothing instrumental
- fight: retaliation, blame others, conflict with hosts, etc.
- change self: reduce dissimilarities- try to escape attention, initiate behaviour, identify more- go native; start to reorganize life, compartmentalize public/ private lives, deepen/ increase interpersonal relationship, job role(s), develop skills, look/listen more, intensify learnings – lang./ norms/ customs/roles
- etc.

→ RETURNEES
→ ESCAPERS
→ BEAVERS
→ TIME SERVERS

OVERCOMING

AFFECTIVE
- self-confidence, start enjoying differences, etc.
- pos. attitude to home/host cultures
- growth in personal flexibility
- etc.

COGNITIVE
- insider awareness, non-judgementalness, then insider understanding
- accept then adapt to then integrate
- cultural relativity
- etc.

BEHAVIORAL
- increasing coping skills, productivity, competence
- strategies/ behaviors/ skills increasing in no. / complexity/ applicability, etc.
- etc.

→ ADJUSTERS
→ PARTICIPATORS

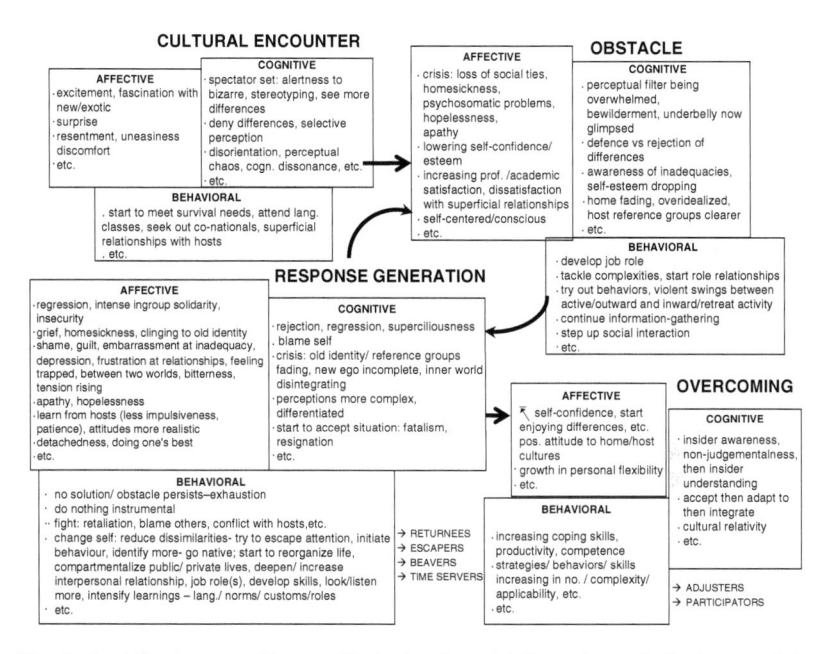

Fig. 1.6 Affective, cognitive, and behavioral model (In order to fit the layout of the book, some of the detailed examples in each box, that is, affective, behavioral, and cognitive have been omitted by the author.) (Source: Anderson 1994, pp. 310–31. Reprinted from *International Journal of Intercultural Relations*, 3/18, Linda E. Anderson, A new look at an old construct: Cross-cultural adaptation, Pages 310–311, Copyright (1994), with permission from Elsevier)

With regard to how international Chinese students adjust to their study abroad contexts, these three dimensions may be in synchronization during the adjustment process, one mediating, potentiating, or accompanying the other. However, they may also be at war, producing dissonance and conflicts within the Chinese student. Depending on the student, these three dimensions may also operate entirely independent of each other. Ultimately, the 'endpoint' of the adjustment is a fluctuating continuum, rather than a fixed point, dividing the sojourner into six discrete categories: returnees, escapers, beavers, timeservers, adjusters, and participators, according to their response and ability to overcome.

Significance of This Research

Chinese Students as Diverse and Heterogeneous Individuals

Much of the previous research exploring the problems of international Asian students treats them as a homogeneous group, neglecting differences present within it (Trice 2003). While it is true that Asian students often share many similarities (Noesjirwan 1970), a comparison of academic success and failure among six Asian-American ethnic groups (Chinese, Filipino, Japanese, Korean, Vietnamese, and other Southeast Asians) show that Asian ethnic groups also have distinctly different attribution profiles (Mizokawa and Ryckman, 1990).

Similarly, in investigating the academic adjustment of Chinese students, a large amount of previous research regards specifically Chinese students as not only a homogeneous group, but also the epitome of *Asian students*. This overgeneralization of the group fails to acknowledge the diversity among individual Chinese students (Zhao and Bourne 2011). Under the umbrella term *Chinese students* or *Chinese learners*, there is a wide and complex diversity of temperaments, academic accomplishments, and social backgrounds (Cortazzi and Jin 2011).

For instance, China is home to fifty-six ethnic groups who weave a complex, heterogeneous Chinese culture. Among them, Han Chinese (汉族 *hanzu*) account for 91.5 per cent of the overall Chinese population, and the other fifty-five ethnic Chinese minorities (少数民族 *shaoshu minzu*) make up the remaining 8.5 per cent according to the Sixth National Population Census of 2010 (NBS 2011). While Mandarin (普通话 *putonghua*) is the official language of China spoken across the country, there are also seven other major dialects spoken simultaneously in different regions. Additionally, most ethnic Chinese minorities have their own distinctly different languages. Accordingly, this book views Chinese students as diverse and heterogeneous individuals, taking into account the variety of their current diverse profiles (e.g. academic disciplines, academic degree pursued, financial resource, etc.).

A Longitudinal Approach

As adjustment is a long-term and dynamic process, this book takes a longitudinal approach in following international students' development. Previous literature has highlighted the importance of undertaking more research on international students' adjustment using this approach in order to fully understand the different phases of adjustment and how student experiences change over time (Klein et al. 1971; Sam and Berry 2010).

However, in spite of the importance of longitudinal research, much of the previous research has only suggested its use, instead of implementing it, due to the time and cost involved. Over 90 per cent of the research on international students' experiences in Germany is based only on their contact with the students during their stay abroad. Thus, a significant component of this research explores Chinese students' academic adjustment in a longitudinal manner, which probes Chinese students' experiences, attitudes, and expectations before, during, and after their stay abroad.

As international Chinese students studying abroad are only at one phase of their adjustment, to some extent, they cannot provide researchers with information about the whole range of the academic adjustment. Thus, this book will also investigate graduates' learning experience in retrospect, in order to enrich the research on Chinese students studying abroad from a broader perspective and in a chronological view, in order to look at the following questions: What benefits Chinese graduates most from the learning experience in the host country? How do they reflect on their academic adjustment and how do they deal with the difficulty?

Hearing Voices from Many Sides

Who decides what makes for a successful study abroad trip—the student or the university? Often, this debate falls in favor of the student, with few ever listening to the side of the faculty and administration who handle Chinese students (Trice 2003). The study of learning across cultures should be composed of subjective perceptions from both staff and students, so as to obtain a wider perspective that transcends culture-bound norms or principles of good learning (Volet 1999). Comments and opinions from academic staff could be compared with those of international students, so as to find out which factors impeded or supported international students' adjustment (Danckwortt 1984). As such, this book will provide perspectives from both Chinese students and lecturers in the host university, in order to obtain an overview of the academic adjustment of Chinese students.

Furthermore, the context of this book is set in Germany for several reasons. First, it is a common host country for international students. After the USA and the UK, Germany is the third largest country in terms of hosting international students. Second, Germany is an ideal model for a non-English-speaking country with a large number of Chinese students. In 2014, 28,381 Chinese students studied in Germany, representing 13.0 per cent of the overall international student population (DAAD & DZHW 2015). As English-speaking countries have the lion's share of Chinese students, much has already been written in this regard, but little is known about Chinese students' learning experiences in non-English-speaking countries, especially non-CHC countries. Furthermore, it is only within the last ten years that Chinese students have become the largest international student group in Germany. As few non-English-speaking countries have a long history of experience with hosting Chinese students, Germany's case can provide guidance to other countries that have also experienced the rapid growth of international Chinese students.

Additionally, while much research on international students has been conducted in Germany, a majority of this research is only available in German. As a result, the current research status of international students in Germany is not widely known in the non-German-speaking world. Germany differentiates itself from other host countries of international students in many aspects. Since German universities charge international students the same fees as German students, research on international students in Germany has not been based on any customer-oriented or market-driven contexts. Although some research has focused on the themes of learning style, adjustment, integration, and social and financial situation (Guan 2007; Guan 2010; Luo 2011; Mao 2011; Zhou 2010) of Chinese students, little empirical research has particularly probed the dynamic academic adjustment of Chinese students in Germany.

Research Question, Methods, and Procedures

Research Question

Compared with their counterparts from other countries studying in Germany, Chinese students achieve the highest academic completion rate out of all the international student groups in Germany. Education statistics indicated that in Germany, the overall drop-out rate among international students enrolled in bachelor's programs in 2012 was 41 per cent, while the drop-out rate of Chinese students was only 16 per cent (Heublein et al. 2014). In contrast, the drop-out rate of students from France and Poland was 59 per cent and 49 per cent, respectively. These results set an interesting backdrop for more discussion on Chinese students in Germany. Coming from arguably more culturally different academic backgrounds, why are Chinese students more able to manage their studies and have a lower dropout rate than their other international counterparts in Germany?

Thus, the main research question of this book is, how do international Chinese students adjust to the educational milieu and intercultural learning environment of a German university? In order to tackle this question, this research study conducted detailed analysis of the process of academic adjustment and learning experience, factors influencing academic adjustment, and educational development and personal growth.

This main, overarching research question comprises three sub-questions. First, what comprises the process of academic adjustment that Chinese students experience at German universities? Since people generally adapt to new situations differently, the question facing Chinese students is not *if* they adapt, but *how* (Kim 1988), especially in terms of new constructs for learning, socializing, and communicating (Holmes 2004). Thus, it is important to trace Chinese students' learning experience and the kind of learning strategy they adopt after arriving at German universities. In this way, universities can better serve their largest international demographic.

Second, why do some Chinese students appear more academically well adjusted compared to their other international counterparts, and what factors facilitate or impede their adjustment? For instance, how do students' background (e.g. language proficiency, previous academic training, etc.), university environment (e.g. academic support, intercultural communication, etc.), and personal factors (e.g. personality, doing part-time jobs, etc.) influence adjustment of Chinese students at German universities?

Third, what kind of educational development and personal growth do Chinese students undergo through their learning experience in Germany? In other words, besides discipline-based knowledge and professional skills, what else have Chinese students learned from studying in an intercultural learning environment?

Research Methods

This study used a mixed methods research design 'that combines or associates both qualitative and quantitative forms' (Creswell 2009, p. 4). Data generated from both quantitative questionnaires and qualitative interviews were compared and combined to enhance the validity and reliability of the findings. For increased depth, this research is composed of three different studies (Fig. 1.7).

Study 1
- **Form**
  Interview (cross-sectional)
- **Purpose**
  Zooming-out: To listen to the experience of Chinese students with different profiles, so as to obtain an overview of their learning experience
- **Participants**
  Chinese students: 18

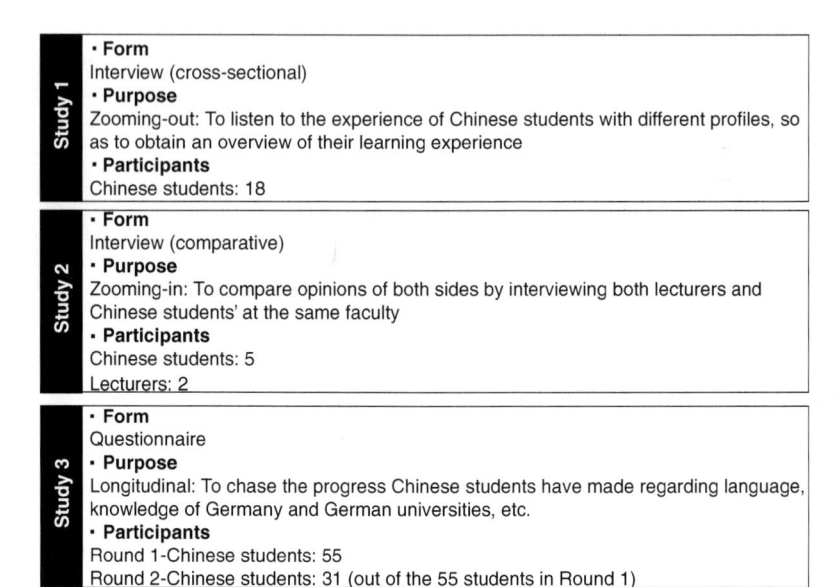

Study 2
- **Form**
  Interview (comparative)
- **Purpose**
  Zooming-in: To compare opinions of both sides by interviewing both lecturers and Chinese students' at the same faculty
- **Participants**
  Chinese students: 5
  Lecturers: 2

Study 3
- **Form**
  Questionnaire
- **Purpose**
  Longitudinal: To chase the progress Chinese students have made regarding language, knowledge of Germany and German universities, etc.
- **Participants**
  Round 1-Chinese students: 55
  Round 2-Chinese students: 31 (out of the 55 students in Round 1)

Fig. 1.7 Methods conducted in this research

Study 1

To get an overall picture of the learning and intercultural experience of Chinese students in Germany, eighteen Chinese students with different profiles (Appendix) were interviewed for Study 1. The Chinese students included as participants differed in terms of degree of completion, academic disciplines (e.g. engineering, natural science, social science, etc.), levels of study (e.g. bachelor's, master's, and doctoral), and sources of funding (e.g. self-funded or with scholarships) of their study in Germany. The purpose of conducting interviews with Chinese students from different backgrounds was to avoid homogenizing representation of Chinese by observing individual Chinese students, while still probing general trends in their experiences. By listening to their stories, this research paints a picture of Chinese students' experiences starting from their first preparations in China to completion of their study in Germany.

Study 2

Since the majority of research on international students' experiences focus mainly on the students' perspectives, this research interviewed both Chinese students and German lecturers at the same faculty, so as to provide a comparative view that included the voices of natives in the intercultural learning environment. Altogether, five Chinese students and two German lecturers from the same faculty in humanities participated in one-on-one interviews (Appendix). Initially, German students were also invited to participate in the interviews, but none ultimately volunteered.

In general, the faculty involved in this study has a noticeable international and intercultural background. Because the faculty has academic exchange programs with Chinese universities, it subsequently has a large percentage of Chinese students. Additionally, the lecturers themselves in this faculty have overseas experience in East Asia, North America, and other European countries.

Study 3

This research comprised two longitudinal questionnaire surveys (Appendix), providing 'a quantitative or numeric description of trends, attitudes, or opinions of a population by studying a sample of that population' (Creswell 2009, p. 145). At the beginning of the first semester, fifty-five Chinese students participated in Round 1 of the questionnaire, which involved academic background, foreign language skills, knowledge about Germany and German universities, and motivation of studying in Germany. At the end of the second semester one year later, thirty-one out of the original fifty-five participants (a return rate of 56.4 per cent) later joined Round 2 of the questionnaire. The results of the questionnaires for Study 3 provided a baseline description of the sample Chinese students' motivations, expectations, and a range of personal, social, and academic challenges that they experienced in the initial phase of their academic adjustment in Germany.

Reliability and Validity

Re-interview

In order to increase the reliability and validity of research findings, the *Re-interview* method (Kvale 1996) was used during data analysis. After analyzing the completed interviews, the interpretations were made available to Chinese participants to give them a chance to comment on the interviewer's interpretations and elaborate on their own original statements. Each interview was usually transcribed immediately afterwards, and the transcriptions, including researchers' interpretations, field notes, and any questions, were sent to interviewees by email. Participants were asked to read through the transcripts and check for any misunderstandings or misrepresentation. Interviewees would later email back to confirm the authenticity and accuracy of the interview data. All interviewees contacted were quick to provide feedback or confirmation, which helped avoid any confusion.

Mixed Method
The mixed method 'involves the intentional collection of both quantitative and qualitative data and the combination of the strengths of each to answer research questions' (Creswell et al. 2011, p. 5). In this research, the mixed method adopted is intended to establish and increase credibility, as both interviews and questionnaires used consistent questions, providing both qualitative and quantitative data for comparison.

Analysis of the Data
Quantitative data from the questionnaire were analyzed by using Statistical Package for the Social Sciences, and qualitative data from the interview transcriptions were processed by MAXQDA, a software for qualitative and mixed method data analysis. The quantitative analysis was conducted in parallel with the initial qualitative data collection to ensure proper synthesis of the data analysis and increase validity and reliability within the limitations of the study.

Ethical and Moral Concerns
Before conducting the three studies, the research purposes were clearly explained to participants. No major identifying information has been included in this publication in order to preserve their anonymity. In terms of the interviews, all participation was completely voluntary, and interviewees were informed that they could refuse to answer any question that they regarded as aggressive, or that otherwise made them uncomfortable.

STRUCTURE OF THE BOOK

This book provides insight into Chinese overseas students' academic adjustment to the intercultural learning environment and details the process for how they deal with the challenges of fulfilling the academic requirements and expectations of German universities.

Chapter 2 first reviews the literature of current empirical research regarding the different stages of students' academic adjustment: pre-departure situation (e.g. motivation, preparation, and previous intercultural experience), overseas learning experience (e.g. general difficulties and specific academic difficulties), psychological wellbeing (e.g. academic stress and cultural and acculturative stress), and intercultural communication (e.g. current situation, reasons for reduced intercultural communication, friendship patterns, and benefit of intercultural communication). The end of the chapter reviews factors influencing adjustment of international students.

Chapter 3 looks at the actual research project on Chinese students' academic adjustment. This chapter mainly describes the experience of Chinese students' pre-departure adjustment, which this study refers to as *an unprepared academic journey*. Previous research, with very few exceptions, regards the very arrival date in a foreign country as the start of the adjustment process for Chinese students. However, this chapter includes the pre-departure phase as the beginning of academic adjustment.

Chapter 4 continues the intercultural academic journey by looking at Chinese students' initial experiences at German universities. As the Chinese proverb says, 'All things are difficult before they become easy', which illustrates how the initial period of studying abroad is the most difficult time for most Chinese students. Students describe their unexpected problems with university life, such as the *Modul-system*, the different academic culture of Germany, and the efforts they took to overcome them.

Chapter 5 probes the process of Chinese students' academic adjustment after they have spent a certain period of time abroad (often two semesters). The experience of this phase can be summarized as *the battle continues*. With all their efforts, Chinese students make substantial progress within several semesters, and some problems do not challenge them any longer. Nevertheless, new problems still occur. Students continue to experience confusion as what was once 'correct or appropriate' student behavior is now 'wrong or unacceptable' within the new study abroad context. This chapter details how Chinese students begin to compare and negotiate the deeper and more nuanced differences between study in China and Germany, and how they change their strategies to deal with their confusion and frustration.

Chapter 6 observes the academic adjustment of Chinese students approaching the end of their study in Germany. In the final phase, Chinese students are able to reflect on and appreciate the different learning tradition in Germany and more easily make necessary changes accordingly. Chinese students' understanding of academic requirement and appreciation of features unique to German universities encourage them to participate and take the initiative more in their academic and social life. Furthermore, students make use of available resources as they become more familiar with the academic resources offered by their institutions.

Chapter 7 discusses different factors influencing Chinese students' academic adjustment and suggestions for Chinese students and host universities regarding intercultural learning. The factors discussed are necessary 'surviving' skills (e.g. language proficiency, knowledge of courses, and intercultural competency) and campus-wide academic support (i.e. long-term orientation courses and intercultural communication skills) offered by lecturers, fellow students, faculty members, and others. These play a decisive role in Chinese students' academic adjustment.

Chapter 8 offers suggestions and advice for Chinese students and German universities at each of the four phases. First, the chapter discusses the importance for Chinese students to pay more attention to the pre-departure phase, and how to develop the necessary surviving skills before departure. Next, it discusses the expectations and attitudes students should have when first arriving to begin their studies. Following that, the chapter discusses how students can reflect on their experience and modify their approach, once they have made initial adjustments. Finally, the conclusion suggests how universities can offer better resources and support for Chinese students, and how the students can take advantage of them.

References

Altbach, P. G., & Knight, J. (2007). The internationalization of higher education: Motivations and realities. *Journal of Studies in International Education, 11*(3–4), 290–305. doi:10.1177/1028315307303542.

Altbach, P. G., & Teichler, U. (2001). Internationalization and exchanges in a globalized university. *Journal of Studies in International Education, 5*(1), 5–25. Retrieved from http://jsi.sagepub.com/content/5/1/5

Altbach, P. G., Kelly, D. H., & Lulat, Y. G.-M. (1985). *Bibliography of foreign students and international study*. New York: Praeger.

Anderson, L. E. (1994). A new look at an old construct: Cross-cultural adaptation. *International Journal of Intercultural Relations, 18*(3), 293–328. doi:10.1016/0147-1767(94)90035-3.

Arkoudis, S., & Tran, L. T. (2007). International students in Australia: Read ten thousand volumes of books and walk ten thousand miles. *Asia Pacific Journal of Education, 27*(2), 157–169. doi:10.1080/02188790701378792.

Biggs, J. B. (1996). Approaches to learning of Asian students: A multiple paradox. In J. Pandey, D. Sinha, D. P. S. Bhawuk, & D. P. S. Bhawuk (Eds.), *Asian contributions to cross-cultural psychology*. New Delhi/Thousand Oaks: SAGE Publications.

Black, J. S., & Gregersen, H. B. (1991). Antecedents to cross-cultural adjustment for expatriates in Pacific Rim assignments. *Human Relations, 44*(5), 497–515. doi:10.1177/001872679104400505.

Bochner, S. (1972). Problems in culture learning. In S. Bochner & P. Wicks (Eds.), *Overseas students in Australia* (pp. 65–81). Randwick: New South Wales University Press.

Brandenburg, U., & Zhu, J. (2007). *Higher education in China in the light of massification and demographic change: Lessons to be learned for Germany. Arbeitspapier / CHE, Centrum für Hochschulentwicklung gGmbH: Vol. 97.* Gütersloh: CHE.

Brown, L., & Holloway, I. (2008). The adjustment journey of international postgraduate students at an English university: An ethnographic study. *Journal of Research in International Education, 7*(2), 232–249. doi:10.1177/1475240908091306.

Campbell, J., & Li, M. (2007). Asian students' voices: An empirical study of Asian students' learning experiences at a New Zealand University. *Journal of Studies in International Education, 12*(4), 375–396. doi:10.1177/1028315307299422.

Chan, S. (1999). The Chinese learner: A question of style. *Education + Training, 41*(6–7), 294–304.

Chan, C. K. K. (2010). Classroom innovation for the Chinese learner: Transcending dichotomies and transforming pedagogy. In C. K. K. Chan & N. Rao (Eds.), *Revisiting the Chinese learner. Changing contexts, changing education* (CERC studies in comparative education, Vol. 25, pp. 169–209). Dordrecht: Springer Science+Business Media B.V.

Chan, D., & Drover, G. (1997). Teaching and learning for overseas students: The Hong Kong connection. In D. McNamara & R. Harris (Eds.), *Overseas students in higher education. Issues in teaching and learning* (pp. 46–61). London: Routledge.

Cheng, X. (2000). Asian students' reticence revisited. *System, 28*(3), 435–446. doi:10.1016/S0346-251X(00)00015-4.

Church, A. T. (1982). Sojourner adjustment. *Psychological Bulletin, 91*(3), 540–572.

Cortazzi, M., & Jin, L. (1996). Cultures of learning: Language classrooms in China. In H. Coleman (Ed.), *Society and the language classroom* (pp. 169–206). Cambridge: Cambridge University Press.

Cortazzi, M., & Jin, L. (1997). Communication for learning across cultures. In D. McNamara & R. Harris (Eds.), *Overseas students in higher education. Issues in teaching and learning* (pp. 76–90). London: Routledge.

Cortazzi, M., & Jin, L. (2011). Conclusions: What are we learning from research about Chinese learners? In L. Jin & M. Cortazzi (Eds.), *Researching Chinese learners. Skills, perceptions and intercultural adaptations* (pp. 314–318). Basingstoke/New York: Palgrave Macmillan.

Creswell, J. W. (2009). *Research design: Qualitative, quantitative, and mixed method approaches* (3rd ed.). Thousand Oaks: SAGE Publications.

Creswell, J., Klassen, A., Plano, C. V., & Smith K. C. for the Office of Behavioral and Social Sciences Research. (2011). *Best practices for mixed methods research in the health sciences*. Retrieved from https://obssr-archive.od.nih.gov/scientific_areas/methodology/mixed_methods_research/pdf/Best_Practices_for_Mixed_Methods_Research.pdf

Danckwortt, D. (Ed.). (1984). *Werkstattberichte: Vol. 11. Auslandsstudium als Gegenstand der Forschung: Eine Literaturübersicht.* Kassel: Geschschule, Wiss. Zentrum f. Berufs- u. Hochschulforschung.

Delgado-Gaitan, C. (1988). Sociocultural adjustment to school and academic achievement. *The Journal of Early Adolescence, 8*(1), 63–82. doi:10.1177/0272431688081005.

Deutscher Akademischer Austauschdienst (DAAD) & Deutsches Zentrum für Hochschul- und Wissenschaftsforschung GmbH (DZHW). (2015). *Wissenschaft weltoffen: Daten und Fakten zur Internationalität von Studium und Forschung in Deutschland [Schwerpunkt: Internationale Masterstudierende an deutschen Hochschulen]*. Bielefeld: Bertelsmann.

Finnish National Board of Education. (2007). *Higher Education in the People's Republic of China*. Retrieved from http://www.oph.fi/download/47688_chinaedu.pdf

Fong, V. L. (2004). *Only hope: Coming of age under China's one-child policy*. Stanford: Stanford University Press.

Gong, Y., & Chang, S. (2007). The relationships of cross-cultural adjustment with dispositional learning orientation and goal setting: A longitudinal analysis. *Journal of Cross-Cultural Psychology, 38*(1), 19–25. doi:10.1177/0022022106295438.

Gu, Q., Schweisfurth, M., & Day, C. (2010). Learning and growing in a 'foreign' context: Intercultural experiences of international students. *Compare: A Journal of Comparative and International Education, 40*(1), 7–23. Retrieved from http://dx.doi.org/10.1080/03057920903115983

Guan, H. (2007). *Anpassung und Integration der chinesischen Studierenden in Deutschland. Eine Untersuchung anhand des Beispiels an der Universität Bremen.* Dissertation. Universität Bremen, Bremen. Retrieved from http://elib.suub.uni-bremen.de/diss/docs/00010886.pdf

Guan, L. (2010). *Anpassung der chinesischen Studenten in Deutschland*. München: Grin Verlag.

Gudykunst, W. B. (1998). Applying anxiety\uncertainty management (AUM) theory to intercultural adjustment training. *International Journal of Intercultural Relations, 22*(2), 227–250. doi:10.1016/S0147-1767(98)00005-4.

Hamilton, A. M. (2009). *From China To Hartford, Elsie Jane Yung's Historic Connection*. Retrieved from http://www.hartfordinfo.org/issues/documents/history/htfd_courant_061409.asp

Harris, R. (1995). Overseas students in the United Kingdom university system. *Higher Education, 29*(1), 77–92. doi:10.1007/BF01384242.
Hechanova-Alampay, R., Beehr, T. A., Christiansen, N. D., & Van Horn, R. K. (2002). Adjustment and strain among domestic and international student sojourners: A longitudinal study. *School Psychology International, 23*(4), 458–474. doi:10.1177/0143034302234007.
Henze, J., & Zhu, J. (2012). Current research on Chinese students studying abroad. *Research in Comparative and International Education, 7*(1), 90. doi:10.2304/rcie.2012.7.1.90.
Heublein, U., Richter, J., Schmelzer, R., & Sommer, D. (2014). *Die Entwicklung der Studienabbruchquoten an den deutschen Hochschulen: Statistische Berechnungen auf der Basis des Absolventenjahrgangs 2012*. Hannover: Deutsches Zentrum für Hochschul- und Wissenschaftsforschung (DZHW).
Holmes, P. (2004). Negotiating differences in learning and intercultural communication: Ethnic Chinese students in a New Zealand university. *Business Communication Quarterly, 67*(3), 294–307. doi:10.1177/1080569904268141.
Huang, J. (2005). Challenges of academic listening in English: Reports by Chinese students. *College Student Journal, 39*(3), 553–569.
Huang, J. (2006). English abilities for academic listening: How confident are Chinese students? *College Student Journal, 40*(1), 218–226.
Institute of International Education (IIE). (2014). *Open doors data: Open doors fact sheet: China*. Retrieved from http://www.iie.org/Research-and-Publications/Open-Doors/Data/Fact-Sheets-by-Country/2014
Jin, B. (2004, April 22). Early educational mission. *China Daily*. Retrieved from http://www.chinadaily.com.cn/english/doc/2004-04/22/content_325340.htm
Kagan, H., & Cohen, J. (1990). Cultural adjustment of international students. *Psychological Science, 1*(2), 133–137.
Kim, Y. Y. (1988). *Communication and cross-cultural adaptation: An integrative theory* (Intercommunication series, Vol. 2). Clevedon: Multilingual Matters Ltd.
Kim, H. S. (2002). We talk, therefore we think? A cultural analysis of the effect of talking on thinking. *Journal of Personality and Social Psychology, 83*(4), 828–842. doi:10.1037//0022-3514.83.4.828.
Kim, Y. Y. (2007). Adapting to an unfamiliar culture. In W. B. Gudykunst (Ed.), *Cross-cultural and intercultural communication* (pp. 243–257). Thousand Oaks: Sage.
Kinginger, C. (2015). Student mobility and identity-related language learning. *Intercultural Education, 26*(1), 6–15. doi:10.1080/14675986.2015.992199.
Kingston, E., & Forland, H. (2008). Bridging the gap in expectations between international students and academic staff. *Journal of Studies in International Education, 12*(2), 204–221. doi:10.1177/1028315307307654.
Klein, M. H., Alexander, A. A., Tseng, K.-H., Miller, M. H., Keh, E.-K., Chu, H.-M., & Workneh, F. (1971). The foreign student adaptation program: Social experiences of Asian students in the U. S. *International Educational and Cultural Exchange, 6*(3), 77–90.

Knight, J., & de Wit, H. (1995). Strategies for internationalisation of higher education: Historical and conceptual perspectives. In H. de Wit (Ed.), *Strategies for internationalisation of higher education. A comparative study of Australia, Canada, Europe and the United States of America* (pp. 5–32). Amsterdam: European Association for International Education.

Kvale, S. (1996). *Interviews: An introduction to qualitative research interviewing.* Thousand Oaks: SAGE Publications.

Lan, F. (2015). A case study into the writing of Chinese postgraduate students in a UK academic environment. *English Language Teaching*, 8(9). doi:10.5539/elt.v8n9p86.

Law, N. W., Yuen, A. H., Chan, C. K., Yuen, J. K., Pan, N. F., Lai, M., & Lee, V. S. (2010). New experiences, new epistemology, and the pressures of change: The Chinese learner in transition. In C. K. K. Chan & N. Rao (Eds.), *Revisiting the Chinese learner. Changing contexts, changing education* (CERC studies in comparative education, Vol. 25, pp. 89–131). Dordrecht: Springer Science+Business Media B.V.

Levin, R. C. (2004, August 02). *Yung Wing 150th Anniversary.* Retrieved from http://communications.yale.edu/president/speeches/2004/08/02/yung-wing-150th-anniversary

Lewthwaite, M. (1996). A study of international students' perspectives on cross-cultural adaptation. *International Journal for the Advancement of Counselling*, 19(2), 167–185. doi:10.1007/BF00114787.

Li (李松涛), S., & Pan (潘圆), Y. (2012, March 16). 囚徒困境下,教育消费何去何从. *The China Youth Daily (*中国青年报*)*. Retrieved from http://zqb.cyol.com/html/2012-03/16/nw.D110000zgqnb_20120316_1-05.htm

Liu, J. (2002). Negotiating silence in American classrooms: Three Chinese cases. *Language and Intercultural Communication*, 2(1), 37–54. doi:10.1080/14708470208668074.

Liu, J. (2015). Reading transition in Chinese international students: Through the lens of activity system theory. *Journal of English for Academic Purposes*, 17, 1–11. doi:10.1016/j.jeap.2014.11.004.

Luo, X. (2011). Gibt es Lernstile, die kulturspezifisch sind? Eine interkulturelle Annäherung an das Lernstilkonzept anhand einer vergleichenden Untersuchung am Beispiel deutscher und chinesischer Studenten. *Interculture Journal*, 10(15). Retrieved from http://www.interculture-journal.com/download/article/luo_kueck_2011_15.pdf

Mao, X. (2011). *Die soziale und wirtschaftliche Lage chinesischer Studierender in Berlin 2010: Umfrage im Auftrag des Studentenwerks Berlin im Rahmen der Teilnahme am "China-Traineeprogramm", einem Kooperationsprojekt von der Robert Bosch Stiftung und dem Deutschen Studentenwerk.* München: Grin Verlag.

Martin, J. N. (1986). Communication in the intercultural reentry: Student sojourners' perceptions of change in reentry relationship. *International Journal of Intercultural Relations*, 10(1), 1–22. doi:10.1016/0147-1767(86)90031-3.

Martin, J. N. (1987). The relationship between student sojourner perceptions of intercultural competencies and previous sojourn experience. *International Journal of Intercultural Relations, 11*(4), 337–355.

Marton, F., & EDB Chinese Language Research Team. (2010). The Chinese learner of tomorrow. In C. K. K. Chan & N. Rao (Eds.), *Revisiting the Chinese learner. Changing contexts, changing education* (CERC studies in comparative education, Vol. 25, pp. 133–163). Dordrecht: Springer Science+Business Media B.V.

Ministry of Education of The People's Republic of China (MoE). (2014). Gross enrolment ratio of Education in China. Retrieved July 23, 2015, from http://www.moe.edu.cn/publicfiles/business/htmlfiles/moe/s8493/201412/181724.html

Mizokawa, D. T., & Ryckman, D. B. (1990). Attributions of academic success and failure: A comparison of six Asian-American ethnic groups. *Journal of Cross-Cultural Psychology, 21*(4), 434–451. doi:10.1177/0022022190214003.

National Bureau of Statistics of China (NBS). (2011). 2010年第六次全国人口普查主要数据公报(第1号) http://www.stats.gov.cn/tjsj/tjgb/rkpcgb/qgrkpcgb/201104/t20110428_30327.html. Retrieved 26 Aug 2015.

National Bureau of Statistics of China (NBS). (2014). Retrieved 26 August 2015 from National Bureau of Statistics of China. China Statistical Year Book 2014 (中国统计年鉴 2014) http://www.stats.gov.cn/tjsj/ndsj/2014/indexeh.htm

National Bureau of Statistics of China (NBS). (2015a). *Education: Number of postgraduates and students study abroad.* Retrieved from http://data.stats.gov.cn/english/easyquery.htm?cn=C01

Noesjirwan, J. (1970). Attitudes to learning of the Asian student studying in the west. *Journal of Cross-Cultural Psychology, 1*(4), 393–397.

Ogburn, W. F., & Nimkoff, M. F. (1964). *A handbook of sociology.* London: Routledge & Kegan Paul LTD.

Organisation for Economic Co-operation and Development (OECD). (2004). *Education at a Glance 2004: OECD indicators. Document—Organisation de coopération et de développement économiques.* Paris: Organisation for Economic Co-operation and Development.

Organisation for Economic Co-operation and Development (OECD). (2005). *Education at a Glance 2005: OECD indicators.* Paris: Organisation for Economic Co-operation and Development.

Organisation for Economic Co-operation and Development (OECD). (2006). *Education at a Glance 2006: OECD indicators.* Paris: OECD.

Organisation for Economic Co-operation and Development (OECD). (2007). *Education at a Glance 2007: OECD indicators. Education at a Glance.* Paris: Organisation for Economic Co-operation and Development.

Organisation for Economic Co-operation and Development (OECD). (2008). *Education at a Glance 2008: OECD indicators.* Washington: Organization for Economic Cooperation & Development.

Organisation for Economic Co-operation and Development (OECD). (2009). *Education at a Glance 2009: OECD indicators*. Paris: Organisation for Economic Co-operation and Development.
Organisation for Economic Co-operation and Development (OECD). (2010). *Education at a Glance 2010: OECD indicators*. Paris: Organisation for Economic Co-operation and Development. Retrieved from http://www.oecd.org/document/52/0,3343,en_2649_39263238_45897844_1_1_1_1,00.html
Organisation for Economic Co-operation and Development (OECD). (2011). *Education at a Glance 2011: OECD indicators*. Paris: Organization for Economic Co-operation and Development
Organisation for Economic Co-operation and Development (OECD). (2012a). *Education at a Glance 2012: OECD indicators*. Paris: OECD.
Organisation for Economic Co-operation and Development (OECD). (2012b). How does class size vary around the world? Retrieved from http://www.oecd.org/edu/skills-beyond-school/EDIF%202012--N9%20FINAL.pdf
Organisation for Economic Co-operation and Development (OECD). (2013). *Education at a Glance 2013: OECD indicators. Education at a Glance 2013*. Paris: OECD Publishing.
Organisation for Economic Co-operation and Development (OECD). (2014a). *PISA 2012 results in focus: What 15-year-olds know and what they can do with what they know*. Retrieved from http://www.oecd.org/pisa/keyfindings/pisa-2012-results-overview.pdf
Organisation for Economic Co-operation and Development (OECD). (2014b). *Education at a Glance 2014: OECD indicators*. Paris: OECD Publishing.
Pearson-Evans, A. (2006). Recording the journey: Diaries of Irish students in Japan. In M. Byram & A. Feng (Eds.), *Living and studying abroad. Research and practice* (Languages for intercultural communication and education, Vol. 12, pp. 38–63). Clevedon/Buffalo: Multilingual Matters Ltd.
Pitts, M. J. (2009). Identity and the role of expectations, stress, and talk in short-term student sojourner adjustment: An application of the integrative theory of communication and cross-cultural adaptation. *International Journal of Intercultural Relations, 33*(6), 450–462. doi:10.1016/j.ijintrel.2009.07.002.
Rao, N., & Chan, C. K. (2010). Moving beyond paradoxes: Understanding Chinese learners and their teachers. In C. K. K. Chan & N. Rao (Eds.), *Revisiting the Chinese learner. Changing contexts, changing education* (CERC studies in comparative education, Vol. 25, pp. 3–31). Dordrecht: Springer Science+Business Media B.V.
Rohrlich, B. F., & Martin, J. N. (1991). Host country and reentry adjustment of student sojourners. *International Journal of Intercultural Relations, 15*(2), 163–182. doi:10.1016/0147-1767(91)90027-E.
Sam, D. L., & Berry, J. W. (2010). Acculturation: When individuals and groups of different cultural backgrounds meet. *Perspectives on Psychological Science, 5*(4), 472–481. doi:10.1177/1745691610373075.
Samuelowicz, K. (1987). Learning problems of overseas students: Two sides of a story. *Higher Education Research & Development, 6*(2), 121–133.

Searle, W., & Ward, C. (1990). The prediction of psychological and sociocultural adjustment during cross-cultural transitions. *International Journal of Intercultural Relations, 14*(4), 449–464. doi:10.1016/0147-1767(90)90030-Z.

Siu, P. C. P. (1952). The sojourner. *The American Journal of Sociology, 58*(1), 34–44.

Smith, P., & Smith, S. N. (1999). Differences between Chinese and Australian students: Some implications for distance educators. *Distance Education, 20*(1), 64–80. doi:10.1080/0158791990200106.

Spencer-Oatey, H., & Xiong, Z. (2006). Chinese students' psychological and sociocultural adjustments to Britain: An empirical study. *Language, Culture and Curriculum, 19*(1), 37–53.

Trice, A. G. (2003). Faculty perceptions of graduate international students: The benefits and challenges. *Journal of Studies in International Education, 7*(4), 379–403. doi:10.1177/1028315303257120.

Turner, Y. (2006). Chinese students in a UK business school: Hearing the student voice in reflective teaching and learning practice. *Higher Education Quarterly, 60*(1), 27–51. doi:10.1111/j.1468-2273.2006.00306.x.

UNESCO Institute for Statistics (UIS). (2010). *Global Education Digest 2010: Comparing education statistics across the world.* Montreal: UIS. Retrieved from http://www.uis.unesco.org/template/pdf/ged/2010/GED_2010_EN.pdf

Volet, S. (1999). Cultural and multicultural perspectives on learning and motivation. *Asia Pacific Journal of Education, 19*(2), 9–14. doi:10.1080/0218879990190202.

Volet, S., & Renshaw, P. (1996). Chinese students at an Australian university: Adaptability and continuity. In D. A. Watkins & J. B. Biggs (Eds.), *The Chinese learner: Cultural, psychological, and contextual influences* (pp. 205–220). Hong Kong: CERC [u.a.].

Waldmeir, P. (2013, December 29). China parents count cost of sending children to overseas universities. *Financial Times.* Retrieved from http://www.ft.com/intl/cms/s/0/98c4a5ac-63c1-11e3-b70d-00144feabdc0.html#axzz3nfjN4Hjt

Wang, W.-h. (2009). *Chinese international students' cross-cultural adjustment in the U.S.: The roles of acculturation strategies, self-construals, perceived cultural distance, and English self-confidence.* Doctoral thesis. The University of Texas at Austin, Texas. Retrieved from http://repositories.lib.utexas.edu/bitstream/handle/2152/6588/wangw58087.pdf?sequence=2

Wang, K.-H. (2015). The use of dialogic strategy clusters for vocabulary learning by Chinese students in the UK. *System, 51,* 51–64. doi:10.1016/j.system.2015.04.004.

Wang(王孙禹), S., Kong(孔钢城), G., Lei(雷环), H., & Shao(邵小明), X. (2008). Gaige kaifang zilai woguo gaoshuiping daxue ji qi yhongdian xueke jianshe de huigu zu sikao (改革开放以来我国高水平大学及其重点学科建设的回顾与思考). *China Higher Education Research (*中国高教研究*), 4,* 1–6.

Ward, C. (2001). *The impact of international students on domestic students and host institutions.* Retrieved from http://www.educationcounts.govt.nz/publications/international/the_impact_of_international_students_on_domestic_students_and_host_institutions

Ward, C., & Kennedy, A. (1999). The measurement of sociocultural adaptation. *International Journal of Intercultural Relations, 23*(4), 659–677. doi:10.1016/S0147-1767(99)00014-0.
Ward, C., Bochner, S., & Furnham, A. (2006). *The psychology of culture shock.* London: Routledge. 2. ed., reprinted.
Watkins, D. A., & Biggs, J. B. (Eds.). (1996). *The Chinese learner: Cultural, psychological, and contextual influences.* Hong Kong: CERC [u.a.].
Xu, B. (2010). Research on mathematics education in China in the last decade: A review of journal articles. *Frontiers of Education in China, 5*(1), 130–155. doi:10.1007/s11516-010-0009-y.
Yung, W. (1909). *My life in China and America.* New York: Henry Holt and Company.
Zha, Q. (2011). Understanding China's move to mass higher education from a policy perspective. In R. Hayhoe, J. Lin, & Q. Zha (Eds.), *Portraits of 21st century Chinese universities in the move to mass higher education // Portraits of 21st century Chinese universities. In the move to mass higher education* (CERC Studies in Comparative Education, Vol. 30, pp. 20–57). Dordrecht: Springer.
Zhang, Z. (2011). A nested model of academic writing approaches: Chinese international graduate students' views of english academic writing. *Language and Literacy, 13*(1).
Zhang, Z., & Brunton, M. (2007). Differences in living and learning: Chinese international students in New Zealand. *Journal of Studies in International Education, 11*(2), 124–140. doi:10.1177/1028315306289834.
Zhao, T. (2007). *An ethnographic study of the intercultural adaption process between Chinese students and their British lecturers and fellow students in the UK.* Doctoral thesis. University of Southampton, Southampton.
Zhao, T., & Bourne, J. (2011). Intercultural adaptation—It is a two-way process: Examples from a British MBA programme. In L. Jin & M. Cortazzi (Eds.), *Researching Chinese learners. Skills, perceptions and intercultural adaptations* (pp. 250–273). Basingstoke/New York: Palgrave MacMillan.
Zheng, X., & Berry, J. W. (1991). Psychological adaptation of Chinese sojourners in Canada. *International Journal of Psychology, 26*(4), 451–470. doi:10.1080/00207599108247134.
Zheng, X., Sang, D., & Wang, L. (2004). Acculturation and subjective well-being of Chinese students in Australia. *Journal of Happiness Studies, 5*(1), 57–72. doi:10.1023/B:JOHS.0000021836.43694.02.
Zhou, J. (2010). *Zwischen "Elite von morgen" und "Liu Xue La Ji" ("Müllstudenten").* Münster: Verl.-Haus Monsenstein und Vannerdat.
Zhou, Y., & Todman, J. (2009). Patterns of adaptation of Chinese postgraduate students in the United Kingdom. *Journal of Studies in International Education, 13*(4), 467–486. doi:10.1177/1028315308317937.

CHAPTER 2

Review of Literature on International Chinese Students

Survival of the fittest.

Herbert Spencer

Research surveys of international students can be traced back almost 100 years. As early as 1915, the Committee on Friendly Relations among Foreign Students began conducting an annual census of foreign students and in 1921, the Institute of International Education (IIE) worked together with the Committee in circulating the census questionnaire (Du Bois 1956). Substantial empirical studies in the late 1950s and 1960s later contributed to the research on adaptation of international students at host universities (Aich 1963; Du Bois 1956; Galtung 1965; Selby and Woods 1966; Selltiz et al. 1963; Sewell and Davidsen 1961; Terhune 1964).

With a dramatic increase in Chinese students abroad in the last decade comes an abundance of new research literature, speaking to a number of questions. Are Chinese students' learning experiences different from those of other international students? Compared with international students from other countries, how have Chinese students' previous learning experiences and learning milieux affected their academic beliefs and styles? How do the host countries influence academic adjustment; that is, how do Chinese students in one country compare to those in another in terms of their adjustment? How do Chinese students compare to their peers from the host country in academic performance? Because research findings on international students apply to Chinese students, while investigation of Chinese students contributes to the overall research on international students, this chapter also considers and refers to the broader background of current research on international students toward investigating these questions. Figure 2.1 illustrates how this chapter considers current literature on 'international students' and 'international Chinese students' respectively.

This chapter reviews the landscape of current research on international Chinese students in terms of their pre-departure situation (motivation, preparation, and previous intercultural experience), overseas learning experience (academic and more general difficulties), psychological situation (academic, cultural, and acculturative stress), and intercultural communication

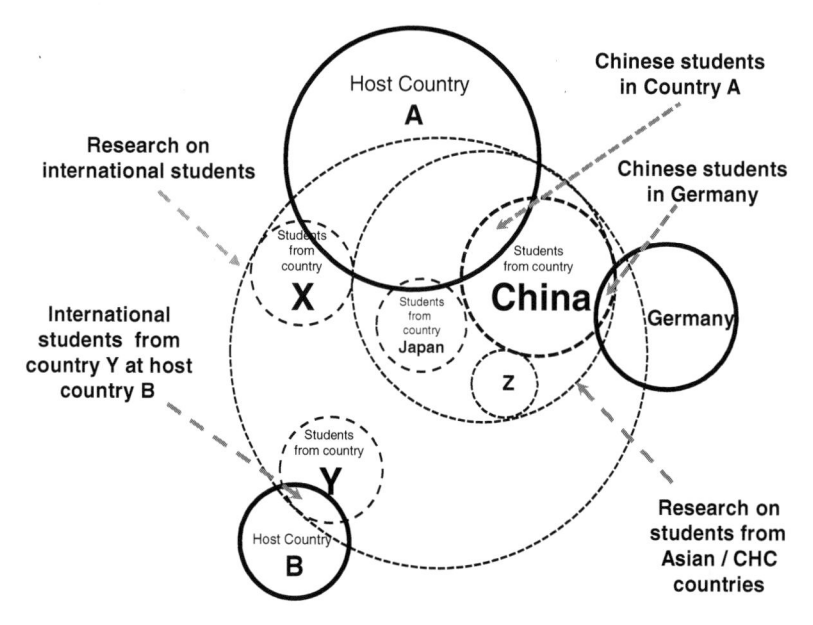

Fig. 2.1 Structure of literature review on Chinese students abroad. Note: The biggest *circle* with *dotted lines* in this figure stands for the overall research on international students and the subsequent *dotted circles* within represent the students from various countries (e.g. China, Japan, Country X, Y), while the *circles* with *solid lines* represent hosting countries (e.g. Germany, Country A, B). The part where the *circles* with *dotted lines* and *solid lines* overlap indicates the specific research on international students from Country X studying in Country A

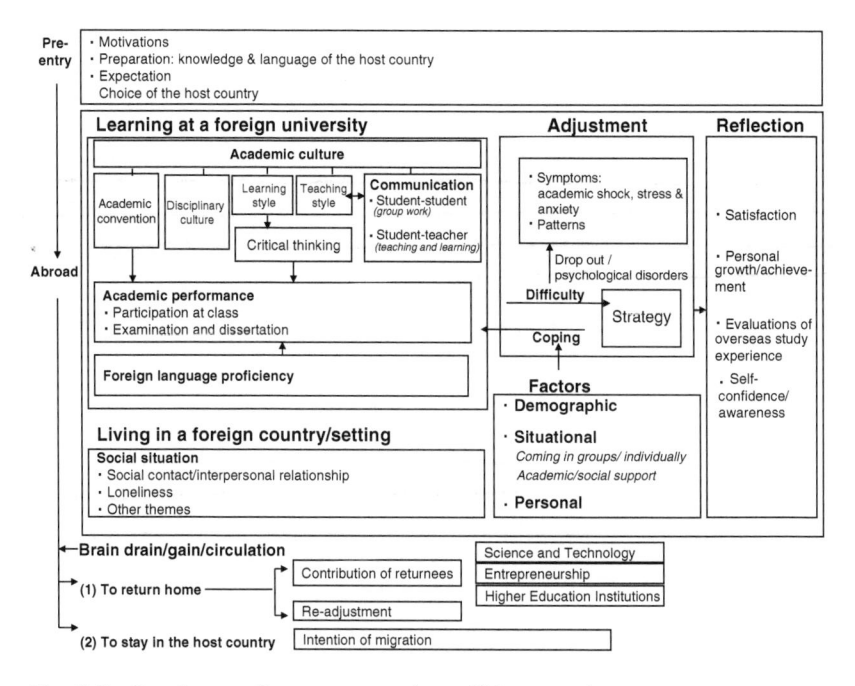

```
Pre-      • Motivations
entry     • Preparation: knowledge & language of the host country
          • Expectation
          • Choice of the host country
```

Learning at a foreign university	Adjustment	Reflection
Academic culture Academic convention / Disciplinary culture / Learning style / Teaching style / **Communication** • Student-student (group work) • Student-teacher (teaching and learning) Critical thinking	• Symptoms: academic shock, stress & anxiety • Patterns Drop out / psychological disorders **Difficulty** **Coping** → Strategy	• Satisfaction • Personal growth/achievement • Evaluations of overseas study experience • Self-confidence/awareness
Academic performance • Participation at class • Examination and dissertation		
Foreign language proficiency	**Factors** • Demographic	
Living in a foreign country/setting **Social situation** • Social contact/interpersonal relationship • Loneliness • Other themes	• Situational Coming in groups/ individually Academic/social support • Personal	

```
←— Brain drain/gain/circulation
                              ┌→ Contribution of returnees    │ Science and Technology
   ┌→ (1) To return home  ────┤                               │ Entrepreneurship
   │                          └→ Re-adjustment                │ Higher Education Institutions
   └→ (2) To stay in the host country    Intention of migration
```

Fig. 2.2 Landscape of current research on Chinese students

(current habits, difficulties, friendship patterns, and benefits). The factors influencing adjustment of international Chinese students are also reviewed. Figure 2.2 shows the scope of the research this chapter discusses.

Pre-departure Period: Student Readiness

A Customer-Based Orientation

Compared with research on international students' learning experience and intercultural communication in the host country, international students' pre-departure status (e.g. their motivation, readiness, previous intercultural experience, expectation, etc.), and so on, has not attracted much attention in the previous literature (Gong and Chang 2007). Moreover, existing studies have mainly been conducted in English-speaking countries, because of their popularity among prospective Chinese students. Chinese students regarded the USA and UK as 'first tier' destinations for their world-renowned reputation, while they viewed Canada, Australia, and New Zealand as 'second tier' for their attractive environment (Mazzarol et al. 2001). Chinese students also chose New Zealand as a secure, English-speaking location (Malcolm et al. 2004).

Because some countries charge international students higher tuition fees than native students, host countries regard Chinese students as important 'customers' or 'part of the commercial aspect of universities' (Montgomery 2010, p. 6). In Australia, where Chinese students accounted for 37.6 per cent of the total international enrolment in 2013 (IIE 2013), the education of Chinese students brings in considerable revenue to higher education institutions. In such a market-driven context, host countries have been paying much attention to the wants and needs of international students, as well as their satisfaction (Pan et al. 2008; Zhang and Brunton 2007). This tendency to focus on Chinese as business clients, however, overshadowed research on international students' personal, social, and individual purposes in pursuing study at a host university (Montgomery 2010).

Pre-departure: The 'Entry Points'

Durkin (2008b) regarded the pre-departure period as the stage for 'entry points' (p. 20) of overseas study, and summarized four factors that would ease these 'entry points' of the learning journey for international students: experience with western teaching methodology/employment; aptitude (e.g. intelligence, mental flexibility); formerly acquired academic skills (e.g. English competence, referencing and structuring essays); enthusiasm (e.g. personal motivation, open-mindedness, willingness to take risks), and so on. Borrowing from this framework, this section reviews the pre-departure situation of Chinese students by examining the following entry points: motivation, pre-departure preparation, and previous intercultural experience.

Motivation: Multifaceted Interests and Concerns
Research on the motivation of international students is valuable, as motivation has an impact on students' potential adjustment. Regarding overseas study, researchers have sought to formulate different theories explaining the multifaceted interests and concerns of international students and their families for going abroad. Based on the theory of migration, Lee (1966) proposed that the area of origin, the area of destination, intervening

obstacles, and personal factors all affected an individual's decision to go abroad. In response to this research, Altbach et al. (1985) argued that there were 'push' and 'pull' factors affecting a person's decision to study abroad. Key factors from the area of origin that may 'push' people to leave included poor quality educational facilities and lack of research facilities, whereas factors from the area of destination that may 'pull' people to study there included good quality education and availability of advanced research facilities. Zeilinger (2006) argued that international students' motivations could be categorized as intrinsic versus extrinsic. Intrinsic may include interest to learn the culture and language of the host country, while extrinsic factors may relate to using the host country as a springboard into further careers. For instance, career-oriented motivation and gaining experience for future employment (Obst and Forster 2006) or bigger chances of being admitted to the host university (Aich 1963) are major factors influencing students' decisions to study abroad.

However, international students from industrialized nations tend to differ from those from developing countries in their motivations to study abroad. According to Altbach et al. (1985), the former are typically motivated to achieve personal and cultural experience, while the latter are motivated for political and economic reasons. Similarly, Feldhaus and Logemann (2002) found that the origins of international students influenced their motivation, as the favorable academic conditions in the host country, such as low tuition fees and wider choices of courses, attracted Asian students most, while job-related reasons had the biggest influence on African students. Baas (2006), an Australian anthropologist, found that Indian students came to Australia not for the academic reputation of Australian universities but for the possibility of applying for permanent residence after graduation. With regard to Chinese students, Chirkov et al. (2007) investigated how the motivational factors of preservation and self-determination played a role in their decisions to study abroad and found that these factors had an independent effect on the cultural adaptation of the students.

Pre-departure Preparation
In addition to language capability, international students' prior knowledge of norms, customs, and values of the host country is also closely related to their adjustment (Church 1982; Kim 1988, Pruitt 1978). With regard to Chinese students, research of pre-departure preparation identified that

before going abroad they lack certain skills to cope with expected challenges. For instance, as Chinese students did not pay enough attention to the host academic culture before departure, they often arrived in a raw and unprepared state (Skyrme 2007). Chinese students often did not have sufficient prior knowledge of academic conventions practiced in the host country before their arrival, which led to difficulty in writing assignments, essays, and reports (Campbell and Li 2007).

Previous Intercultural Experience
International students' former intercultural experience is another important aspect which has not drawn enough attention in the research on the pre-departure period. Based on an eleven-country study of university exchange students, Klineberg and Hull (1979) indicated that international students who had overseas travel experience, or other prior foreign experiences with people local to the host culture, tended to have fewer problems in establishing contacts in the host country, enhancing international students' adjustment. Regarding Chinese students, they often have little intercultural experience, as studying abroad is their first time overseas. In this context, observation of Chinese students' previous intercultural experience is limited.

STUDYING IN AN INTERCULTURAL MILIEU

General Difficulties Challenging International Students

Student mobility[1] brings not only opportunities, but some challenges as well. Moving out of the familiar 'cultural comfort zone' (Kingston and Forland 2008, p. 211) and entering into a brand new educational milieu, international students often encounter difficulties in new social and academic environments. Problems that challenge international students were first acknowledged by two Christian associations[2] in the USA in 1922. The two associations organized committees to conduct a Survey of Foreign Students. The results identified seven major problems concerning international students' adjustment: academic or curriculum issues;

---

[1] Student mobility in this case refers to any opportunity for students to work or study abroad while undertaking their degree program—whether undergraduate or postgraduate.

[2] The two associations are the International Committee of the Young Men's Christian Association and the National Board of the Young Women's Christian Association.

language; economic problems; housing difficulties; inability to be socially accepted; health and recreation; and racial prejudice (Wheeler et al. 1925). It is worth noting that in comparing the difficulties pointed out by international students previously, difficulties reported by international students today have remained essentially the same over the last nine decades.

Difficulties Challenging Both Domestic and International Students
Church (1982) divided the common problems that international students encounter into three types: academic problems, personal problems, and sociocultural problems. Based on the different roles of international students abroad, Bochner (1972) summarized the problems challenging overseas students into four categories: the student as a foreigner living in an unfamiliar environment, as a representative of one's home country, as a university student facing unfamiliar demands, and as an adolescent encountering puzzles on the way toward becoming an adult. However, presenting these challenges in this way may actually be somewhat misleading. Except for Bochner's first two categories (i.e. the role as a foreigner and the representative of one's own nation), international students actually face problems more similar to their counterparts in the host country than many realize (Evans et al. 2009). Klein et al. (1971) argued that previous 'research focused on a special array of problems unique to international students (such as culture shock) may be potentially misleading or misguided' (p. 80). Both international students and students of the host country encounter challenges in adjusting to the demands of being a university student (Bochner 1972). Both sets of students need to transition from secondary to tertiary education and settle into the new academic environments (Sovic 2009), as well as take care of themselves through routine tasks, such as cooking and laundry (Turner 2002).

Nevertheless, some problems are particularly challenging for international students. Just because they face the same problems as domestic students does not mean they are equally equipped to face them. A longitudinal study undertaken in the USA found that international students, compared with their domestic counterparts, had greater difficulty in adjusting to their university at the beginning (Hechanova-Alampay et al. 2002); similarly, problems reported by international students in coping with the US education style, cultural differences, and language challenges seldom challenged domestic students (Zhai 2002). For instance, international doctoral students in the USA reported they were less informed about their degree programs than their American counterparts (Robinson

2005). Meanwhile, first-year international students in Australia reported more stress and anxiety (Ramsay et al. 1999) and felt less adjusted to university life than their domestic counterparts (Ramsay et al. 2007). Compared with local students, many international students also reported that they encountered more difficulties in seeking the appropriate type of assistance (Kaczmarek et al. 1994); practicing time management, study, revision, and examination skills; using the language of the host country; joining in class discussions; and embracing cultural values related to questioning authority figures (Burns 1991).

At the same time, lecturers in the host country observed that the mastery of foreign language, social interaction with home students, intercultural adaptation, and achieving academic goals were the main challenges to international students (Trice 2003). It is important to note that some problems are common to all international students, regardless of different cultural, religious, and educational backgrounds (McAdam 1972); yet Church (1982) pointed out that students from different cultures differ in the degree to which they experience certain problems. Asian international students encountered many common problems, such as pressure from academic demands, language barriers, financial concerns, depression, loneliness, and bicultural conflicts (Lin and Yi 1997).

Language Difficulties
Concerning difficulties challenging international students, foreign language proficiency is most likely the first problem, or at least the most common academic stressor, encountered by international students (Lin and Yi 1997). One study in Germany indicated that over four-fifths of international students pursuing their first degree at a tertiary level (e.g. traditional German first degrees such as *Magister* or *Diplom*) complained that they encountered language problems, and one-fourth indicated that this problem was 'serious or very serious' (Heublein et al. 2004). For international students, foreign language skills primarily affect aspects of their academic life, such as reading and writing skills and understanding and participation in class (Barker et al. 1991; Evans et al. 2009). Moreover, additional research suggests that foreign language proficiency affects international students' intercultural communication competence (Nishida 1985), social lives, and understanding of the host culture (Pan et al. 2008). International students who believed their English was adequate reported fewer academic difficulties (Xu 1991) and perceived less academic stress (Wan et al. 1992).

Academic Challenges

International students often are not familiar with the academic rituals or educational system of the host country, as well as the rules that apply in specific social or academic situations (Barker et al. 1991). In the host learning environment, the forms of lecture styles, assignments, assessments, and the grading system; study regulation; and the relationship between students and lecturers are totally new to most international students (Campbell and Li 2007; Ehlers and Hemmingsen 2011; Evans et al. 2009; Griffiths et al. 2005; Li et al. 2010; Maxwell 1974). Gu et al. (2010) also identified that over one-third of international students regarded their exposure to new pedagogies, such as answering questions in class or speaking up in class discussions, as a big challenge in the host country.

Scope and Intensity of Difficulties

The scope and intensity of difficulties that international students meet vary. First, in terms of duration, some problems may be for a short term and solved soon after students' arrival, while others may be longer lasting (Hammer 1992). Inspired by this, this section considers both daily and academic-based problems and includes a table to indicate their 'stubbornness' (Table 2.1).

Concerning short-term, daily problems, before departure international students are worried about finding accommodation, orienting themselves to the city, especially in terms of public transportation system, supermarkets, and shops, as well as mastering daily conversation for survival. Concerning academic-based difficulties in their new learning surroundings, international students must orient to themselves the facilities and structures of a new campus, and learn about the organization and processes

Table 2.1 Duration of difficulty based on daily life and academic situations

	Short-term difficulties	*Long-lasting difficulties*
Daily life-based difficulty	Accommodation Orientation in the city Survival language Visa issues	Intercultural communication with people in the host country Financial difficulty (Advanced) daily foreign language
Academic-specific difficulty	Getting oriented to the new campus Getting familiar with the expectation in the new learning surrounding (choice of courses)	Academic-based foreign language skills (writing and reading)

of a new university system. Though these problems are urgent, international students are typically able to obtain more information shortly after arrival and solve the problems quickly.

Long-term difficulties, whether specific to daily or academic challenges, might accompany some international students throughout their overseas experience. Take foreign language as an example: one-third of international students studying in Germany reported that they were challenged by German language difficulties during their entire study in Germany (Danckwortt 1984). Nevertheless, students found that their academic-based German language gradually improved, and they faced less difficulty in understanding class lectures, talking in seminars, and writing academic papers (Heublein 2009). Chinese students reported that the longer they were in Germany, the fewer new difficulties they would come across. Only 17 per cent of Chinese students who studied for one to two years in Germany regarded their German as 'very good or good'. For those who stayed for three to four years, the percentage increased to 22.2 per cent. Meanwhile, for Chinese students who study for 5–7 years in Germany, 100 per cent of them regard their German language as 'very good or good' (Guan 2007).

In spite of the difficulties discussed above, a large number of scholars are optimistic about the result of international students' adjustment and maintain that the majority of sojourners successfully manage the adjustment (Gu et al. 2010; Kim 1988; Sussman 2002). Most international students are capable and promising candidates, and temporary unsatisfying academic performance, especially during the first semester, does not tell the true potential of these students' academic competence. Though the enthusiasm for studying abroad is increasing, only those students who meet strict admission requirements are admitted. In terms of grades, Kingston and Forland (2008) reported that from 2003 to 2005, 51 per cent of international students and 53.8 per cent of domestic students achieved a satisfactory mark on their degrees at a London university. Another empirical study indicated first-year international students reported more frequency in terms of academic challenge, active and collaborative learning, student-faculty interaction, and technology use than their American counterparts (Zhao et al. 2005). Church (1982) estimated that approximately 80 per cent of international students made reasonable adjustments to their new cultural and institutional demands.

Specific Difficulties Challenging Chinese Students

Silence, Reticence, and Low Level of Participation

Regarding Chinese students, one of the focuses of the current research is on their academic experience in new educational settings. Much of the previous research documents that silence and low levels of participation in class have long been regarded as standard classroom communication behaviour for international Chinese students (Liu 2002). Some regard foreign language proficiency as one of the biggest barriers (Zhu 2007) causing this silence and preventing Chinese students from participating in class activities, particularly in the initial phase of overseas study. For instance, Chinese students studying in Australia encounter difficulties in dealing with tutorials, as they do not know how to behave or express their opinions in English confidently (Barker et al. 1991). However, reasons for such silence are obviously more complicated than simply insufficient foreign language in general.

In addition to lack of general foreign language proficiency, international Chinese students also lack knowledge of foreign language specific to their academic studies and major disciplines. Though most Chinese students meet the minimum language requirement before being admitted to enroll in courses, they lack the necessary specialized language skills for participating in the discussions. Holmes (2004) pointed out that difficulties in listening, understanding, and interacting were related to Chinese students' lack of familiarity with the skills of how to involve themselves in discussions. Lewthwaite (1996) further explained that international students lacked unspoken social and language skills such as 'rules for speaking' and 'turn taking'.

Second, there are many who believe silence cannot be attributed solely to language. The concept of class participation that Chinese students hold is very different from that practiced in western cultures, where expressing one's own opinion, challenging the teacher, and thinking critically is highly valued (Holmes 2004). Growing up in a teacher-oriented educational system, Chinese students are used to obeying authority and respecting 'class harmony' (Holmes 2008). Because of this, they tend to avoid offending a supervisor's senior and superior role (Stephens 1997). Additionally, showing respect to teachers is regarded as a virtue in Chinese culture. Zhou et al. (2005) attributed students' silence to the 'reciprocal cultural familiarity and power differentials between different languages, cultures and knowledge' (p. 307). Liu (2001) further suggested that this silence was caused by Chinese students' perception of 'face',[3] politeness, and social identity. Moreover, Cheng (2000) warned of the danger of overgeneralizing such silence, suggesting that most Chinese students, as well as students from other East Asian countries, were willing to participate in class discussions. However, one study further identified that Chinese students' silence occurred when they first encountered group work with Western students in class, but changed after a year (Wang 2012). Thus, such silence is not always a long-term occurrence for Chinese students.

Academic Culture
Mongillo (1995) defines academic culture as 'all those rules, practices, expectations, and behaviors of the teaching and learning process which are either implicitly or explicitly agreed upon by those involved in an educational setting' (p. 33). Although, in most cases, this learning culture works in its own environment, problems often emerge when a student transfers from his or her home academic culture to a new one.

Currently, many researchers argue that the difficulties Chinese students encounter results from the differences between Confucian and Socratic cultures in terms of academic discourse expectations regarding critical thinking and argumentation (Durkin 2011; Wan et al. 1992), expectation of teaching and learning styles (Choo 2007; Jin and Cortazzi 1997; Lin 2002; Wang and Byram 2011), perception of cultural adjustment problems (Jenkins and Galloway 2009), and perception of the dissertation process (Pilcher et al. 2011) between Chinese students and the lecturers of the host country. In dealing with the different academic cultures between the home and host countries, the majority of Chinese students opted for a *'Middle Way'* (Durkin 2008a), a strategy that synergized the traditional cultural academic values held by many Chinese students with Western academic norms, or demonstrated a concept of *'third space'* (Feng 2009), which contested binary or polar opposites between Confucian and Socratic cultures of learning.

Academic Writing
International Chinese students frequently have difficulty with 'referencing rules in academic writing' (Arkoudis and Tran 2007, p. 165), and they are often accused of committing plagiarism. Often, Chinese students commit

---

[3] Either translated as 面子 *mianzi* or 脸 *lian*. 'Face' can be interpreted as a person's reputation and feelings of prestige within multiple spheres, including the workplace, the family, personal friends, and society at large.

plagiarism unintentionally. Holmes (2004) regarded the allegiance to the established authorities in Chinese learning culture as a main cause of plagiarism. Students who could not master the foreign language also tended to write in a manner close to the original text. Another important point concerning academic writing is the culture of writing. Kavan and Wilkinson (2003) reviewed the differences of paragraphs and essay structure between Chinese and English writing, and further noted 'Chinese writing is more likely to be circular, looking at the subject from several angles and building up a foundation for later stating one's point' (p. 120). In this instance, it is important to keep in mind that academic writing problems are not unique to international students, but are experienced by domestic students in the host country, as well (Kingston and Forland 2008).

Autonomous Learning and Critical Thinking
Another two aspects that challenge Chinese students in particular are autonomous learning and critical thinking. Sun, J. (2010) compared German and Chinese universities and indicated that the former emphasized the self-organization of studies, while the latter was centrally organized. This difference becomes a big challenge for Chinese students, as one study reported that over 45 per cent of Chinese students had difficulty in organizing their studies, and 43.5 per cent were not confident of how they were managing their studies in Germany (Zhou 2010).

To many Chinese students, arguing and debating in class is a completely alien practice. They often view lecturers and authors as 'the ultimate authorities on "truth"' (Durkin 2008b, p. 21), and seldom challenge their views by raising questions. However, this 'good' practice in China often turns out to be unappreciated in western countries, where critical thinking and active questioning in class are highly valued. International Chinese students reported encountering difficulty in understanding the concept of critical thinking and in applying critical thinking in their studies (Huang 2008).

Intercultural Communication

Intercultural communication between international students and both lecturers and students of the host country composes a very important part of the learning experience for international students. Current research on intercultural communication on campus mainly focuses on quality and quantity of contact, friendship patterns, social support networks, and the functional roles of intercultural interactions.

Quantity and Quality

Quantity and Quality of Intercultural Communication Matters
Kim (1988) emphasizes two important attributes of sojourners' networks in the host country: the size and proportion of host ties and the strength of host ties. First, the size and proportion of host ties increases over time. Given time, sojourners will gradually increase communication with people in the host country, which is an important consideration often neglected in research. One empirical study confirmed this proposition and found that senior international students participated in diversity-related activities more frequently than their junior counterparts (Zhao et al. 2005). Second, the quality of intercultural communication is another important consideration often neglected in research. Kim (1988) criticized the 'normal practice' of studies on host and ethnic relations simply asking sojourners' number of ethnic and nonethnic friends in their interpersonal networks, emphasizing 'the strength of host ties' (p. 110). Brein and David (1971) shared Kim's opinion and believed that occurrence of contact or interaction was not the most important characteristic of a relationship; they further proposed that research should pay more attention to what actually happened during contact.

Intercultural Communication with Lecturers
In terms of student-teacher communication, international Chinese students tended to use vague language and indirect requests when communicating with lecturers (Yan and Berliner 2009). It is suggested that low contact between international Chinese students and their Australian lecturers accounted for Chinese students' difficulties in integrating to the host academic communities (Hui 2005). In addition to the foreign language insufficiency, which discourages Chinese students from communicating with their supervisors, division of the curriculum and time in the semester were the major variables influencing the student-faculty interaction (Cornelius et al. 1990).

Intercultural Communication with Peer Students: 'Hi-bye friends'
Another problem international students face is having few friends in the host country. Sovic (2009) described the intercultural relationship between many international and domestic students as *'Hi-bye friends'*, where these two groups of students say little more than 'hi' and 'bye' to each other, but have no deeper connection with each other. A nation-wide study in

the UK (UKCOSA 2004) found that 59 per cent of international students kept close contact either with co-nationals or with other international students; 43 per cent complained that it was hard to get to know UK students. Strikingly, only 15 per cent of international Chinese students in the UK reported they had any British friends. Apparently, Chinese students' insufficient intercultural communication with peers is more severe than for other international students. Chinese students' social interactions with non-Chinese were consistently identified as problematic (Spencer-Oatey and Xiong 2006). Instead of establishing contacts and relationships with the domestic students in the host country, Chinese students often stayed with their co-national friends (Klein et al. 1971; Turner 2002).

However, a situation of 'gravitation toward compatriots' (Brown 2009, p. 446) is not exclusive to Chinese students: international students from other countries are also inclined to have friends from the same culture (Bochner 1981; Church 1982). One classic study with over 2,500 international students in eleven countries conducted by Klineberg and Hull (1979) demonstrated that a majority of international students had primary bonds with co-nationals. For example, Japanese students in the USA spent 88 per cent of their study time and 82 per cent of their social time with other Japanese (Trice and Elliott 1993). Another study reported that 70 per cent of international Japanese students regarded their compatriots as their 'first three closest persons' in the UK, a tendency which stays stable over the year (Ayano 2006).

However, this inability to make cross-cultural friendships can be found in the German context, as well. In Germany, one survey conducted at four universities indicated that four-fifths of international students complained they had insufficient contact with their German counterparts or lecturers; about one-third of international students reported poor contact with lecturers and domestic students at German universities as a 'big' or 'very big' challenge to them (Heublein et al. 2004). Another study conducted in Germany identified that merely one-third of international students regarded their contact with German students as 'very good' or 'good' (38.3 per cent) and about 7.4 per cent of them had no contact with German students at all (Peroz 2008).

Reasons for Limited Intercultural Communication
There are many reasons for limited intercultural communication, including lack of foreign language proficiency and motivation, cultural differences, worry about affecting relationships in the co-national circle, and psychological

self-defense. These factors have a significant influence on the development of student relationships, and thus play an important role throughout the study abroad experience.

First, foreign language skills diminish the distance between international students and their host counterparts (Brown 2009). This does not only refer to the language skills of the international students. In some non-English speaking countries, local students' foreign language capacity can also be a decisive factor promoting intercultural communication (Heublein et al. 2007).

Students' motivations to engage with the community also matters, both in terms of the school environment specifically and the host country community as a whole. As the motivation to study abroad may be primarily instrumental rather than integrative (Grimshaw 2011), some international students have little motivation for interacting with domestic students. At the same time, students in the host country may also lack motivation to interact with international students. Surveys indicate that students in host countries often do not realize the benefits of intercultural contact with international students (e.g. interaction with international students can increase domestic students' intercultural skills without needing to go abroad). Thus, they demonstrate little motivation in interacting with international students (Brown 2009; UNITE 2006).

International students often reported cultural differences as another primary factor influencing the intercultural communication with their native counterparts throughout the process of relationship development (Bochner et al. 1976; Chen 2007). International and domestic student groups may believe they have few things to share with each other. For example, Chinese students studying in the USA reported that they did not have common topics or interests with their native peers (Feng 1991; Lin 2002). American students tended to talk about sports like football and basketball, which Chinese students knew little about. Similarly, Japanese students studying in the UK reported frustration in communicating with British peers, as they both lacked interesting ideas to share with each other (Ayano 2006). Furthermore, international students studying in the UK commented negatively that 'pub culture' (i.e. the prevalence of heavy drinking and the role of alcohol in social activities in the UK) was a substantial barrier for those who did not drink alcohol when getting to know UK peers outside the classroom (Turner 2002; UKCOSA 2004).

Some international students were afraid of making friends with local students in the host country and kept a distance so as to avoid causing jealousy in their co-national circle. Klein et al. (1971) suggested 'withdrawal is enforced by the noticeable lack of tolerance that exists within the subculture (p. 85)'. For instance, Japanese students reported that friendships with co-national Japanese students and British students were 'often incompatible' with each other. Having British friends often caused other Japanese students to be jealous, which sometimes then led to exclusion from the co-national network (Ayano 2006).

The jealousy in co-national circles actually reveals how international students may have paradoxical attitudes toward intercultural communication. On the one hand, they admire co-national friends who are able to establish good relationships with local students; on the other hand, their insufficient foreign language proficiency and intercultural communication skills prevent them from forming these relationships themselves. To deal with their own stress and frustration, members of the co-national community may exert pressure on those these 'traitors', which jeopardizes the opportunity for intercultural communication between international students and students of the host country. Compared with other international students, Chinese students have more powerful ties in their co-national circles and thus often encounter this dilemma. British students mentioned that the Chinese student community is 'apparently inward-looking and even unwelcoming when individuals have made overtures of friendship' (Turner 2002, p. 18).

Another important factor that limits intercultural communication is that international students feel uncertain and anxious about contact with the students in the host country. Gudykunst (2004) proposed Anxiety and Uncertainty Management theory, which explains how higher uncertainty and anxiety leads to less effective interpersonal and intergroup communication. Another similar theory that explains the problem is the protecting-mechanism/defensive reactions theory. Kim (1988) argued that human beings have a tendency to keep a variety of variables ordered in their internal meaning structure; whenever they receive messages that disrupt this internal order, they feel anxious and unbalanced. Thus, in order to prevent feelings of anxiety or uncertainty, some international students simply avoid communicating with their counterparts in the host nation.

Friendship Patterns: A Functional Model

Bochner et al. (1977) suggested a functional model for the development of foreign students' friendship patterns from a social psychology perspective. They identified sojourners as belonging to three social networks: a primary, mono-cultural (i.e. co-national) network; a secondary, bi-cultural (i.e. foreign student-host national) network; and a third multi-cultural (i.e. friendship between non-compatriot foreign students) network.

Co-national Networks
International students are inclined to have friends from the same culture (Bochner 1981). The 'mono-culture network' is 'a type of extended ethnic network' that emphasizes the contact with friends and family at home. This plays a significant role in adjustment abroad (Pearson-Evans 2006, p. 44). First, co-national friends serve a protective function and provide international students with 'psychological security, self-esteem, and a sense of belonging' (Church 1982, p. 551–52). According to Bochner and his colleagues (1977), co-national friends in the host country played the role of *'gatekeeper'*, *'patronage'*, or *'culture broker'*. After all, people prefer the familiar when seeking safety and stability in the world (Maslow 1943).

Co-national friendships provided international students with important elements such as structure in the new world, mutual esteem and approval, suitable marriage partners, substitutes for parents in courting, and relief from the stresses of coping with new ways and a strange tongue (Klein et al. 1971). Such 'material, informational, emotional, educational, and entertainment services' (Kim 1988, p. 64) facilitates sojourners' adaptation in the initial phase.

Second, co-national friends play a role as reference groups. For instance, within their co-national network, international students refine and create new expectations for studying abroad (Pitts 2009). Sharing similar experiences together makes students feel closer to each other and reduces expectation gaps, enabling sojourners to adjust better over time. In short, contact with co-nationals provides 'the reassurance of instrumental and emotional support that was unforthcoming on the part of the host community' (Brown 2009, p. 246). With this in mind, though the overwhelming majority of research encourages intercultural communication between international and host students and regards co-national friendship as a negative influence on adjustment, contact with fellow country persons in dormitories, clubs, and living arrangements should not be discouraged (Pedersen 1980).

Bi-cultural Networks
Bochner et al. (1977) argued that international students' networks with local students were based on professional and career-oriented purposes, as the native peers 'control the desired academic resources' (p. 279). Through

contact with locals, the sojourner learns patterns, trends, consistencies, and inconsistencies in the host environment (Kim 1988), which facilitates the academic or professional aspirations of international students. Although some senior co-national students may also provide significant information and share their personal experience in detail, host national friends provide more firsthand 'insider' information. Some international students regard the establishment of relationships with host students as 'more difficult' and 'more demanding' (Pearson-Evans 2006, p. 45). Nevertheless, initial utilitarian relationships may later turn out to be long-lasting friendships.

Multi-cultural Networks
In a multi-cultural[4] environment, international students interact with students from many countries, not just the home country. In many ways, non-compatriot international students have a shared 'international' identity. One study conducted at a German university indicated that over one-third of international students regarded their communication with German students as poor. In contrast, over half of them viewed their communication with other international students (57.1 per cent) or with co-national students (56.2 per cent) as either 'good' or 'very good' (Peroz 2008). However, Bochner and his colleagues (1977) indicated 'the impetus for the formation of multi-cultural bonds is usually quite weak' (p. 280).

Benefits of Intercultural Communication

Several points support the value of intercultural communication for the positive adjustment of sojourner students in the host country. Sovic (2009) affirmed that international students benefited from intercultural communication in terms of 'better academic achievement, a lower drop-out rate, better self-motivation, better usage of campus services, less alienation and homesickness, a better sense of identity, improved fluency in English, greater satisfaction with courses, and greater enjoyment of university and of life generally' (p. 748).

Second, intercultural communication with host nationals increases degree of satisfaction. A good social interaction with local counterparts facilitates international students' personal adjustment and general sojourn satisfaction (Hull 1978; Klineberg and Hull 1979). Swell and Davidsen

---

[4] For purposes of this study, multi-culture is defined as bonds between non-compatriot foreign students.

(1961) also found a direct correlation between the quality and quantity of social interaction between Scandinavian and Americans students and overall satisfaction with their sojourn. Similarly, international students with local friends were more likely to feel satisfied with their stay in the UK (UKCOSA 2004). Pruitt (1978) also indicated that African students who spent their leisure time with American families and white American students held more positive attitudes toward American culture. Chinese students who failed to establish close relationships with local people in the USA held an unfriendly view of Americans and regarded the local people as 'insincere, superficial, and incapable of making real friendships' (Klein et al. 1971).

Third, intercultural communication helps international students to maintain psychological well-being. Research shows that positive and frequent contact with host counterparts facilitates international students' psychological well-being. Ramsay et al. (2007) found that freshmen who felt well adjusted reported higher levels of social companionship support than those who felt less adjusted. International students who mainly interact with non-natives are likely to experience more acculturative stress (Poyrazli et al. 2004), while those who keep closer contact with native people achieve self-confidence, well-being, and satisfaction (Antler 1970; Klein et al. 1971; Klineberg and Hull 1979; Wang 2009). This in turn generates a more direct impact on their sociocultural adaptation.

Psychological Issues: The Fight Against Stress

International students feel stressed and anxious for multiple reasons: foreign language anxiety, academic demands and other educational stressors, sociocultural stressors, cultural distance, loneliness and homesickness, psychosociocultural issues, financial issues, political concerns, and so on (Brown and Holloway 2008; Chen 1999; Cheng and Erben 2011; Pan et al. 2008; Yeh and Inose 2003). International Chinese students' psychological health has also caught researchers' attention, as Wei et al. (2007) found a positive association between acculturative stress and depression among Chinese students.

Academic Shock

Although the term *cultural shock* (Oberg 1960) has been frequently used to describe the initial experience of adjustment to a new cultural environment, not much research is available on how international students experience their adjustment to, specifically, a new learning environment specifically (Griffiths et al. 2005). Nevertheless, academic difficulty is the main form of stress experienced by international students (Wan et al. 1992) and Buddington (2002) found that stress and grade point average were significantly inversely correlated. At the beginning of their study abroad, international students often encounter information overload and unfamiliarity with the educational institution (Westwood and Barker 1990). Some scholars refer to this phenomenon as *academic shock* (Ehlers and Hemmingsen 2011), *learning shock* (Griffiths et al. 2005; Gu 2011), or *academic culture shock* (Li et al. 2010, p. 394). All these terms can be interpreted as 'some unpleasant feelings and difficult experiences' (Gu 2011, p. 221) or 'experiences of acute frustration, confusion and anxiety' (Griffiths et al. 2005, p. 275) that international students encounter when they are exposed to a new learning environment.

A primary reason for academic shock is the difference between expectations and learning traditions in the home and host country, which international students seldom foresee. Pitts (2009) pointed out that the gap between international students' expectations and the reality of the sojourn was one contributor to adjustment stress, and Brown (2008a, b) further found that academic tasks that reflect academic cultural differences or that demand language ability were closely related to stress. For instance, many international students have difficulty in understanding the highly decentralized and autonomous nature of American education (Yan and Berliner 2009) or they have 'mismatched cross-cultural educational expectations' (Zhou et al. 2011, p. 234). Chinese students studying in the USA encountered high academic stress (Yan and Berliner 2009), and reported higher levels of anxiety than their counterparts in the host country (Lin et al. 2001). In particular, Chinese students are more likely than others to be concerned about academic failure (Smith and Smith 1999).

Griffiths et al. (2005) identified three coping strategies adopted by international students to deal with academic shock: talking to others; diversion or self-care; and planning, rationalizing, and contemplation. Chen (1995) focused on East Asian students and found that they often tried to overcome discouragement through reading, meeting friends, and getting involved in a hobby.

Acculturative Stress, Symptoms, and Support

Berry et al. (1987) defined the concept of *acculturative stress* as 'one kind of stress, that in which the stressors are identified as having their source in the process of acculturation; in addition, there is often a particular set of stress behaviors which occurs during acculturation' (p. 492). Acculturative stress has a significant effect on international students' depression (Wei et al. 2007). Given this, international students' stress deserves more attention in research.

Acculturative Stress and Symptoms
Being far away from parents and friends, international students encounter clinical depression and loneliness at a significantly higher rate than students in the host country do (Oei and Notowidjojo 1990). For instance, international students in Australia experienced cultural stress, especially in relation to issues of separation from family and a familiar way of life (Thomson et al. 2006). Based on 200 intensive interviews, Sawir et al. (2008) found that two-thirds of the international students in Australia experienced problems of loneliness, particularly in the early months. Jabeen Khan (1988) explored the critical life situation of international students from a psychological perspective and found that about 65 per cent suffered from 'sadness' and 51 per cent felt 'lonely'.

Research has also shed light on Chinese students' acculturative stress, and considerable research probes the psychological health of international Chinese students in terms of their acculturation and subjective well-being (Zheng et al. 2004), psychological and sociocultural adjustment (Wang 2009), psychological adaptation (Zheng and Berry 1991), anxiety (Lin et al. 2001), transitional stress (Jou and Fukada 1996a), and social self-efficacy (Lin and Betz 2007). Based on both quantitative and qualitative data, Spencer-Oatey and Xiong (2006) found that Chinese students' social interaction with non-Chinese and difficulties in adjusting to daily life were correlated with Chinese students' psychological stress. Similarly, Pak et al. (1985) found that confidence with English was positively related to linguistic assimilation into local community and to several components of psychological adjustment. Like other international students, Chinese students experienced homesickness as a common psychological reaction while studying in the UK (Lu 1990).

Support for Fighting Against Stress
Research has shed light on solutions for coping with stress at the same time that social and academic support systems for international students attract increasing attention. Research has reviewed the forms (traditional and online) of support networks (Ye 2006) and analyzed the effect of social support on students' adjustment (Jou and Fukada 1995a, b, 1996b).

Jou and Fukada (1997) discussed stress and support of mental and physical health of Chinese students in Japan and suggested that Chinese students with higher levels of perceived or received support often reported greater happiness. Poyrazli et al. (2004) found that social support and English proficiency were primary factors in international students' different levels of acculturative stress in the USA.

Failing to Adjust: Dropouts and Psychiatric Disorders

Dropouts

Surprisingly, international student retention statistics are not provided in government higher education reports (Evans et al. 2009). For example, in the UK, only information about the national dropout rate among all students is available—it is 21 per cent (Loveys 2011)—while specific statistics on international student dropout rates are unavailable. Evans et al. (2009) attributed the lack of data to the low ratio of international students on campus and a lack of consideration of the dropout rates specific to international students. Nevertheless, available research does indicate that for international students, failing to meet psychological or academic challenges leads to dropping out.

There are two prominent exceptions to the general lack of statistics comparing the dropout rate between international students and all other students in the host country. Germany presents statistics of international students' dropout rates[5] (in German: *Studienabbruchraten*) in its annual report *Wissenschaft weltoffen*.[6] In the latest publication, the dropout rate of first-year international students[7] (in German: *Studienanfängerjahrgang*)

---

[5] According to *Wissenschaft weltoffen*, the term 'student dropout' refers to 'former students who commenced a first degree at a German higher education institution, but ultimately left the German higher education system without completing the degree. Students who changed their subjects or their higher education institution are not taken into consideration' (DAAD and DZHW 2015, p. 37).

[6] *Wissenschaft weltoffen* presents data on the international nature of studies and research in Germany, including themes as foreign students in Germany, German students abroad, and international mobility of students.

[7] It is paramount to clarify the definition of 'international students' in Germany. In the German language, international students are called *Ausländische Studierende*. According to the criteria of whether students received their higher education entrance qualification in Germany or in another country, official government statistics have differentiated between *Bildungsausländer* (mobile international students) and *Bildungsinländer* (non-mobile international students). The differentiation between these two groups of international students is important: the criterion for applying to the university and applying for the financial support

at the bachelor's level in 2008–2009 was 41 per cent, which decreased by 6 per cent from 2006 to 2007. The rate for German students for the 2008–2009 academic year was 33 per cent at universities and 23 per cent at universities of applied sciences. Thus, international students are less likely to successfully complete a bachelor's program than their German counterparts. However, the results of master's programs are far more positive. Here, the dropout rate for international students in 2010 was 9 per cent, which is more similar to the figure for German students (11 per cent at universities and 7 per cent at universities of applied sciences) (DAAD and DZHW 2015). Chinese students, together with other students from East Asian countries, have the lowest dropout rate among all international students in Germany.

Another exception is research that identifies the retention rates of international students and all students in the USA as roughly equivalent (Andrade 2009). In looking at 'First-Year Persistence' (2006–2007) and 'Six-Year Graduation' (1999), international students' persistence over the first year is 80.2 per cent compared to 80.1 per cent for all students, while their six-year graduation rate is 58.7 per cent, compared to 57.8 per cent for all students. Andrade (2009) further attributed the parity in retention and graduation rates between international and host country students to the numerous programs developed by host institutions, which attached importance to the adjustment of international students.

Psychiatric Disorders
Mental illness is an even more acute result for international students who are unable to adjust to life and study in the host country. The percentage of international students suffering depression or other psychiatric disorders is limited, and mental health of international students requires further research.

For Chinese students, this issue is particularly urgent: in contrast with their native peers in the host country, Chinese students experiencing mental health issues will not take advantage of the counseling and wellness

according to *Bundesausbildungsförderungsgesetz* (Federal Education and Trainings Assistance Act for supporting university students in Germany) between *Bildungsausländer* and *Bildungsinländer* is different: the latter can apply for it while the former cannot. In addition, although *Bildungsinländer* have a lower university participation rate than German students, the learning and living situation of *Bildungsinländer* is more similar to the German students than to *Bildungsausländer*. Unless specified, in this book, the term 'international students' in Germany refers to the *Bildungsausländer*.

services in the host university. Such means of support is new to Chinese students, who hold that unless their problems are very severe, it is shameful for them to use the services and talk about their problems. Chinese students who experience mental health challenges may often appear inconspicuous and are not easy to be identified. They may self-isolate to heal the 'wound' by avoiding communication with others or by playing computer games. Failure to seek professional treatment or therapy can lead to an even worse psychological situation. Some news reports over the past few decades detailed incidents involving international Chinese students who had difficulty adapting to their academic life abroad, and developed mental illnesses that led to terrible consequences. In 1991, a Chinese graduate student shot people in his department after his dissertation did not achieve an academic award. In 2000, a Chinese graduate student shot his advisor after learning his research contract would not be renewed. Nine years later, a Chinese student with mental illness murdered another Chinese student while trying to help the latter with the adjustment process at the beginning of the school year.[8]

Factors Influencing Adjustment

Scholars have long been exploring the possible factors that affect the adjustment of international students—why some international students successfully deal with the academic and cultural challenges in the host country, while others fail to manage the transition. Researchers have probed these factors from the perspectives of psychology, sociology, social psychology, and so on. Church (1982) summarized the variables influencing adjustment into three categories: (1) background variables (nationality, status, language proficiency, age, educational level, and previous cross-cultural experience), (2) situational variables (social interaction and overlapping membership conflict), and (3) personality variables. Inspired by Church's categories, factors influencing international students' adjustment will be reviewed from background, situational, and personal perspectives.

---

[8] The source of news retrieved 30 August 2015 from http://www.nytimes.com/1991/11/04/us/iowa-gunman-was-torn-by-academic-challenge.html; http://www.washington.edu/alumni/columns/sept00/choices.html; and http://www.washingtonpost.com/wp-dyn/content/article/2009/01/22/AR2009012200943.html respectively.

Background Factors

The most widely studied background variables are demographic factors (gender, age, nationality, culture, among others), foreign language proficiency, education level, and previous cross-cultural experience (Church 1982; Kim 1988). The main focus here is on how gender, foreign language proficiency, and academic disciplines have an impact on international students' adjustment.

Gender

Some studies suggest that female international students report more adjustment problems than their male counterparts (Church 1982). According to these studies, females appear to have a different stress-symptom structure (Dyal and Chan 1985) or greater behavioral and physiological reactions to academic stressors (Misra and Castillo 2004). Misra and Castillo (2004) further explained that this might result from their gender role in society, as women are expected to express their emotion. Nevertheless, some empirical research indicates that female students actually have an easier time than male students in adjusting to the host country. For instance, Zheng et al. (2004) found that female Chinese students were happier and more psychologically adjusted than males in Australia, and Guan (2007) similarly indicated that male Chinese students had more difficulty in transferring to the German educational system. Kim (1988) held that gender itself did not qualify as a theoretically sound explanatory factor for the observed differences in adaptation.

Foreign Language Proficiency

Studies do not agree on whether foreign language proficiency can predict academic success or adjustment. Some research indicates that acquisition of the host language facilitates sojourners' participation in the new environment. A good mastery of the foreign language promotes better academic achievement and performance (Kim 1988). For instance, Chinese students' Korean language proficiency proved to have a moderate effect on their academic success at Korean universities (Yan and Cheng 2015). Lecturers' observations also indicated the positive influence of foreign language skill on international students' success in the host country (Trice 2003). However, Pearson-Evans (2006) argued that in spite of the fact that good foreign language skills provided potential for deeper communication with people in the host culture, foreign language proficiency did not automatically facilitate adjustment.

Academic Disciplines

Becher (1987) proposed that different academic disciplines had their own cultures and held that there were identifiable patterns within the relationship between the 'knowledge focus' and 'knowledge communities' of each discipline. Disciplines differently relate to international students' adjustment to the new academic environment, in part because of how foreign language skills relate to success in a discipline. Feng (1991) explored the role of foreign language proficiency in academic disciplines and suggested that natural and applied science students adjusted better than social science students did in general, as hard science majors are not expected to have as high a competence in language skills as social science majors. Hu (2004) drew a similar conclusion that high proficiency in French (i.e. the host country language of the study) was more important in some disciplines (e.g. humanities) than in others (e.g. Science, Technology, Engineering, and Mathematics, STEM). Chen (1992) found that, for science students, oral and written language skills were less difficult than for humanities students and believed that science students adapted to academic tasks more easily than humanities students.

Situational Factors

Klein et al. (1971) pointed out that situational variables including intercultural communication, cultural distance and geographic proximity, and support from the host environment exerted an important influence on students' adaptations and behaviors.

Intercultural Communication

Kim (1988) held that successful adaptation of sojourners was related to their ability to communicate in a given cultural environment. Empirical research indicates that friends in the host culture provide international students with encouragement, support, and advice (Wan et al. 1992); at the same time, they play a role as interpreters of the host culture to the international student and are regarded as 'the best source of information about host cultural norms' (Brown 2009, p. 442). Likewise, Furnham Bochner, and Lonner (1986) regarded social contact with local people as one of the most important factors influencing the coping process of students at a foreign university. Thus, intercultural communication facilitates international students' academic adjustment, improves their foreign language proficiency and knowledge of the host culture, and lowers the probability of dropping out (Brown 2009; Westwood and Barker 1990). Brown and Holloway (2008) contended that international students who more frequently interacted with native networks and practiced foreign language reached adjustment more quickly than those who only stayed in the co-national group. Accordingly, international students who felt isolated or were unable to make friends were very likely to have difficulty in academic adaptation (Zhou and Todman 2009).

Cultural Distance and Geographic Proximity
Although the construct 'cultural distance' is often applied in the field of international business (Shenkar 2001), Sussman (2002) proposed that cultural distance between the home and host country had an influence on adjustment, and particularly on the cultural values that the sojourners held. Kim (1988) believed that the greater the disparity between the two cultures, the larger the cultural gap to be bridged. Furnham and Bochner (1982) likewise reached the conclusion that cultural distance and social difficulty were strongly related. Further empirical research supports this cultural distance hypothesis. Furukawa (1997) found that cultural distance had a strong influence on the psychological adjustment of international exchange students: the greater the difference between the host country and international students' home country, the more the students demonstrated psychological distress. Redmond (2000) found that intercultural competencies differed among international students based on respective cultural distance between home and host cultures. The result of an international comparative study suggested that geographic proximity and rate of social mobility had an influence on international students' adjustments and degrees of acceptance of the foreign culture (Galtung 1965). For instance, Sewell and Davidsen's (1961) finding echoed Galtung's assumption, reporting that Scandinavian students had little difficulty in adjusting to life in the USA, while Asian international students in New Zealand reported significantly more difficulty than their European counterparts did (Ward 2004).

Support from the Host Environment
Kim (1988) identified two host environmental conditions: receptivity and conformity. The former condition describes an attitude of acceptance in the host culture, while the latter describes an expectation that the newcomers will follow and observe the cultural and communication norms of the host. Leung (2001) found supportive social relationships were important for overseas students' psychological and academic adaptation; and Ramsay et al. (2007) pointed out that well-adjusted international students significantly

benefitted from higher levels of social companionship support. Additionally, academic support plays an important role in facilitating international students' adjustment. Wilcox et al. (2005) examined the type of support international students received from friends and tutors in their courses as well as support provided by friends alone and found the former to be more instrumental and informational oriented. A longitudinal study undertaken by Boyer and Sedlacek (1987), covering eight semesters, indicated that availability of a support person and self-confidence were important determinants of adjustment to academic demands and attainment of academic success.

Nevertheless, results indicated that some lecturers at the host university were neither ready for the cultural differences nor able to provide help to international students. Universities, in the meantime, have made little effort to provide advisory services (Danckwortt 1984). For instance, in Germany, a mere 26 per cent of international students reported having received help and service from German lecturers (Breitenbach and Danckwortt 1961).

Personal Factors

In addition to the background and situational factors, factors closely related to the international students' personal issues, such as personality and duration of stay in the host country, also have an impact on students' adjustment overseas.

Personality
Ward et al. (2004) suggested that psychological adaptation was associated with extraversion, agreeableness, conscientiousness, and neuroticism, while sociocultural adaptation was linked to greater extraversion and less neuroticism. Klein et al. (1971) also regarded self-confidence and self-esteem as significant predictors of adaptation. Specifically, emotional stability appears to be a positive predictor for academic performance and psychological well-being, and a negative predictor for experienced difficulties. In contrast, cultural empathy, open-mindedness, and social initiative are more important predictors for indicators of social adjustment, such as having friends and receiving social support (Long et al. 2009). Other researchers emphasized the importance of an open attitude held by international students to adjustment. Kim (1988) proposed that those who held an open attitude to the host culture were likely to deal with the uncertainties and challenges in the host country better.

Duration of Stay

Wang (2009) suggested that length of residence is an important factor concerning Chinese students' cross-cultural adjustment. Zheng et al. (2004) suggested that the acculturation process resulted in acculturative stress initially, but that adaptation might reduce Chinese students' acculturative stress after a span of residence in the host country. Similarly, Wei et al. (2007) found that length of time in the USA, acculturative stress, and maladaptive perfectionism were the predictors of depression of Chinese students.[9]

LIVING IN A FOREIGN COUNTRY

Studying abroad is a challenging task academically for international students, but simply living in a foreign country is not easy either. In addition to academic and psychological problems, other challenges referenced in research on Chinese students are managing finances and daily life in the host country.

Financial Problems

One problem that typically challenges some international students from developing countries is financial difficulty (Chen 1995; Feng 1991). The majority of Chinese students are self-funded, and depend on their parents or part-time jobs to finance their study abroad. Financial difficulties can also often have negative side effects on Chinese students' adjustment. In order to meet their financial needs, some Chinese students take part-time jobs on the weekends. As a result, they have little time to participate in other social activities. Furthermore, in order to save money, some students choose to live together with other Chinese students, which in turn leaves them few opportunities to practice the language or interact with host people (Feng 1991).

Daily Life

There are a large number of widely scattered research topics concerning the daily life of international students. For example, studies have examined topics including international students' accommodation and living situa-

---

[9] Results indicated that low maladaptive perfectionism played a buffering effect for those who had been in the USA longer, but had the opposite effect for those who had been in the USA for a shorter period. In contrast, the effect of high maladaptive perfectionism shows no significant difference between the two groups (Wei et al. 2007).

tions (Deutscher Städtetag 2000; Krüger 2001), internet use and loneliness (Wang and Sun 2009), social contact and discrimination (Feldhaus and Logemann 2002; Krüger 2001; Peroz 2008), and financing for studies (Deutscher Städtetag 2000; Peroz 2008).

Concerning Chinese students, there are a large number of research topics, seemingly even more wide ranging, discussing their cultural identities (Ding 2009), cultural values (Lowe and Corkindale 1998), gambling (Li and Tse 2015; Li et al. 2006), holiday behaviors (Ryan and Zhang 2007), name change (Kang 1971), eating problems (Davis and Katzman 1999), changes in eating patterns after living abroad (Pan et al. 1999), and online learning (Zhao and McDougall 2008).

Finishing the Overseas Study

Upon completion of their degrees, international students must decide whether to return home, stay in the host country, or even go to another country. As with research on pre-departure situations of international students, however, the influence of overseas learning experience on students' professional and personal lives after returning is under-researched (Gu and Schweisfurth 2015) but receiving increasing attention.

Returning Home

The latest statistics announced by the Ministry of Education of the People's Republic of China (MOE) indicates that from 1978 to 2014, a total of 1.8 million overseas Chinese students returned to China after completing their studies (Fig. 2.3). The number of returnees increased from 248 in 1978 to 364,800 in 2014 (MoE 2015), with an average annual growth rate of 37 per cent. Although the number of Chinese students going abroad has increased much faster than that of those returning, the trends of students going out and coming back generally parallel each other. As the number of Chinese students and scholars has increased, so has the research that sheds light on returnees' experiences.

Returnees and Their Impact on Modern and Contemporary China: A Retrospect/Historical View

In the 1950s and 1960s, China sent over 15,000 students to the former Soviet Union. These Chinese students later made many contributions to the development and building of modern China after they returned

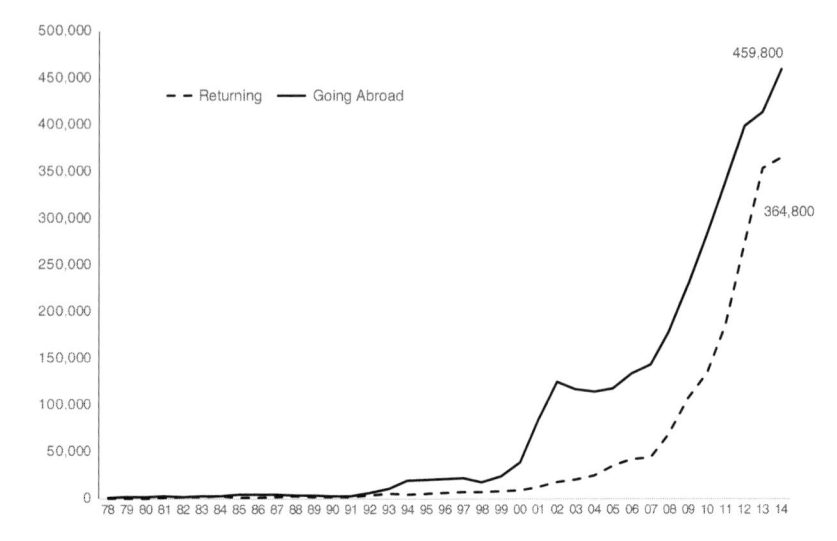

Fig. 2.3 Number of Chinese students going abroad and returning (1978–2014) (Source: National Bureau of Statistics of the People's Republic of China)

(Sun, G. 2010, October 30). Similarly, Chinese students who studied in Japan and the USA brought back many advanced technologies and new ideas to China after their studies concluded. Against this background, much research on returned Chinese students conducted by Chinese scholars emphasizes their contributions in many fields, including aviation, naval science and technology, geology, biology, physics, chemical industry, agriculture, education, mathematics, architecture, and medicine. All of these students and their contributions have played a decisive role in the construction of modern China.

Chinese returnees to the academic fields make further contributions in terms of scientific research. A recent survey of academics revealed that between 1955 and 2009, about 37 per cent of academicians employed by the Chinese Academy of Sciences and the Chinese Academy of Engineering (two of the leading prestigious academic institutions in China) had overseas learning or research experience.[10] Among them, 42 per cent once

[10] Among these 700 academicians who obtained an overseas degree, 79.05 per cent of them received a doctoral degree, 13.55 per cent received a master's degree, and 7.26 per cent received a bachelor's degree.

studied in the USA, followed by 22 per cent in the former Soviet Union, and 12 per cent in the UK. Others studied in Germany, Japan, France, Canada, Switzerland, Australia, and Poland (CUAA 2009). In addition, 77 per cent of the presidents of the MoE-administrated universities (教育部直属高校 *jiaoyubu zhishu gaoxiao*) have overseas learning experience (Wang 2011).

Xu et al. (2014) held that the returned Chinese students and scholars working at universities played an important role in promoting the globalization of higher education, because they would bring back advanced pedagogical methods, establish academic networking and academic exchange, offer courses in English, and recruit international students. Returnees contribute to government as well as academics: among sixty-eight national leaders and 101 provincial officials (including ministries and commissions under the State Council and main Party and Executive Heads of the 31 provinces), thirty-one of them (accounting for 18 per cent) had studied abroad, with fifteen completing academic degrees (Liu et al. 2014, April 17).

Another trend of research focuses on returned Chinese student entrepreneurship (创业 *chuangye*). China launched initiatives such as 'The Recruitment Program of Global Experts' (also called the '1000 Talent Plan') in 2008, so as to bring in the top talents from overseas to China. In 2013, over 260 'start-up parks' (创业园 *chuangyeyuan*) (Xinhuanet 2014) were aimed at attracting more Chinese students who graduated abroad. This development indicates that China's return migration has exerted unexpected influence on domestic development by introducing new management concepts and ways of financing businesses, benefitting the overall development of entrepreneurship in China (Wang 2013).

Readjustment

After returning home, most international students had to undergo a period of 'readjustment' to the home country. Research has probed returned Chinese students' readjustment, re-adaptation (Zhang 2013), cultural identity, and reverse culture shock (Yin 2008). For instance, one of the focuses is on returned Chinese students and scholars currently working in the Chinese academic system. Scholars have investigated the living situation of returnee teachers (Liu 2010), their experience and perception, individual efforts to adapt to this academic system and environment (Li 2013; Yuan 2014), and job satisfaction (Xu 2009). In general, results indicated that returned Chinese scholars experienced readjustment difficulties. In terms of an effective academic culture that supported high-quality teaching and research, returned Chinese scholars often complained about the bureaucracies of university administration, the non-transparency of China's funding system, and complicated interpersonal relationships in the universities (Chen and Li 2013).

Staying Abroad

Intent to Return and Factors Influencing the Decision

Another focus of research is probing international students' intention of staying or returning after completing their studies, and factors that influence their decisions. Zweig (1997) pointed to background variables such as age, sex, social background in China, and students' views about returning when they first left China as factors that affect their decision to go home. Similarly, investigating migrant intention among Chinese students in Canada, Lu et al. (2009) revealed students' demographic characteristics, pre-move traits, Canadian experiences, parental expectations, and related aspirations influenced students' intent to stay. Similarly, Alberts and Hazen (2005) found that upon completion of their degrees, students decided whether to stay in the host country or return home based on professional, societal, and personal factors. Zhang (2014) found that the disparity between the academic environments of China and the USA is the most important factor deciding whether Chinese doctoral students in the USA would like to return to China. Those students regarded the academic environment in China as much worse than that found in the USA. Another survey conducted in the USA indicated that, compared with political and sociocultural factors, academic and economic factors have a bigger deterrent effect on Chinese students' return intention (Cheung and Xu 2014). However, making the decision either to return or to stay is never an easy job for Chinese students, as Qin (1999) found that both push and pull factors coexisted for Chinese students in the USA.[11]

In the context of the competitive 'war for talent' (Beechler and Woodward 2009) worldwide, research tends to focus on international Chinese students who are majoring in science and technology as well as on doctoral students. Based on a survey of 662 Chinese overseas gradu-

---

[11] For example, inadequate graduate education in China, limited opportunities for career development, and so on, are push factors from the Chinese side; advanced graduate education, positive aspects of individual life in the USA, and so on, are pull factors from the American side; while Chinese students' limited English language proficiency, difficulties in cultural adjustment, and so on, are push factors from the USA.

ates who were currently working in the USA, Gao (2012) identified four important factors that impacted their willingness to return, namely: the occupational situation for Chinese talents in science and technology; the talent-absorbing power of the USA; the international economic situation; and China's economic, science, and technology development. For science and engineering majors, academic factors (including continuation of research, the teacher-student relationship, academic exchange and research cooperation with China, and career development) were important in the decision to immigrate (Gao 2014).

Brain Gain, Brain Drain, or Brain Circulation?

With the increase in student mobility, 'brain drain' and 'brain gain' has been much studied in the last few decades. Research has demonstrated that the impact of the movement of international students is more complicated than a simple tally of brain gain or brain drain (Qin 1999, Zweig and Chen 1995) based on current physical location. Realizing that the movement of people is at the heart of this process, scholars have moved away from the limited concepts of brain drain and brain gain to a broader view: 'brain circulation' (DeVoretz and Zweig 2008; Saxenian 2005). China and many other countries have adopted strategies based on the brain circulation concept. Since 2001, China has encouraged overseas mainlanders to contribute to China's modernization, even if they remain abroad, by outlining various ways they could continue to help their home country (Zweig et al. 2008). Researchers increasingly view these overseas students and scholars as part of an 'international migration of human capital' (Blachford and Zhang 2013), or, alternatively, as 'transnational human capital' (Zweig et al. 2004). For instance, Blachford and Zhang (2013) interviewed naturalized Chinese-Canadian professors and found that although they stayed in the host country, they made significant contributions to both Canadian and Chinese societies in economic, academic, and sociocultural dimensions.

STUDENTS' REFLECTIONS: ACHIEVEMENT AND SATISFACTION

In spite of the initial challenges or hardships, international students who are called upon to reflect on their learning experience abroad, judging their achievements and satisfaction during their academic journey, overwhelmingly hold a positive attitude toward the experience of studying abroad.

A longitudinal study in the UK indicated that international students made academic and personal achievements and developed new perceptions of cultures and acceptance of differences. They encountered 'new' pedagogy and learning styles in the host country and became comfortable in small-group discussions (Gu et al. 2010). Most of the Chinese students who returned to China from the UK achieved new transnational competencies, skills, and worldviews (Gu and Schweisfurth 2015). Furthermore, regarding specific professional skills like academic writing, Chinese international students regarded themselves as having moved from being 'outsiders', in terms of the discourse of their discipline to 'insiders' who were now more familiar with the discourse of their world (Arkoudis and Tran 2007).

Concerning personal growth, Gu et al. (2010) compared the experience of studying overseas to 'a further step on a journey of self-discovery', as students 'must rely upon themselves to survive and flourish' (p. 19). Likewise, Murphy-Lejeune (2003) regarded the experience of learning abroad as 'a maturing process' which was 'a personal expansion, an opening of one's potential universe'. Yeh (1976) believed that crises encountered by Chinese students were worthwhile in that they strengthened ego identity and psychosocial maturity. Similarly, Wang (2004) concluded that through encountering various difficulties in their adjustment, international Chinese students made encouraging progress in their academic and personal development. Empirical research indicated that, compared with first-year international students, senior international students reported greater gains in personal and social aspects (Zhao et al. 2005). Wang (2004) interviewed twenty-one international graduate students in the USA and concluded that the adaptation process promoted students' psychological and emotional growth.

Furthermore, Ro (2006) probed East Asian students' satisfaction of studying in Germany, and suggested that expectation of academic discipline-based study and personal development had an effect on international students' satisfaction.

Reflection on Research Methods and Perspectives of Chinese Students

As researchers' understanding of Chinese students has grown, research topics and methodologies have changed accordingly. For instance, themes concerning Asian students are no longer limited to culture shock (Henderson et al. 1993) and do not regard lack of English proficiency as the major problem (Nicholson 2001).

Current research pays more attention to Chinese students' identities as sojourners, while academic adjustment has not been the focus of the discussion. Much has been written regarding their intercultural experience as 'foreigners', while their experience of struggling and surviving in an intercultural learning environment is widely neglected. Little research on adjustment and the concept of intercultural competency has been conducted from a learning perspective (Taylor 1994). Given the pivotal role of academic adjustment for students, however, it is important to investigate the process of their academic adjustment and learning experiences at host universities.

As English-speaking countries have the lion's share of Chinese students, much of the research on Chinese students has been contributed from these countries. Compounding this, the research on international Chinese students that has been conducted in non-English countries is not well known outside its native language boundaries. For example, even though Chinese students in 2012 accounted for 73.5 per cent and 64.1 per cent of international students in South Korea and Japan respectively, little is known about the academic literature in English. The few exceptions include a couple of research studies introducing Chinese students in France (Francis and Jean-François 2010) and in Korea (Jon 2012; Yan and Cheng 2015).

Furthermore, non-English-speaking countries often have little experience hosting Chinese students. For instance, Chinese students have only become the largest international student group in Germany in the last ten years. The absence of research on Chinese students conducted in non-English-speaking countries leads to great difficulty when trying to draw international comparisons using international Chinese students.

Research Methodologies

Qualitative Analysis: The Suitable Research Method for the Analysis of International Chinese Students

Quantitative approaches have dominated the research on Chinese and international students. The focus of these studies has been themes of international students' learning and intercultural communication. Standardized indexes, inventories, scales of psychological and sociocultural adjustments are frequently employed to collect data. For instance, much research has been conducted based on the psychological and sociocultural adjustment model developed by Colleen Ward and her associates (Searle and Ward 1990; Ward and Kennedy 1999; Ward and Rana-Deuba 1999) to explore the adjustment of Chinese students in the USA (Wang 2009; Ye 2006), the UK (Spencer-Oatey and Xiong 2006), and Australia (Zheng et al. 2004). In addition, based on the principles of the classic models,[12] many researchers used inventories or checklists and undertook qualitative and/or quantitative studies on international students' adjustment (Feng 2009). Some were even inclined to combine various psychological scales to test their models (Tsang 2001). Some researchers combined interviews with the standardized scales of psychological and sociocultural adjustments (Spencer-Oatey and Xiong 2006) or used multiple data-gathering techniques (survey questionnaires, individual interviews, and focus group discussions) to explore experiences of Chinese students' studying abroad (Zhang and Zhou 2010).

In spite of the contribution to research on Chinese students' adjustment by using these indexes, inventories, or scales, the results of quantitative research often presented a static situation, which failed to tell us about the dynamic processes of adjustment. Church (1982) did not support using simple survey tools (e.g. survey questionnaires, problem checklists, etc.) to measure adjustment, as he believed such studies failed to relate sojourners' behavior and adjustment difficulties. He further suggested scholars exert more effort to conduct research through more diverse methods, in view of the dynamic features of sojourner adjustment. Moreover, a large number of these scales are developed by western psychologists and based on western academic cultures. Thus, the application of these tools to non-western students and contexts may not be appropriate, and requires further validation.

Ethnographic Approach
Qualitative approaches facilitate a deep understanding of Chinese students' adjustment. For example, Wang (2004) used case studies to explore four Chinese graduates' individual experiences in the sociocultural and academic environment in the USA. Li (2004) conducted a narrative inquiry to record the challenges Chinese students face in brand new educational,

---

[12] See models developed by Bennett (A developmental model of intercultural sensitivity 1993), Berry et al. (Psychology of acculturation 1987), and Kim (Communication and cross-cultural adaptation 1988), which describe the developmental stages of acculturation and intercultural sensitivity or adaptation.

cultural, and social environments. Spurling (2006) used in-depth interviews to investigate the adjustment of first-year Chinese students in the UK.

There is also a remarkable tendency to adopt ethnographic approaches to explore international students' adjustment. Ethnographic approaches come largely from the field of anthropology and the term ethnography 'has come to be equated with virtually any qualitative research project where the intent is to provide a detailed, in-depth description of everyday life and practice' (Hoey 2014, p. 1). Ethnographic approaches enable the researcher to 'keep an open mind about the groups or cultures' (Fetterman 2010, p. 1). Brown and Holloway (2008) believed that this approach offered the opportunity to study students in a natural setting over a long period. Much ethnographic research adopts naturalistic methods, such as observations, in-depth interviews, or informal meetings (Brown 2008b; Brown and Holloway 2008; Jackson 2006; Pitts 2009). Concerning Chinese students, some research adopting ethnographic approaches explores their learning experience and intercultural communication (Holmes 2004; Lam 2006; Liu 2002; Zhao 2007; Zhao and Bourne 2011). Furthermore, some scholars do not limit themselves to formal interviews or observations, but adopt more creative research approaches. For example, Pearson (2006) analyzed the diaries of Irish students studying in Japan, and Ayano (2006) combined interviews with collecting imagery and metaphors in the narratives of Japanese students studying in the UK. Burnett and Gardner (2006) asked Chinese students to describe their experience in the UK by spontaneously drawing diagrams with different colors. Jackson (2006) collected data from participant observations, reflective diary entries, critical incident reports, informal ethnographic discussions, and photographs/videotapes to explore the intercultural experience of Hong Kong Chinese students studying in England. Such visual material provides international students a non-verbal method to depict their experience abroad.

Longitudinal Method
In regarding adjustment as a process instead of the result of a checklist, there is an increasing trend of adopting a longitudinal method. Currently, the time span of the longitudinal research on international students ranges from twenty-one weeks (Cemalcilar and Falbo 2008) to eight semesters (Boyer and Sedlacek 1987). One longitudinal study even managed to interview international students ten years after their time abroad, exploring the lasting influence of one year overseas on their careers, international identities, and intercultural competency (Alred and Byram 2006).

Most longitudinal research divides the length of stay into three periods (Cemalcilar and Falbo 2008; Hechanova-Alampay, et al. 2002; Wang 2010; Ward, et al. 1998; Ward and Kennedy 1999; Zhao 2007; Zhou and Todman 2009) or four periods (Jou and Fukada 1996c; Skyrme 2005; Zhang and Xu 2007). Some research extended the start of longitudinal research even before arrival (Cemalcilar and Falbo 2008; Zhou and Todman 2009). Some longitudinal research starts following the experience of international students shortly after arrival, sometimes within the first twenty-four hours (Ward et al. 1998) or within the first week (Gong and Chang 2007). Longitudinal research methods enable depictions of the dynamic change of international students in different periods of their adjustment, such as patterns of strain (Hechanova-Alampay, et al. 2002), psychological well-being, adopted identification with the host culture, and stable identification with the home culture (Cemalcilar and Falbo 2008). Moreover, Zhou and Todman (2009) suggested two main strands of longitudinal investigation for student sojourners: predictive studies and monitoring studies. The former focused on how pre-departure variables predicted successful post-arrival adaptation, while the latter sought to find the patterns of sojourner adjustment over time.

Since a longitudinal approach is time-consuming, most longitudinal research gathers and measures data based on psychological scales or inventories, with few exceptions using interviews (Skyrme 2005; Wang 2010; Zhang and Xu 2007) or participant observation (Zhao 2007). In spite of the fact that longitudinal research can demonstrate international students' adjustment in a dynamic manner, the amount of research using longitudinal research is still quite small.

It is also worth noting that the results of longitudinal methods are not always identical. Some international students may encounter their greatest adjustment problems at the entry point (Ward et al. 1998) or their greatest stress in the initial stage (Brown and Holloway 2008). Other research found the pattern of strain peaked three months after the start of the semester (Hechanova-Alampay et al. 2002).

Perspectives

Perspective from Lecturers in the Host Countries

In contrast to the trend that the majority of research on international students probes problems mainly from student perspectives, some studies view international students' learning experiences as 'reciprocal adaptation'

(Tran 2011, p. 80; Zhou and Todman 2008, p. 223), and explore the issue from the perspectives of both students and lecturers. Durkin (2004) conducted in-depth interviews with forty-one students from China and other East Asian countries, while also interviewing twelve host country lecturers and six native students from the same courses. Similarly, Francis and Jean-François (2010) adopted qualitative methods to probe instructional staff's attitudes and opinions toward teaching Chinese students foreign language at a French university, as well as how instructors adapt to an unfamiliar milieu. Arkoudis and Tran (2007) interviewed two Chinese students and asked their opinions of writing their first assignment; simultaneously, they asked two Australian academics to make comments on the two essays. The results indicated there were certain mismatches between what the students perceived as important in their writing and the academics' views of the strengths and weaknesses in the students' work. Furthermore, Huang (2008) interviewed both international Chinese students and lecturers in the UK, exploring the understanding of critical thinking from both perspectives.

Including lecturers' perspectives is important, because lecturers provide the other side of the story of international students' adjustment to an intercultural learning environment. One study conducted in Canada probed Chinese overseas graduate students' adjustment by interviewing both international Chinese students and university administrative staff and student leaders (Mongillo 1995). By doing so, it is much easier to compare the disparity between students' understandings of what is required and the actual expectations of academics in the host country. All these contributions of 'others' opinions' has facilitated a 'panoramic view' of research on Chinese students' adjustment in an intercultural learning environment.

Comparative Perspective
Conducting comparative research facilitates understanding Chinese students and reveals whether certain problems are unique to Chinese students or to common college students in general. When exploring Chinese students' adjustment, researchers often arrange 'control groups', so as to compare the learning experience of Chinese students either with local peers or with international students from other countries. For instance, one study found that Chinese students achieved higher scores in categories like 'deep approach', 'relating ideas', and 'use of evidence' than Australian students.[13] This research indicated that Asian students were not rote learners

---

[13] However, at the same time, Chinese students scored significantly higher than Australian students in 'fear of failure', 'negative attitude to study', and 'disorganized study'.

and had a strong orientation toward the development of understanding (Smith and Smith 1999). Another common method is to compare Chinese students with students from other Asian or CHC countries, like students from Indonesia, Japan, Thailand, Hong Kong, and Taiwan (Nicholson 2001) or with students from Vietnam (Tran 2011), so as to identify both the similarities and differences between international students from Asia.

Perspectives from Chinese Scholars Overseas and Indigenous Researchers
Chinese scholars abroad also conduct research on other international Chinese students. These scholars are typically doctoral (Chen 2004; Guan 2007; Liang and Wen 2013; Song 2009; Wang 2009, 2010; Zhao 2007) or master's students (Gao 2006; Guan 2010; Zhu 2008). Because of their shared Chinese language and co-national identities, Chinese students can more freely share their overseas experience without any language barrier. Moreover, the co-national relationship engenders trust and encourages Chinese students to share their experience freely, facilitating the research (Li 2004). So far, indigenous researchers have explored international Chinese students' acculturation or cross-cultural adjustment in the USA (Fan 2004; Li 2011; Zhang 2008), the UK (Liu 2008), Germany (He 2009), France (Xu, L. 2010), and Finland (Cai 2009).

It is important to include this indigenous research on Chinese students. From an etic perspective, this type of research interprets international Chinese students' beliefs and thought processes to others in detail, and associates their current thinking and behaviors with their previous learning experience, contributing to the overall research on international Chinese students.

SITUATING THIS STUDY

Following the theoretical review of adjustment and the landscape of current research on international students, this research study establishes a framework of academic adjustment for Chinese students in Germany, transitioning from learning in China to learning in Germany.

First, examining adjustment as a dynamic process, the research presented in this book explores the development of Chinese students' academic adjustment throughout the duration of their study. It follows Chinese students enrolling in a German university through the pre-departure, initial, developing, and finishing phases. Second, taking different forms of learning and assessment between Chinese and German universities into consideration, this study discusses how Chinese students adjust themselves to

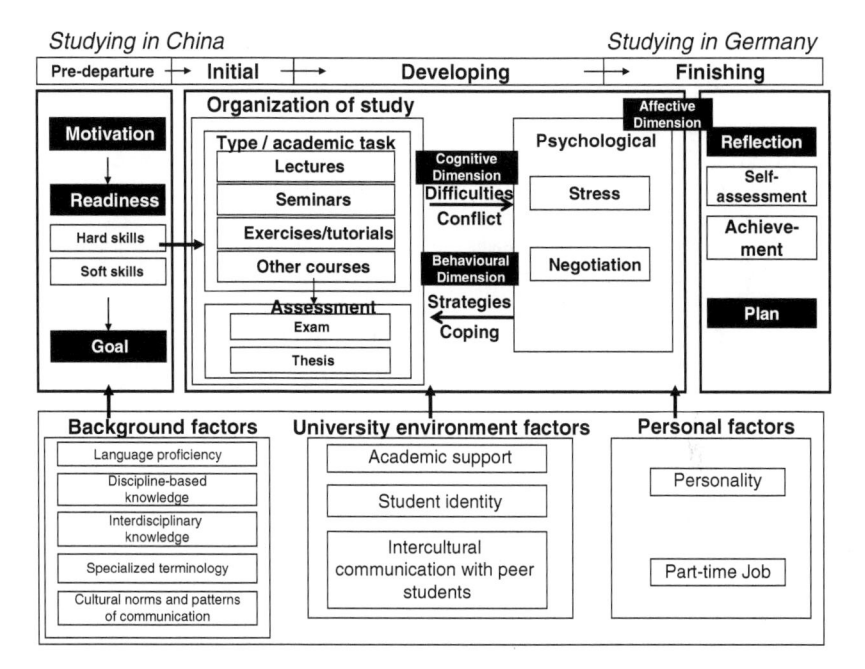

Fig. 2.4 Framework of Chinese students' academic adjustment in Germany

meet their new expectations. Third, in exploring the learning experiences of Chinese students at German universities, this research applies the 'affective, cognitive, and behavioral' model (Fig. 2.4) put forward by Anderson (1994): when facing difficulty, what do students perceive as the problem, how do they feel about it, and what kind of strategies do they adopt to solve it? Fourth, this study probes factors influencing the academic adjustment of international Chinese students, analyzing the factors from background, situational, and personal dimensions.

References

Aich, P. (1963). *Farbige unter Weißen*. Köln: Verlag Kiepenheuer & Witsch.
Alberts, H. C., & Hazen, H. D. (2005). "There are always two voices…": International students' intentions to stay in the United States or return to their home countries. *InternationalMigration,43*(3),131–154.doi:10.1111/j.1468-2435.2005.00328.x.
Alred, F., & Byram, M. (2006). British students in France: 10 years on. In M. Byram & A. Feng (Eds.), *Living and studying abroad. Research and practice* (Languages

for intercultural communication and education, Vol. 12, pp. 210–231). Clevedon/Buffalo: Multilingual Matters Ltd.

Altbach, P. G., Kelly, D. H., & Lulat, Y. G.-M. (1985). *Bibliography of foreign students and international study*. New York: Praeger.

Anderson, L. E. (1994). A new look at an old construct: Cross-cultural adaptation. *International Journal of Intercultural Relations, 18*(3), 293–328. doi:10.1016/0147-1767(94)90035-3.

Andrade, M. S. (2009). The international student picture. In M. S. Andrade & N. W. Evans (Eds.), *International students. Strengthening a critical resource* (pp. 1–24). Lanham: Rowman & Littlefield Education.

Antler, L. (1970). Correlates of home and host country acquaintanceship among foreign medical residents in the United States. *Journal of Social Psychology, 80*(1), 49–57.

Arkoudis, S., & Tran, L. T. (2007). International students in Australia: Read ten thousand volumes of books and walk ten thousand miles. *Asia Pacific Journal of Education, 27*(2), 157–169. doi:10.1080/02188790701378792.

Ayano, M. (2006). Japanese students in Britain. In M. Byram & A. Feng (Eds.), *Living and studying abroad. Research and practice* (Languages for intercultural communication and education, Vol. 12, pp. 11–37). Clevedon/Buffalo: Multilingual Matters Ltd.

Baas, M. (2006). Students of migration: Indian overseas students and the question of permanent residency. *People and Place, 14*(1), 9–24.

Barker, M., Child, C., Gallois, C., Jones, E., & Callan, V. J. (1991). Difficulties of overseas students in social and academic situations. *Australian Journal of Psychology, 43*(2), 79–84. doi:10.1080/00049539108259104.

Becher, T. (1987). The disciplinary shaping of the profession. In B. R. Clark (Ed.), *The academic profession. National, disciplinary, and institutional settings* (pp. 271–303). Berkeley: University of California Press.

Beechler, S., & Woodward, I. C. (2009). The global "war for talent". *Journal of International Management, 15*(3), 273–285. doi:10.1016/j.intman.2009.01.002.

Bennett, M. J. (1993). Towards Ethnorelativism: A developmental model of intercultural sensitivity. In R. M. Paige (Ed.) *Education for the intercultural experience*. Yarmouth, ME: Intercultural Press.

Berry, J. W., Kim, U., Minde, T., & Mok, D. (1987). Comparative studies of acculturative stress. *International Migration Review, 21*(3), 491–511.

Blachford, D. R., & Zhang, B. (2013). Rethinking international migration of human capital and brain circulation: The case of Chinese-Canadian academics. *Journal of Studies in International Education, 18*(3), 202–222. doi:10.1177/1028315312474315.

Bochner, S. (1972). Problems in culture learning. In S. Bochner & P. Wicks (Eds.), *Overseas students in Australia* (pp. 65–81). Randwick: New South Wales University Press.

Bochner, S. (1981). The social psychology of cultural mediation. In S. Bochner (Ed.), *The mediating person. Bridges between cultures* (pp. 6–36). Boston/ Cambridge: G.K. Hall; Schenkman Pub. Co.

Bochner, S., Buker, E. A., & McLeod, B. M. (1976). Communication patterns in an international student dormitory: A modification of the "small world" method1. *Journal of Applied Social Psychology, 6*(3), 275–290. doi:10.1111/ j.1559-1816.1976.tb01331.x.

Bochner, S., McLeod, B. M., & Lin, A. (1977). Friendship patterns of overseas students: A functional model. *International Journal of Psychology, 12*(4), 277–294.

Boyer, S. P., & Sedlacek, W. E. (1987). *Noncognitive predictors of academic success for international students: A longitudinal study*. Retrieved from http://www.eric. ed.gov/ERICWebPortal/search/detailmini.jsp?_nfpb=true&_&ERICExtSearch_ SearchValue_0=ED284499&ERICExtSearch_SearchType_0=no&accno =ED284499

Brein, M., & David, K. H. (1971). Intercultural communication and the adjustment of the sojourner. *Psychological Bulletin, 76*(3), 215–230.

Breitenbach, D., & Danckwortt, D. (1961). *Studenten aus Afrika und Asien als Stipendiaten in Deutschland: Eine sozialwissenschaftliche Studie*. Berlin: Deutscher Akademischer Austauschdienst Berlin.

Brown, L. (2008a). The incidence of study-related stress in international students in the initial stage of the international sojourn. *Journal of Studies in International Education, 12*(1), 5–28. doi:10.1177/1028315306291587.

Brown, L. (2008b). *The adjustment journey of international postgraduate students at a university in England: An ethnography*. Doctoral thesis. Bournemouth University, England, UK. Retrieved from http://eprints.bournemouth.ac. uk/10305/1/Lorraine_Brown.pdf

Brown, L. (2009). A failure of communication on the cross-cultural campus. *Journal of Studies in International Education, 13*(4), 439–454. doi:10.1177/10283 15309331913.

Brown, L., & Holloway, I. (2008). The adjustment journey of international postgraduate students at an English university: An ethnographic study. *Journal of Research in International Education, 7*(2), 232–249. doi:10.1177/14752 40908091306.

Buddington, S. A. (2002). Acculturation, psychological adjustment (stress, depression, self-esteem) and the academic achievement of Jamaican immigrant college students. *International Social Work, 45*(4),447–464.doi:10.1177/00208728020450040401.

Burnett, C., & Gardner, J. (2006). The one less travelled by… : The experience of Chinese students in a UK university. In M. Byram & A. Feng (Eds.), *Living and studying abroad. Research and practice* (Languages for intercultural communication and education, Vol. 12, pp. 64–90). Clevedon/Buffalo: Multilingual Matters Ltd.

Burns, R. B. (1991). Study and stress among first year overseas students in an Australian university. *Higher Education Research & Development, 10*(1), 61–77. Retrieved from http://dx.doi.org/10.1080/0729436910100106

Cai, L. (2009). *An Investigation into Chinese students' adaptation to a new cultural environment.* Master's thesis. Yunnan Normal University, Yunnan.

Campbell, J., & Li, M. (2007). Asian students' voices: An empirical study of Asian students' learning experiences at a New Zealand University. *Journal of Studies in International Education, 12*(4), 375–396. doi:10.1177/1028315307299422.

Cemalcilar, Z., & Falbo, T. (2008). A longitudinal study of the adaptation of international students in the United States. *Journal of Cross-Cultural Psychology, 39*(6), 799–804. doi:10.1177/0022022108323787.

Chen, C.-P. (1992). *Language proficiency and academic achievement: An ethnographic investigation of language demands and problems confronted by Chinese graduate students functioning in university classrooms.* Ed.D. Dissertation. Boston University, Massachusetts.

Chen, Y.-s. (1995). *Ausländische Studierende in der BRD: Anpassung fernostasiatischer Studierender an das Leben in Deutschland.* Univ., Diss.—Trier, 1994. *Kulturkontakte: Vol. 2.* Münster: Waxmann.

Chen, C. P. (1999). Common stressors among international college students: Research and counseling implications. *Journal of College Counseling, 2*, 49–65.

Chen, X. (2004). *Lü ju zhe he "wai guo ren": Sojourners and "foreigners" : A study on Chinese students' intercultural interpersonal relationships in the United States (in Chinese: 旅居者和"外国人")* (1st ed.). Beijing: Educational Science Publishing House

Chen, L. (2007). Communication in intercultural relationships. In W. B. Gudykunst (Ed.), *Cross-cultural and intercultural communication* (pp. 225–242). Thousand Oaks: Sage.

Chen, Q., & Li, M. (2013). Globalization, internationalization and world-class movement: The Chinese experience. In T. Seddon & J. S. Levin (Eds.), *World yearbook of education 2013. Educators, professionalism and politics: Global transitions, national spaces, and professional projects* (World yearbook of education series, pp. 236–251). Abingdon: Routledge.

Cheng, X. (2000). Asian students' reticence revisited. *System, 28*(3), 435–446. doi:10.1016/S0346-251X(00)00015-4.

Cheng, R., & Erben, A. (2011). Language anxiety: Experiences of Chinese graduate students at U.S. higher institutions. *Journal of Studies in International Education.* doi:10.1177/1028315311421841.

Cheung, A. C. K., & Xu, L. (2014). To return or not to return: Examining the return intentions of mainland Chinese students studying at elite universities in the United States. *Studies in Higher Education, 40*(9), 1605–1624. doi:10.1080/03075079.2014.899337.

Chinese Universities Alumni Association (CUAA). (2009). Report on academicians of the Chinese Academy of Sciences and the Chinese Academy of Engineering

2009 (in Chinese: 2009中国两院院士调查报告出炉，清华大学包揽新科院士两项第一). Retrieved from http://www.cuaa.net/cur/2009ysdc/

Chirkov, V., Vansteenkiste, M., Tao, R., & Lynch, M. (2007). The role of self-determined motivation and goals for study abroad in the adaptation of international students. *International Journal of Intercultural Relations, 31*(2), 199–222. doi:10.1016/j.ijintrel.2006.03.002.

Choo, K. L. (2007). The implications of introducing critical management education to Chinese students studying in UK business schools: Some empirical evidence. *Journal of Further and Higher Education, 31*(2), 145–158. doi:10.1080/03098770701267614.

Church, A. T. (1982). Sojourner adjustment. *Psychological Bulletin, 91*(3), 540–572.

Cornelius, R. R., Gray, J. M., & Constantinople, A. P. (1990). Student-faculty interaction in the college classroom. *Journal of Research & Development in Education, 23*(4), 189–197.

Danckwortt, D. (Ed.). (1984). *Werkstattberichte: Vol. 11. Auslandsstudium als Gegenstand der Forschung: Eine Literaturübersicht.* Kassel: Gesamthochschule, Wiss. Zentrum f. Berufs- u. Hochschulforschung.

Davis, C., & Katzman, M. A. (1999). Perfection as acculturation: A study of the psychological correlates of eating problems in Chinese male and female students living in the United States. *International Journal of Eating Disorders, 25*(1), 65–70.

Deutscher Akademischer Austauschdienst (DAAD) & Deutsches Zentrum für Hochschul- und Wissenschaftsforschung GmbH (DZHW). (2015). *Wissenschaft weltoffen: Daten und Fakten zur Internationalität von Studium und Forschung in Deutschland [Schwerpunkt: Internationale Masterstudierende an deutschen Hochschulen].* Bielefeld: Bertelsmann.

Deutscher Städtetag (Ed.). (2000). *"Ausländische Studierende—willkommene Gäste!?": Dokumentation einer Fachtagung zur Situation ausländischer Studierender in deutschen Hochschulstädten.* : C 26. Köln.

DeVoretz, D., & Zweig, D. (2008). An overview of twenty-first-century Chinese "brain circulation". *Pacific Affairs, 81*(2), 171–173.

Ding, H. (2009). East meets west: Chinese students making sense of their cultural identity in London. *Changing English, 16*(3), 313–321. doi:10.1080/13586840903194771.

Du Bois, C. (1956). *Foreign students and higher education in the United States. Studies in universities and world affairs.* Washington, DC: American Council on Education.

Durkin, K. (2004). *Adapting to western norms of academic argumentation and debate.* Doctorate thesis. Bournemouth University.

Durkin, K. (2008a). The middle way: East Asian master's students' perceptions of critical argumentation in U.K. universities. *Journal of Studies in International Education, 12*(1), 38–55. doi:10.1177/1028315307302839.

Durkin, K. (2008b). The adaptation of East Asian masters students to western norms of critical thinking and argumentation in the UK. *Intercultural Education, 19*(1), 15–27. doi:10.1080/14675980701852228.

Durkin, K. (2011). Adapting to western norms of critical argumentation and debate. In L. Jin & M. Cortazzi (Eds.), *Researching Chinese learners. Skills, perceptions and intercultural adaptations* (pp. 274–291). Basingstoke/New York: Palgrave Macmillan.

Dyal, J. A., & Chan, C. (1985). Stress and distress: A study-of Hong Kong Chinese and Euro-Canadian students. *Journal of Cross-Cultural Psychology, 16*(4), 447–466. doi:10.1177/0022002185016004003.

Ehlers, S., & Hemmingsen, L. (2011). Academic schock: The joint move towards a transnational academic culture. *Adult Learning: Teachers as Learners, 6*, 31–40.

Evans, N. W., Carlin, D. B., & Potts, J. D. (2009). Adjustment issues. In M. S. Andrade & N. W. Evans (Eds.), *International students. Strengthening a critical resource* (pp. 25–41). Lanham: Rowman & Littlefield Education.

Fan, L. (2004). *Acculturation strategies among Chinese Overseas students in America.* Master thesis. Huazhong University of Science and Technology, Huhan.

Feldhaus, M., & Logemann, N. (2002). Student sein—Ausländer sein: Eine Replikationsstudie über die soziale Situation und Integration ausländischer Studierender an der Universität Oldenburg. Oldenburg: Bibliotheks- und Informationssystem der Univ. Retrieved from http://docserver.bis.uni-oldenburg.de/publikationen/bisverlag/2003/felstu02/felstu02.html

Feng, J. (1991, March). *The adaptation of students from the People's Republic of China to an American academic culture.* Retrieved from http://www.eric.ed.gov/PDFS/ED329833.pdf

Feng, A. (2009). Becoming intercultural competent in a third space. In A. Feng, M. Byram, & M. Fleming (Eds.), *Becoming interculturally competent through education and training* (pp. 71–91). Bristol/Buffalo: Multilingual Matters.

Fetterman, D. M. (2010). *Ethnography: Step-by-step* (Applied social research methods series 3rd ed., Vol. 17). Los Angeles: Sage.

Francis, B., & Jean-François, B. (2010). Teaching French as a second language to Chinese students: Instructional staff adaptation and intercultural competence development. *International Journal of Intercultural Relations, 34*(6), 561–570. doi:10.1016/j.ijintrel.2010.01.003.

Furnham, A., & Bochner, S. (1982). Social difficulty in a foreign culture: An empirical analysis of culture shock. In S. Bochner (Ed.), *Cultures in contact. Studies in cross-cultural interaction* (International series in experimental social psychology, pp. 161–190). Oxford: Pergamon Press.

Furnham, A., & Bochner, S. (1986). *Culture shock: Psychological reactions to unfamiliar environments.* London u.a: Methuen. 1.

Furukawa, T. (1997). Cultural distance and its relationship to psychological adjustment of international exchange students. *Psychiatry and Clinical Neurosciences, 51*(3), 87–91. doi:10.1111/j.1440-1819.1997.tb02367.x.

Galtung, I. E. (1965). The impact of study abroad: A three-by-three-nation study of cross-cultural contact. *Journal of Peace Research,* 2(3), 258–275. doi:10.1177/002234336500200304.

Gao, X. (2006). Understanding changes in Chinese students' uses of learning strategies in China and Britain: A socio-cultural re-interpretation. *System, 34*(1), 55–67.

Gao (高子平), Z. (2012). Changing of returning willing of American Chinese S&T talents and the transition of China's policy to absorb overseas talents (在美华人科技人才回流意愿变化与我国海外人才引进政策转型). *Science & Technology Progress and Policy* (科技进步与对策), 29(19), 145–150.

Gao (高子平), Z. (2014). Analysis on wishes of inverse flow of science and engineering rencai studying aboard in the dimension of academic correlation (学术相关性维度的海外理工科留学人才回流意愿研究). *Studies in Dialectics of Nature* (自然辩证法研究), 74–81.

Gong, Y., & Chang, S. (2007). The relationships of cross-cultural adjustment with dispositional learning orientation and goal setting: A longitudinal analysis. *Journal of Cross-Cultural Psychology,* 38(1), 19–25. doi:10.1177/0022022106295438.

Griffiths, D. S., Winstanley, D., & Gabriel, Y. (2005). Learning shock: The trauma of return to formal learning. *Management Learning,* 36(3), 275–297. doi:10.1177/1350507605055347.

Grimshaw, T. (2011). Concluding editorial: 'The needs of international students rethought—implications for the policy and practice of higher education'. *Teachers and Teaching,* 17(6), 703–712.

Gu, Q. (2011). An emotional journey of change: The case of Chinese students in UK higher education. In L. Jin & M. Cortazzi (Eds.), *Researching Chinese learners. Skills, perceptions and intercultural adaptations* (pp. 212–232). Basingstoke/New York: Palgrave Macmillan.

Gu, Q., & Schweisfurth, M. (2015). Transnational connections, competences and identities: Experiences of Chinese international students after their return 'home'. *British Educational Research Journal,* 1–24. doi:10.1002/berj.3175.

Gu, Q., Schweisfurth, M., & Day, C. (2010). Learning and growing in a 'foreign' context: Intercultural experiences of international students. *Compare: A Journal of Comparative and International Education,* 40(1), 7–23. Retrieved from http://dx.doi.org/10.1080/03057920903115983

Guan, H. (2007). *Anpassung und Integration der chinesischen Studierenden in Deutschland. eine Untersuchung anhand des Beispiels an der Universität Bremen.* Dissertation. Universität Bremen, Bremen. Retrieved from http://elib.suub.uni-bremen.de/diss/docs/00010886.pdf

Guan, L. (2010). *Anpassung der chinesischen Studenten in Deutschland.* München: Grin Verlag.

Gudykunst, W. B. (2004). *Bridging differences: Effective intergroup communication* (4th ed.). Thousand Oaks: SAGE Publications.

Hammer, M. R. (1992). Research, mission statements, and international student advising offices. *International Journal of Intercultural Relations, 16,* 217–236.

He, J. (2009). *Investigating the acculturation strategies and adaptation outcomes of Chinese students in Germany.* Master's thesis, Shanghai International Studies University, Shanghai.

Hechanova-Alampay, R., Beehr, T. A., Christiansen, N. D., & Van Horn, R. K. (2002). Adjustment and strain among domestic and international student sojourners: A longitudinal study. *School Psychology International, 23*(4), 458–474. doi:10.1177/0143034302234007.

Henderson, G., Milhouse, V., & Cao, L. (1993). Crossing the gap: An analysis of Chinese students' culture shock in an American university. *College Student Journal, 27*(3), 380–389.

Heublein, U. (2009, January). *Aspekte der Studiensituation ausländischer Studierender,* Bonn.

Heublein, U., Sommer, D., & Weitz, B. (2004). *Studienverlauf im Ausländerstudium: Eine Untersuchung an vier ausgewählten Hochschulen. Dokumentationen und Materialien* (Vol. 55). Bonn: DAAD.

Heublein, U., Özkilic, M., & Sommer, D. (2007). *Aspekte der Internationalität deutscher Hochschulen: Internationale Erfahrungen deutscher Studierender an ihren heimischen Hochschulen* (Vol. 63). Bonn: Hrsg. der Reihe Dok & Mat, Dokumentationen & Materialien: DAAD, Deutscher Akademischer Austausch Dienst.

Hoey, B. A. (2014). *A simple introduction to the practice of ethnography and guide to ethnographic fieldnotes.* Retrieved from http://works.bepress.com/cgi/viewcontent.cgi?article=1022&context=brian_hoey

Holmes, P. (2004). Negotiating differences in learning and intercultural communication: Ethnic Chinese students in a New Zealand university. *Business Communication Quarterly, 67*(3), 294–307. doi:10.1177/1080569904268141.

Holmes, P. (2008). Foregrounding harmony: Chinese international students' voices in communication with their New Zealand peers. *China Media Research, 4*(4), 102–110.

Hu, Y. (2004). *Le métier d'étudiant étranger : le cas des étudiants chinois non spécialistes de français en France.* Doctoral dissertation. Paris 3.

Huang, R. (2008). Critical thinking: Discussion from Chinese postgraduate international students and their lecturers. *Hospitality, leisure, sport and tourism network: Enhancing series: Internationalisation,* 1–12. Retrieved from https://www.heacademy.ac.uk/sites/default/files/e2_critical_thinking.pdf

Hui, L. (2005). Chinese cultural schema of education: Implications for communication between Chinese students and Australian educators. *Issues in Educational Research, 15*(1), 17–36.

Hull, W. F. (1978). *Foreign students in the United States of America: Coping behavior within the educational environment.* New York: Praeger.

Institute of International Education (IIE). (2013). Retrieved from http://www. iie.org/en/Services/Project-Atlas/Australia/International-Students-In-Australia 16 April 2015

Jabeen Khan, K. (1988). *Auslandsstudium als kritisches Lebensereignis: Eine empirische Untersuchung zur psychosozialen Situation ausländischer Studenten in der Bundesrepublik Deutschland. Bildung, Repression, Befreiung.* Wiesbaden: World Univ. Service.

Jackson, J. (2006). Ethnographic pedagogy and evaluation in short-term study abroad. In M. Byram & A. Feng (Eds.), *Living and studying abroad. Research and practice* (Languages for intercultural communication and education, Vol. 12, pp. 134–156). Clevedon/Buffalo: Multilingual Matters Ltd.

Jenkins, J. R., & Galloway, F. (2009). The adjustment problems faced by international and overseas Chinese students studying in Taiwan universities: A comparison of student and faculty/staff perceptions. *Asia Pacific Education Review, 10*(2), 159–168. doi:10.1007/s12564-009-9020-5.

Jin, L., & Cortazzi, M. (1997). Expectations and questions in intercultural classrooms. *Intercultural Communication Studies, 4*(2), 37–58.

Jon, J.-E. (2012). Power dynamics with international students: From the perspective of domestic students in Korean higher education. *Higher Education, 64*(4), 441–454. doi:10.1007/s10734-011-9503-2.

Jou, Y. H., & Fukada, H. (1995a). Effect of social support from various sources on the adjustment of Chinese students in Japan. *The Journal of Social Psychology, 135*(3), 305–311.

Jou, Y. H., & Fukada, H. (1995b). Effects of social support on adjustment of Chinese students in Japan. *The Journal of Social Psychology, 135*(1), 39–47. doi: 10.1080/00224545.1995.9711400.

Jou, Y. H., & Fukada, H. (1996a). The causes and influence of transitional stress among Chinese students in Japan. *The Journal of Social Psychology, 136*(4), 501–509.

Jou, Y. H., & Fukada, H. (1996b). Comparison of differences in the association of social support and adjustment between Chinese and Japanese students in Japan: A research note. *Psychological Reports, 79*(1), 107–112.

Jou, Y. H., & Fukada, H. (1996c). Influences of social supports and personality on adjustment of Chinese students in Japan. *Journal of Applied Social Psychology, 26*(20), 1795–1802. doi:10.1111/j.1559-1816.1996.tb00098.x.

Jou, Y. H., & Fukada, H. (1997). Stress and Social Support in Mental and Physical Health of Chinese Students in Japan. *Psychological Reports, 81,* 1303–1312

Kaczmarek, P. G., Matlock, G., Merta, R., Ames, M. H., & Ross, M. (1994). An assessment of international college student adjustment. *International Journal for the Advancement of Counselling, 17*(4), 241–247. doi:10.1007/BF01407740.

Kang, T. S. (1971). Name change and acculturation: Chinese students on an American campus. *The Pacific Sociological Review, 14*(4), 403–412.

Kavan, H., & Wilkinson, L. (2003). Dialogues with dragons: Assisting Chinese students' academic achievement. In V. Young & M. Brown (Eds.). *Association of Tertiary Learning Advisors of Aotearoa New Zealand (ATLAANZ) Conference 2003 Proceedings: Vol. 8. Learning talk* (pp. 119–131). Hamilton, New Zealand.

Kim, Y. Y. (1988). *Communication and cross-cultural adaptation: An integrative theory* (Intercommunication series, Vol. 2). Clevedon: Multilingual Matters Ltd.

Kingston, E., & Forland, H. (2008). Bridging the gap in expectations between international students and academic staff. *Journal of Studies in International Education, 12*(2), 204–221. doi:10.1177/1028315307307654.

Klein, M. H., Alexander, A. A., Tseng, K.-H., Miller, M. H., Keh, E.-K., Chu, H.-M., & Workneh, F. (1971). The foreign student adaptation program: Social experiences of Asian students in the U. S. *International Educational and Cultural Exchange, 6*(3), 77–90.

Klineberg, O., & Hull, W. F. (1979). *At a foreign university: An international study of adaptation and coping.* New York: Praeger.

Krüger, L. (2001). *Die soziale Situation ausländischer Studierender: Ergebnisse einer schriftlichen Befragung an der Universität Trier im Wintersemester 2000/2001.* Trier. Retrieved from http://www.uni-trier.de/fileadmin/forschung/ZES/Schriftenreihe/051.pdf

Lam, C. M.-H. (2006). Reciprocal adjustment by host and sojourning groups: Mainland Chinese students in Hong Kong. In M. Byram & A. Feng (Eds.), *Living and studying abroad. Research and practice* (Languages for intercultural communication and education, Vol. 12, pp. 91–107). Clevedon/Buffalo: Multilingual Matters Ltd.

Lee, E. S. (1966). A theory of migration. *Demography, 3*(1), 47–57.

Leung, C. (2001). The psychological adaptation of overseas and migrant students in Australia. *International Journal of Psychology, 36*(4), 251–259. doi:10.1080/00207590143000018.

Lewthwaite, M. (1996). A study of international students' perspectives on cross-cultural adaptation. *International Journal for the Advancement of Counselling, 19*(2), 167–185. doi:10.1007/BF00114787.

Liang, X., & Wen, Y. (2013). Academic *Adaptation: Mainland Chinese students in graduate programs at a Canadian university* (中国大陆学生在加拿大研究生项目中的学术表现). Changsha: Hunan shifan daxue chubanshe (湖南师范大学出版社).

Li, Y. (2004). Learning to live and study in Canada: Stories of four EFL learners from China. *TESL Canada Journal, 22*(1), 25–43.

Li, X. (2011). *An analysis of overseas Chinese students' cultural acculturation and solution. Case study of the Chinese overseas students in Oklahoma University in the United States of America.* Master thesis. Chongqing University, Chongqing, China.

Li(李广旭), G. (2013). *A study on un-adaptation of overseas returnees in Chinese universities: A case of teacher M (高校"海归"教师职业不适应问题的研究——以上海某高校M老师为例).* Master thesis. East China Normal University, Shanghai, China.

Li, M., & Bray, M. (2006). Social class and cross-border higher education: Mainland Chinese students in Hong Kong and Macau. *Journal of International Migration and Integration, 7*(4), 407–424. doi:10.1007/BF02934902.

Li, W. W., & Tse, S. (2015). Problem gambling and help seeking among Chinese international students: Narratives of place identity transformation. *Journal of Health Psychology, 20*(3), 300–312. doi:10.1177/1359105314566611.

Li, G., Chen, W., & Duanmu, J.-L. (2010). Determinants of international students' academic performance: A comparison between Chinese and other international students. *Journal of Studies in International Education, 14*(4), 389–405. doi:10.1177/1028315309331490.

Lin, L. (2002, March). *The learning experiences of Chinese graduate students in American social sciences programs.* Annual conference of the comparative and international education society, Orlando, FL, USA. Retrieved from http://www.eric.ed.gov/PDFS/ED474163.pdf

Lin, S.-P., & Betz, N. E. (2007). Factors related to the social self-efficacy of Chinese international students. *The Counseling Psychologist, 37*(3), 451–471. doi:10.1177/0011000009332474.

Lin, J.-C. G., & Yi, J. K. (1997). Asian international students' adjustment: Issues and program suggestions. *College Student Journal, 31*(4), 473–479.

Lin, M. C., Endler, N. S., & Kocovski, N. L. (2001). State and trait anxiety: A cross-cultural comparison of Chinese and Caucasian students in Canada. *Current Psychology, 20*(1), 95–111.

Liu, J. (2001). *Asian students' classroom communication patterns in U.S. universities: An emic perspective. Contemporary studies in second language learning.* Westport: Ablex Pub. Retrieved from http://www.gbv.de/dms/bowker/toc/9781567506204.pdf

Liu, J. (2002). Negotiating silence in American classrooms: Three Chinese cases. *Language and Intercultural Communication, 2*(1), 37–54. doi:10.1080/14708470208668074.

Liu, W. (2008). *A study on the relationship among Chinese overseas students' acculturation, social support and life satisfaction in Britain.* Master's thesis. Fujian Normal University, Fujian, China.

Liu (刘蓉洁), R. (2010). The Study about Living Environment and State of Overseas Returnees in Chinese Universities (高校"海归"教师生存环境与生存状态研究) (Master thesis). Shanghai Jiao Tong University, Shanghai.

Liu(刘斌), B., Tan(谭畅), C., & Zhao(赵栋), D. (2014, April 17). 中国"海归"从政现状报告:"怎么到政府里的人越来越少". *Nanfang Zhoumo (*南方周末*).* Retrieved from http://www.infzm.com/content/99893

Long, J.-H., Yan, W.-H., Yang, H.-D., & Van Oudenhoven, J. P. (2009). Cross-cultural adaptation of Chinese students in the Netherlands. *US-China Education Review, 6*(9), 1–9.

Loveys, K. (2011). *Scandal as a THIRD of students drop out of university*. Retrieved from http://www.dailymail.co.uk/news/article-1371989/Scandal-college-drop-outs-Record-numbers-students-failing-finish-degrees.html

Lowe, A. C.-T., & Corkindale, D. R. (1998). Differences in "cultural values" and their effects on responses to marketing stimuli: A cross-cultural study between Australians and Chinese from the People's Republic of China. *European Journal of Marketing, 32*(9/10), 843–867. doi:10.1108/03090569810232291.

Lu, L. (1990). Adaptation to British universities: Homesickness and mental health of Chinese students. *Counselling Psychology Quarterly, 3*(3), 225–232.

Lu, Y., Zong, L., & Schissel, B. (2009). To stay or return: Migration intentions of students from People's Republic of China in Saskatchewan, Canada. *Journal of International Migration and Integration, 10*(3), 283–310. doi:10.1007/s12134-009-0103-2.

McAdam, K. (1972). The Study Methods and Academic Results of Overseas Students. In S. Bochner & P. Wicks (Eds.), *Overseas students in Australia* pp. 97–104. Randwick N.S.W.: New South Wales University Press.

Malcolm, P., Ling, A., & Sherry, C. (2004). *Why do Chinese students study in New Zealand and how can they be helped to succeed?* Retrieved from http://www.herdsa.org.au/wp-content/uploads/conference/2004/PDF/P018-jt.pdf

Maslow, A. H. (1943). A theory of human motivation. *Psychological Review, 50*, 370–396.

Maxwell, M. J. (1974). Foreign students and American academic ritual. *Journal of Reading, 17*(4), 301–305.

Mazzarol, T., Soutar, G. N., Smart, D., & Choo, S. (2001). *Perceptions, information and choice: Understanding how Chinese students select a country for overseas study*. Canberra: Australian Education International.

Ministry of Education of The People's Republic of China (MoE). (2015). 2014 年度我国出国留学人员情况. Retrieved from 23 July, 2015 from http://www.moe.gov.cn/publicfiles/business/htmlfiles/moe/s5987/201503/184499.html

Misra, R., & Castillo, L. G. (2004). Academic stress among college students: Comparison of American and international students. *International Journal of Stress Management, 11*(2), 132–148.

Mongillo, A. M. (1995). *Beyond the winter coat: Adjustment experiences of graduate students from the People's Republic of China*. Master thesis. McGill University, Montreal.

Montgomery, C. (2010). *Understanding the international student experience*. Basingstoke/New York: Palgrave Macmillan.

Murphy-Lejeune, E. (2003). An experience of interculturality: Student travellers abroad. *Intercultural experience and education*, 101–113.

Nicholson, M. W. (2001). *Adaptation of Asian students to American culture*. Retrieved from http://files.eric.ed.gov/fulltext/ED453751.pdf

Nishida, H. (1985). Japanese intercultural communication competence and cross-cultural adjustment. *International Journal of Intercultural Relations, 9*(3), 247–269. doi:10.1016/0147-1767(85)90028-8.
Oberg, K. (1960). Cultural shock: Adjustment to new cultural environments. *Practical Anthropology, 7,* 170–179.
Obst, D., & Forster, J. (2006). *Perceptions of European higher education (Country Report: USA).* Retrieved from http://ec.europa.eu/education/programmes/mundus/doc/us.pdf
Oei, T. P. S., & Notowidjojo, F. (1990). Depression and loneliness in overseas students. *International Journal of Social Psychiatry, 36*(2), 121–130. doi:10.1177/002076409003600205.
Pak, A. W.-p., Dion, K. L., & Dion, K. K. (1985). Correlates of self-confidence with English among Chinese students in Toronto. *Canadian Journal of Behavioural Science, 17*(4), 260–378.
Pan, Y.-L., Dixon, Z., Himburg, S., & Huffman, F. (1999). Asian students change their eating patterns after living in the United States. *Journal of the American Dietetic Association, 99*(1), 54–57. doi:10.1016/S0002-8223(99)00016-4.
Pan, J.-Y., Wong, D. F. K., Joubert, L., & Chan, C. L. W. (2008). The protective function of meaning of life on life satisfaction among Chinese students in Australia and Hong Kong: A cross-cultural comparative study. *Journal of American College Health, 57*(2), 221–231.
Pearson-Evans, A. (2006). Recording the journey: Diaries of Irish students in Japan. In M. Byram & A. Feng (Eds.), *Living and studying abroad. Research and practice* (Languages for intercultural communication and education, Vol. 12, pp. 38–63). Clevedon/Buffalo: Multilingual Matters Ltd.
Pedersen, P. B. (1980). Role learning as a coping strategy for uprooted foreign students. In G. V. Coelho (Ed.), *Uprooting and development. Dilemmas of coping with modernization* (Current topics in mental health, pp. 295–319). New York: Plenum Press.
Peroz, N. (2008). *Auswertung der Fragebogen für ausländische Studierende an der Fakultät IV.* Retrieved from http://www.flp.tu-berlin.de/fileadmin/fg53/ZiiK/ZiiK_Reports/Report_Nr9.pdf
Pilcher, N., Cortazzi, M., & Jin, L. (2011). Different waves crashing into different coastlines? Mainland Chinese learners doing postgraduate dissertations in the UK. In L. Jin & M. Cortazzi (Eds.), *Researching Chinese learners. Skills, perceptions and intercultural adaptations* (pp. 292–313). Basingstoke/New York: Palgrave Macmillan.
Pitts, M. J. (2009). Identity and the role of expectations, stress, and talk in short-term student sojourner adjustment: An application of the integrative theory of communication and cross-cultural adaptation. *International Journal of Intercultural Relations, 33*(6), 450–462. doi:10.1016/j.ijintrel.2009.07.002.

Poyrazli, S., Kavanaugh, P. R., Baker, A., & Al-Timimi, N. (2004). Social support and demographic correlates of acculturative stress in international students. *Journal of College Counseling, 7*(1), 73–82.
Pruitt, F. J. (1978). The adaptation of African students to American society. *International Journal of Intercultural Relations, 2*(1), 90–118. doi:10.1016/0147-1767(78)90030-5.
Qin, W. (1999). *China's brain drain: A study of the factors affecting Chinese students' and scholars' decisions to remain in the United States and not to return to China.* Dissertation. Boston University.
Ramsay, S., Barker, M., & Jones, E. (1999). Academic adjustment and learning processes: A comparison of international and local students in first-year university. *Higher Education Research & Development, 18*(1), 129–144. doi:10.1080/0729436990180110.
Ramsay, S., Jones, E., & Barker, M. (2007). Relationship between adjustment and support types: Young and mature-aged local and international first year university students. *Higher Education Research & Development, 54*(2), 247–265.
Redmond, M. V. (2000). Cultural distance as a mediating factor between stress and intercultural communication competence. *International Journal of Intercultural Relations, 24*(1), 151–159. doi:10.1016/S0147-1767(99)00028-0.
Ro, H.-K. (2006). *Zufriedenheit ausländischer Studierender an deutschen Hochschulen: Eine empirische Untersuchung am Beispiel ostasiatischer Studierender. Schriften zur Arbeits-, Betriebs- und Organisationspsychologie* (Vol. 23). Hamburg: Kovač.
Robinson, S. C. (2005). *When hope and fear collide: Expectations and experiences of first-year doctoral students in the natural sciences.* Doctoral thesis. University of Wisconsin—Madison.
Ryan, C., & Zhang, Z. (2007). Chinese students: Holiday behaviours in New Zealand. *Journal of Vacation Marketing, 13*(2), 91–105. doi:10.1177/1356766707074734.
Sawir, E., Marginson, S., Deumert, A., Nyland, C., & Ramia, G. (2008). Loneliness and international students: An Australian study. *Journal of Studies in International Education, 12*(2), 148–180. doi:10.1177/1028315307299699.
Saxenian, A. (2005). From brain drain to brain circulation: Transnational communities and regional upgrading in India and China. *Studies in Comparative International Development, 40*(2), 35–61. doi:10.1007/BF02686293.
Searle, W., & Ward, C. (1990). The prediction of psychological and sociocultural adjustment during cross-cultural transitions. *International Journal of Intercultural Relations, 14*(4), 449–464. doi:10.1016/0147-1767(90)90030-Z.
Selby, H. A., & Woods, C. M. (1966). Foreign students at a high-pressure university. *Sociology of Education, 39*(2), 138–154.
Selltiz, C., Christ, J. R., Cook, S., & Havel, J. (1963). *Attitudes and social relations of foreign students in the United States.* Minneapolis: University of Minnesota Press.
Sewell, W. H., & Davidsen, O. M. (1961). *Scandinavian students on an American campus.* Minneapolis: University of Minnesota Press.

Shenkar, O. (2001). Cultural distance revisited: Towards a more rigorous conceptualization and measurement of cultural differences. *Journal of International Business Studies, 32*(3), 519–535.

Skyrme, G. (2005). *The reflective learner: Chinese international students' use of strategies to enhance university study.* Retrieved from http://www.crie.org.nz/research-papers/G.Skyrme%20WP%2016.pdf

Skyrme, G. (2007). Entering the university: The differentiated experience of two Chinese international students in a New Zealand university. *Studies in Higher Education, 32*(3), 357–372. doi:10.1080/03075070701346915.

Smith, P., & Smith, S. N. (1999). Differences between Chinese and Australian students: Some implications for distance educators. *Distance Education, 20*(1), 64–80. doi:10.1080/0158791990200106.

Song, J. (2009). *Cultural experiences of German and Chinese exchange students and implications for a target group-oriented intercultural training program.* Albert-Ludwigs-Universität Freiburg, Freiburg, Germany. Retrieved from http://www.freidok.uni-freiburg.de/volltexte/6821/pdf/Diss_final_Freidok.pdf

Sovic, S. (2009). Hi-bye friends and the herd instinct: International and home students in the creative arts. *Higher Education, 58*(6), 747–761. doi:10.1007/s10734-009-9223-z.

Spencer-Oatey, H., & Xiong, Z. (2006). Chinese students' psychological and sociocultural adjustments to Britain: An empirical study. *Language, Culture and Curriculum, 19*(1), 37–53.

Spurling, N. (2006). Exploring adjustment: The social situation of Chinese students in UK higher education. *LATISS—Learning and Teaching in the Social Sciences, 3*(2), 95–117.

Stephens, K. (1997). Cultural stereotyping and intercultural communication: Working with students from the People's Republic of China in the UK. *Language and Education, 11*(2), 113–124. doi:10.1080/09500789708666722.

Sun, J. (2010). *Die Universität als Raum kultureller Differenzerfahrung: Chinesische Studenten an einer deutschen Hochschule.* Frankfurt, M. [u.a.]: Lang.

Sun(孙国徽), G. (2010, October 30). 如何看待海归当官. *People's Daily Overseas Edition.* Retrieved from http://paper.people.com.cn/rmrbhwb/html/2010-10/30/content_662076.htm

Sussman, N. M. (2002, August). *Sojourners to another country: The psychological rollercoaster of cultural transitions.* Online Readings in Psychology and Culture (Unit 8, Chapter 1). Retrieved from https://csivc.csi.cuny.edu/Nan.Sussman/files/publications/Online_Readings_The_Psychological_Rollercoaster_of_Cultural_Transitions.pdf

Taylor, E. W. (1994). Intercultural competency: A transformative learning process. *Adult Education Quarterly, 44*(3), 154–174. doi:10.1177/074171369404400303.

Terhune, K. W. (1964). Nationalism among foreign and American students: An exploratory study. *Journal of Conflict Resolution, 8*(3), 256–270. doi:10.1177/002200276 400800304.

Thomson, G., Rosenthal, D., & Russell, J. (2006). *Cultural stress among international students at an Australian university.* Retrieved from http://aiec.idp.com/uploads/pdf/Thomson%20(Paper)%20Fri%201050%20MR5.pdf

Tran, L. T. (2011). Committed, face-value, hybrid or mutual adaptation? The experiences of international students in Australian higher education. *Educational Review, 63*(1), 79–94. doi:10.1080/00131911.2010.510905.

Trice, A. G. (2003). Faculty perceptions of graduate international students: The benefits and challenges. *Journal of Studies in International Education, 7*(4), 379–403. doi:10.1177/1028315303257120.

Trice, A. D., & Elliott, J. (1993). Japanese students in America: II. College friendship patterns. *Journal of Instructional Psychology, 20*(3), 262–264.

Tsang, E. W. K. (2001). Adjustment of mainland Chinese academics and students to Singapore. *International Journal of Intercultural Relations, 25*(4), 347–372. doi:10.1016/S0147-1767(01)00010-4.

Turner, Y. (2002). Chinese students in Europe: The influence of culture and society. In W. Cox & D. Cameron (Eds.), *Chinese students in Ireland: New opportunities, new needs, new challenges. Papers from the ICOS seminar January 26, 2001,* (pp. 12–21).

UKCOSA. (2004). *Broadening our horizons: International students in UK universities and colleges.* London: UKCOSA

UNITE. (2006). *The international student experience report.* Retrieved from http://www.unite-group.co.uk/binaries/917/695/international-student-experience-report-2006.pdf

Wan, T.-y., Chapman, D. W., & Biggs, D. A. (1992). Academic stress of international students attending U.S. universities. *Research in Higher Education, 33*(5), 607–623. doi:10.1007/BF00973761.

Wang, Z. (2004). *Studying in the United States: Chinese graduate students' experiences of academic adjustment.* Dissertation. University of Illinois at Urbana-Champaign, Illinois, USA.

Wang, W.-h. (2009). *Chinese international students' cross-cultural adjustment in the U.S.: The roles of acculturation strategies, self-construals, perceived cultural distance, and English self-confidence.* Doctoral thesis. The University of Texas at Austin, Texas. Retrieved from http://repositories.lib.utexas.edu/bitstream/handle/2152/6588/wangw58087.pdf?sequence=2

Wang, L. (2010). *Chinese postgraduate students in a British university: Their learning experiences and learning beliefs* Doctoral thesis. Durham University, Durham, England, UK. Retrieved from http://etheses.dur.ac.uk/196/

Wang, Y. (2011, March 15). 2010中国留学市场呈现六大特征. *Beijing Youth Daily* (北京青年报). Retrieved from http://www.chinanews.com/lxsh/2011/03-15/2907000.shtml

Wang, Y. (2012). Mainland Chinese students' group work adaptation in a UK business school. *Teaching in Higher Education, 17*(5), 523–535. doi:10.1080/13562517.2012.658562.

Wang, H. (2013). China's return migration and its impact on home development. *UN Chronicle,* L(3). Retrieved from http://unchronicle.un.org/article/chinas-return-migration-and-its-impact-home-development/

Wang, L., & Byram, M. (2011). 'But when you are doing your exams it is the same as in China'—Chinese students adjusting to western approaches to teaching and learning. *Cambridge Journal of Education, 41*(4), 407–424. doi:10.1080/0305764X.2011.625001.

Wang, Y., & Sun, S. (2009). Examining Chinese students' Internet use and cross-cultural adaptation: Does loneliness speak much? *Asian Journal of Communication, 19*(1), 80–96. doi:10.1080/01292980802618494.

Ward, C. (2004). Psychological theories of culture contact and their implications for intercultural training and interventions. In D. Landis, J. M. Bennett, & M. J. Bennett (Eds.), *Handbook of intercultural training* (3rd ed.). Thousand Oaks: SAGE Publications.

Ward, C., & Kennedy, A. (1999). The measurement of sociocultural adaptation. *International Journal of Intercultural Relations, 23*(4), 659–677. doi:10.1016/S0147-1767(99)00014-0.

Ward, C., & Rana-Deuba, A. (1999). Acculturation and adaptation revisited. *Journal of Cross-Cultural Psychology, 30*(4), 422–442.

Ward, C., Okura, Y., Kennedy, A., & Kojima, T. (1998). The U-curve on trial: A longitudinal study of psychological and sociocultural adjustment during cross-cultural transition. *International Journal of Intercultural Relations, 22*(3), 277–291. doi:10.1016/S0147-1767(98)00008-X.

Ward, C., Leong, C.-H., & Low, M. (2004). Personality and sojourner adjustment: An exploration of the big five and the cultural fit proposition. *Journal of Cross-Cultural Psychology, 35*(2), 137–151. doi:10.1177/0022022103260719.

Wei, M., Heppner, P. P., Mallen, M. J., Ku, T.-Y., Liao, K. Y.-H., & Wu, T.-F. (2007). Acculturative stress, perfectionism, years in the United States, and depression among Chinese international students. *Journal of Counseling Psychology, 54*(4), 385–394. doi:10.1037/0022-0167.54.4.385.

Westwood, M. J., & Barker, M. (1990). Academic achievement and social adaptation among international students: A comparison groups study of the peer-pairing program. *International Journal of Intercultural Relations, 14*(2), 251–263. doi:10.1016/0147-1767(90)90008-K.

Wheeler, W. R., Henry, H. K., & Davidson, A. B. (Eds.). (1925). *The foreign student in America: A Study by the commission on Survey of Foreign Students in the United*

States of America. Under the Auspices of the Friendly Relations Committees of the Young Men's Christian Association and the Young Women's Christian Association. New York: Association Press.

Wilcox, P., Winn, S., & Fyvie-Gauld, M. (2005). 'It was nothing to do with the university, it was just the people': The role of social support in the first-year experience of higher education. *Studies in Higher Education, 30*(6), 707–722. doi:10.1080/03075070500340036.

Xinhuanet. (2014). 全国已建成各类留学人员创业园超过260家. Retrieved from http://news.xinhuanet.com/2014-11/26/c_1113418899.htm

Xu, M. (1991). The impact of English-language proficiency on international graduate students' perceived academic difficulty. *Research in Higher Education, 32*(5), 557–570.

Xu(徐笑君), X. (2009). Hai Gui Jiaoshi gongzuo manyidu diaocha fenxi("海归"教师工作满意度调查分析). Human Resources(人力资源), 21, 35–37.

Xu, L. (2010). *The Interrelated Factors of Chinese Students' Adaptation in France: Emotion Regulation, Social Support & Acculturative Stress* (Master's thesis). Shanghai International Studies University, Shanghai, China.

Xu (徐蓉), R., Li(李伟), W., & Liu(刘晓侠), X. (2014). A case study of overseas returnees' role in university globalization (海归教师对高校国际化建设的作用探讨). *Journal of Ningbo University (Educational Science Edition) (*宁波大学学报(教育科学版)), 36*(1), 54–56.

Yan, K., & Berliner, D. C. (2009). Chinese international students' academic stressors in the United States. *College Student Journal, 43*(4), 939–960.

Yan, W., & Cheng, L. (2015). How language proficiency contributes to Chinese students' academic success in Korean universities. *Language Testing in Asia, 5*(1), 973. doi:10.1186/s40468-015-0016-2.

Ye, J. (2006). Traditional and online support networks in the cross-cultural adaptation of Chinese international students in the United States. *Journal of Computer-Mediated Communication, 11*(3), 863–876. doi:10.1111/j.1083-6101.2006.00039.x.

Yeh, E.-K. (1976). Cross-cultural adaptation and personal growth: The case of Chinese students. *Acta Psychologica Taiwanica, 18*, 95–104.

Yeh, C. J., & Inose, M. (2003). International students' reported English fluency, social support satisfaction, and social connectedness as predictors of acculturative stress. *Counselling Psychology Quarterly, 16(1), 15–28.*

Yin(殷实), S. (2008). *Cultural identity and reverse cultural shock: A research based on the social cognition theory.* Master thesis. East China Normal University, Shanghai, China.

Yuan(袁凤凤), F. (2014). *A study on the adaptation of junior returnee teachers to China's current academic system (*高校青年海归教师对中国现行学术体制的适应研究*).* East China Normal University, Shanghai.

Zeilinger, M. (2006). Beratung von ostasiatischen Studierenden. *Zeitschrift für Interkulturellen Fremdsprachenunterricht [Online], 11*(2). Retrieved from http://zif.spz.tu-darmstadt.de/jg-11-2/beitrag/Zeilinger1.htm

Zhai, L. (2002). *Studying international students: Adjustment issues and social support.* Retrieved from http://www.eric.ed.gov/PDFS/ED474481.pdf

Zhang, J. (2008). *Chinese students' cross cultural adaptation in the US.* Master's thesis. Yunnan Normal University, Yunnan, China.

Zhang(张欣), X. (2013). *The research on cultural re-adaptation of Chinese returned students from overseas.* Master thesis. Shanxi University of Finance & Economics.

Zhang(张东海), D. (2014). Academic environment and returning inclination: A questionnaire study among Chinese Ph.D. students studying in the U.S. (学术环境与归国意愿——对留美博士生的调查研究). 复旦教育论坛 *(Fudan Education Forum), 12*(5), 45–49, 102.

Zhang, Z., & Brunton, M. (2007). Differences in living and learning: Chinese international students in New Zealand. *Journal of Studies in International Education, 11*(2), 124–140. doi:10.1177/1028315306289834.

Zhang, Z., & Xu, J. (2007). Understanding Chinese international graduate students' adaptation to learning in North America: A cultural perspective. *Higher Education Perspectives, 3*(1), 45–59.

Zhang, Z., & Zhou, G. (2010). Understanding Chinese International Students at a Canadian University: Perspectives, Expectations, and Experiences. *Canadian and International Education / Education canadienne et internationale, 39*(3), 43–58.

Zhao, C.-M., Kuh, G. D., & Carini, R. M. (2005). A Comparison of International Student and American Student Engagement in Effective Educational Practices. *The Journal of Higher Education, 76*(2), 209–231.

Zhao, T. (2007). *An ethnographic study of the intercultural adaption process between Chinese students and their British lecturers and fellow students in the UK.* Doctoral thesis. University of Southampton, Southampton.

Zhao, T., & Bourne, J. (2011). Intercultural adaptation—It is a two-way process: Examples from a British MBA programme. In L. Jin & M. Cortazzi (Eds.), *Researching Chinese learners. Skills, perceptions and intercultural adaptations* (pp. 250–273). Basingstoke/New York: Palgrave MacMillan.

Zhao, N., & McDougall, D. (2008). Cultural influences on Chinese students' asynchronous online learning in a Canadian university. *Journal of Distance Education, 22*(2), 59–79.

Zheng, X., & Berry, J. W. (1991). Psychological adaptation of Chinese sojourners in Canada. *International Journal of Psychology, 26*(4), 451–470. doi:10.1080/00207599108247134.

Zheng, X., Sang, D., & Wang, L. (2004). Acculturation and subjective well-being of Chinese students in Australia. *Journal of Happiness Studies, 5*(1), 57–72. doi:10.1023/B:JOHS.0000021836.43694.02.

Zhou, J. (2010). *Zwischen "Elite von morgen" und "Liu Xue La Ji" ("Müllstudenten")*. Münster: Verl.-Haus Monsenstein und Vannerdat.

Zhou, Y., & Todman, J. (2008). Chinese postgraduate students in the UK: A two-way reciprocal adaptation. *Journal of International and Intercultural Communication, 1*(3), 221–243. doi:10.1080/17513050802101799.

Zhou, Y., & Todman, J. (2009). Patterns of adaptation of Chinese postgraduate students in the United Kingdom. *Journal of Studies in International Education, 13*(4), 467–486. doi:10.1177/1028315308317937.

Zhou, R. Y., Knoke, D., & Sakamoto, I. (2005). Rethinking silence in the classroom: Chinese students' experiences of sharing indigenous knowledge. *International Journal of Inclusive Education, 9*(3), 287–311. doi:10.1080/13603110500075180.

Zhou, Y., Topping, K., & Jindal-Snape, D. (2011). Intercultural adaptation of Chinese postgraduate students and their UK tutors. In L. Jin & M. Cortazzi (Eds.), *Researching Chinese learners. Skills, perceptions and intercultural adaptations* (pp. 233–249). Basingstoke/New York: Palgrave Macmillan.

Zhu, J. (2007). *A cross-cultural learning case study: Comprehending Chinese international students' adapting and learning strategies at Canadian universities*. Master thesis. Halifax, Nova Scotia, Canada, Halifax, Nova Scotia, Canada. Retrieved from http://dc.msvu.ca:8080/xmlui/bitstream/handle/10587/282/JiaZhu-MAED-2007.pdf?sequence=3&isAllowed=y

Zhu(朱佳妮), J. (2008). *A study on Chinese overseas students' academic adjustment (*中国出国留学生教育适应状况的研究*)*. Master thesis. Shanghai Jiao Tong University, Shanghai, China.

Zweig, D. (1997). To return or not to return? Politics vs. economics in China's brain drain. *Studies in Comparative International Development, 32*(1), 92–125. doi:10.1007/BF02696307.

Zweig, D., & Changgui, C. (1995). *China's Brain Drain to the United States: Views of Overseas Chinese Students and Scholars in the 1990s*. Berkeley: Institute of East Asian Studies, University of California.

Zweig, D., Chen, C., & Rosen, S. (2004). Globalization and transnational human capital: Overseas and returnee scholars to China. *The China Quarterly, 179*, 735–757. doi:10.1017/S0305741004000566.

Zweig, D., Fung, C. S., & Han, D. (2008). Redefining the brain drain: China's 'diaspora option'. *Science Technology & Society, 13*(1), 1–33. doi:10.1177/097172180701300101.

CHAPTER 3

An Unprepared Academic Journey: Pre-departure Adjustment

Precise knowledge of self and precise knowledge of the threat leads to victory.
知己知彼,百战不殆

— *The Art of War (孙子兵法 sunzi bingfa)*

The journey of academic adjustment for international Chinese students begins in China, influenced by students' motivations and readiness for study abroad and the process of applying to programs.

MOTIVATION

Motivation for studying abroad influences the success of student sojourns (Klineberg 1980). Given that 'the motivations impelling overseas students [...] are complex, diverse, multi-faceted, not always "rational"' (Bochner 1972, p. 6), it is necessary to discriminate between Chinese students' motivation for going abroad in general and their specific reasons for choosing Germany as a host country.

General Motivations: The 'Dream of Studying Abroad'

Like most new college graduates after their first degree, Chinese students must decide whether to continue their studies or find a job (Fig. 3.1). In China, these graduates face a furiously competitive job market in which the reputation of one's alma mater and the possession of an advanced degree confer distinct advantages. Students pursuing a graduate degree in China, however, need to take the competitive entrance exam for graduate school (考研 *kaoyan*). In 2014 over 1.72 million students took the exam of which 0.57 million—just one-third—were admitted to graduate programs (Han and Li 2014, December 27). In the face of this competition, Chinese students look to go abroad for further study. Furthermore, as long as they can afford the tuition fee and living expenses, parents often encourage their children to study abroad. They visit educational fairs together with their children, collect brochures given by overseas universities, and compare programs. Ultimately, the decision for Chinese students to study abroad is made collectively by the family.

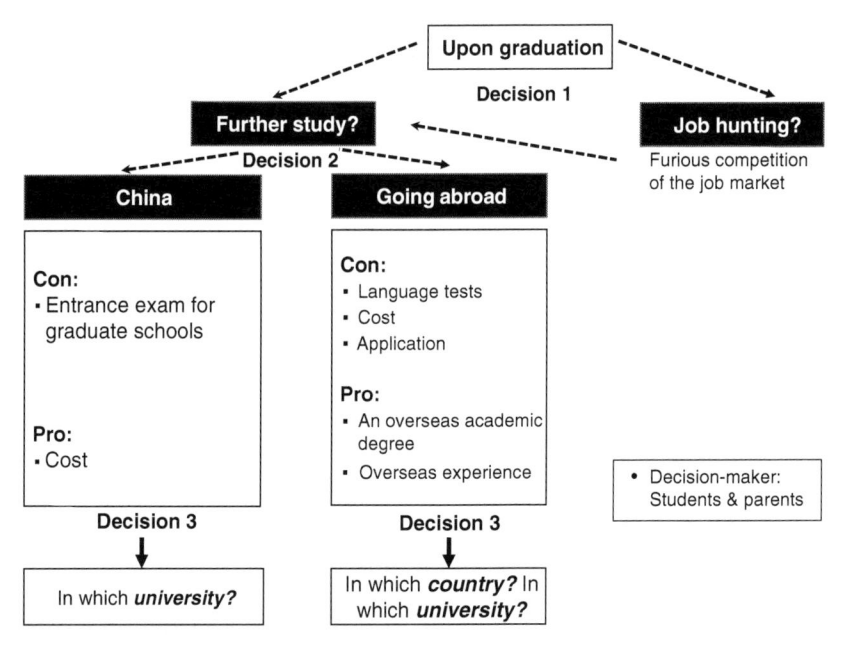

Fig. 3.1 Decision-making process of new Chinese graduates

Moreover, Chinese students in general harbor 'a dream of studying abroad' (留学梦 *liuxue meng*), with 'study abroad fever' (出国热 *chuguo re*) being another common term. Indeed, 'with the rarest of exceptions, they [overseas students] all go willingly, and in many cases enthusiastically' (Klineberg 1980, p. 273). Many of the international Chinese students in the studies that inform this book also showed the same strong determination for going abroad. For some, their dreams to study abroad started as early as their first year of university, because they simply longed to explore and have a look at the outside world (出国看看 *chuguo kankan*) (mentioned by Interviewees 7 and 13). Others began later, forming specific plans near the end of their undergraduate study or even after having already obtained a job (Interviewee 6).

Nevertheless, the survey of 55 Chinese students in Study 3 indicates that 'to pursue academic knowledge' (31 votes), 'to improve the foreign language skills' (31 votes), and 'to obtain an overseas degree' (24 votes) were the three most important reasons motivating Chinese students going abroad in general (Table 3.1).

All of these factors serve to improve students' competitiveness in the job market in China, especially for students who graduate from less-prestigious universities that do not fall under Project 211 or Project 985; they hope an overseas master's degree will make them more competitive candidates (mentioned by Interviewees 5 and 11). Comparatively few students considered variety or courses or academic freedom as an important motivational factor in the decision to study abroad.

Table 3.1 Reasons for going abroad in general according to respondents in Study 3

No.	Reasons for going abroad in general	1st reason[a]	2nd reason	3rd reason	Total
(1)	To pursue academic knowledge	14	13	4	31
(2)	To improve foreign language skills	8	11	12	31
(3)	To obtain an overseas degree	7	11	6	24
(4)	Exchange programs are available	11	4	3	18
(5)	To experience the learning environment abroad	4	3	9	16
(6)	To obtain better learning environment	4	3	3	10
(7)	To gain research experience	2	1	7	10
(8)	More courses are available at foreign university	0	2	5	7
(9)	More academic freedom is available	2	3	0	5
(10)	Others	3	1	1	5
	Total	55	52	50	–

[a]Respondents are allowed to give more than one reason

Specific Motivations for Studying in Germany

Chinese students who choose Germany do so because of its excellent academic reputation, affordable tuition and living expenses, and relatively easy application requirements. This finding is consistent with another study conducted with over 6,000 prospective, current, and recently graduated international students, for whom affordability (37.3 per cent), employment prospects (34.0 per cent), and international recognition of the degree (24.9 per cent) were the three most important factors in choosing a study abroad destination (Lawrence, 2009).

Both qualitative (Study 1 and Study 2) and quantitative (Study 3) results support academic reputation as a topic of influence in attracting Chinese students to study in Germany, a country known for strong programs in classical engineering sciences. In Study 3, for example, 35 out of 55 respondents agreed that the reputation of German universities was an important reason attracting them to choose Germany (Table 3.2). One recent survey (Apolinarski and Poskowsky 2013) conducted among 985 international students in Germany similarly indicated international students specifically chose Germany for the following reasons: (1) 'to improve German language proficiency' (65 per cent), (2) because 'Germany is

Table 3.2 Reasons for studying in Germany according to respondents in Study 3

No.	Reasons for choosing Germany	1st reason[a]	2nd reason	3rd reason	Total
(1)	German universities have a good reputation	15	15	5	35
(2)	Low/no tuition fee	4	11	12	27
(3)	A cooperation program is available	19	3	3	25
(4)	Good career prospects	3	6	7	16
(5)	Germany is an industrialized country	1	7	7	15
(6)	The specific major in Germany enjoys a good reputation	7	4	3	14
(7)	Interested in German culture and history	2	2	7	11
(8)	Going abroad to change the current learning environment	1	2	2	5
(9)	Some friends studying in Germany	1	2	1	4
(10)	Part-time job is allowed	0	1	1	2
(11)	Others	2	0	0	2
	Total	55	53	48	–

[a]Respondents are allowed to give more than one reason

a technologically advanced country' (61 per cent), (3) 'to learn about Germany' (54 per cent), or (4) because 'my financial situation can afford studying in Germany' (46 per cent).

The results of the interviews undertaken for this book were consistent with those of the questionnaires. Chinese students in the interviews clearly demonstrated admiration for specific subjects at German universities, such as mechanical engineering (mentioned by Interviewee 16) and electrical engineering (mentioned by Interviewee 14). Although these two students were admitted to schools in the USA and the UK as well, they chose Germany for its perceived research reputation.

> In the research of natural science, especially in the field of physics, the German researchers have done substantial contribution in the last 200 years, for example, Einstein and Max Planck. There must be something worth learning from its research system and attitude of doing research. (Interviewee 2)

In addition, interviewees also indicated that they came to Germany not just for an overseas degree, but to gain 'genuine' knowledge that is meaningful, useful, and concrete—even if that meant turning down programs elsewhere that could be accomplished in as little as one year.

> Most Chinese parents send their children abroad in the hope that their children can learn the genuine knowledge there, instead of just an overseas degree. If one just aims at achieving an overseas degree, he would probably choose the UK or other English-speaking country (where the length of study is relatively short). (Interviewee 14)

Affordable tuition and living expenses also attracted Chinese students to study in Germany, as indicated by about two-thirds of Chinese students in one study (Zhou 2010). Table 3.2 indicates that free or low-cost tuition was the second most important reason that Chinese students chose Germany as the host country. Student interviews support these results, as Chinese students (Interviewees 3, 7, 10, 11, and 14) emphasized that the low cost of tuition fees or living expenses was a big factor in choosing to study in Germany. For most Chinese families, overseas study is a luxury, often unaffordable. The National Bureau of Statistics of China (NBS) reports the annual disposable income in 2010 in urban areas as 28,844 RMB (about 4,154 euros), while the net annual income in rural areas is 10,489 RMB (about 1,510 euros)

(NBS 2015b). Compared with the relatively high tuition fees in the USA and the UK, costs in Germany allow Chinese students from the working class the opportunity to realize their 'dreams of studying overseas'.

The savings can be significant. According to a recent survey conducted by The College Board, a non-for-profit organization that connects students to college success and opportunity, public four-year colleges in the USA averaged $9,139 (8,137 euros) in tuition and fees for in-state students and $22,958 (about 20,440 euros) for full-time out-of-state students for the 2014–2015 school year (The College Board 2015). According to *U.S. News & World Report*, the average tuition at private universities was $31,381 in 2014–2015 (Snider 2014, October 28), with the tuition at prestigious universities that attract many Chinese students significantly higher. In the UK, figures for 2014–2015 show that the average annual cost of study for non-EU students at the undergraduate level is £11,987 (about 16,850 euros) and £12,390 (about 17,416 euros) at the postgraduate level (QS 2015a). In contrast, international students in Germany pay what domestic German students do, no more than 250 euros per semester. This fee covers administration, student support services, and other costs (QS 2015b) as well as public transportation fees in some federal states. Moreover, since August 2012, non-EU students in Germany have been allowed to work for 120 whole days or 240 half days annually (Deutsches Studentenwerk 2015) making it possible for Chinese students to finance their daily expenses. German prices are much more in line with those in China, where an undergraduate student pays 5,000–10,000 RMB (about 720–1,440 euros) annually, depending on the discipline of study.

A desire to improve German language proficiency also motivates Chinese students to study in Germany. Interviewees majoring in German language and literature studies naturally considered Germany as their first choice (mentioned by Interviewees 17 and 20), but others were motivated to learn German as a second foreign language (mentioned by Interviewees 2, 6, and 13); while English is the dominant foreign language in China, German, French, and Spanish are regarded as important 'minority foreign languages'. Picking up a second foreign language brings Chinese students more opportunities when they enter the job market back home.

Although a large number of interviewees had regarded the USA as their first choice, Chinese students were attracted to easier application requirements in Germany (门槛低 *menkan di*, literally, 'low threshold of admission') and a wide choice of programs for international students taught in English as well as German. Several interviewees mentioned that universities in the USA were difficult to get into (门槛高 *menkan gao*, 'high threshold of admission'), with the time and energy required to prepare for the Graduate Record Examination, a common entrance exam, mentioned by every interviewee who had once considered studying in the USA. In comparison, Germany does not require such an examination. One interviewee (Interviewee 11) also expressed the fear that, because her home university in China was not that 'famous', her chances of being admitted to any 'good' university in the USA were slim. Although the German language became a challenge to those Chinese students with limited proficiency, German universities offer a large choice of master's degree courses in English. According to Deutscher Akademischer Austauschdienst (DAAD), in 2015, about 1,712 international programs are available to international students, including 142 bachelor's programs, 815 master's programs, and 326 doctoral programs (DAAD 2015).

Finally, parents of Chinese students play a very important role (Bodycott and Lai 2012) in making the decision to study in Germany. For some study participants, Germany was either suggested or urged by their friends or relatives. Zhou (2010) found that about one-fifth of Chinese students studied in Germany through their parents' decision. Parents of two interviewees (Interviewees 10 and 11) had had positive experiences in Germany; similarly, in Study 3, 65.5 per cent of participants reported that someone in their family or circle of friends had visited, worked, or studied in Germany.

Clearly, Chinese students choose to study in Germany for a variety of interconnecting reasons, certainly not limited to those given above. Some interviewees were motivated by German culture, history, and art (mentioned by Interviewee 8) or philosophy (e.g. Interviewee 7 mentioned Nietzsche). Some aimed primarily for academic knowledge; others, driven abroad by passion, desire, and curiosity, did not have a concrete goal in mind. Ultimately, the decision to study in Germany was a compromise between dreams and reality. As Chirkov et al. (2007) stated, the goals of international students 'are not their life-guiding principles but more specific situational objectives that are shaped by their situation in the home country, relationships with families, future career goals and other conditions' (pp. 204–205).

APPLICATION

Unlike German students, *Bildungsinländer*—or international students from other EU countries (who legally enjoy the same rights as German citizens)—like other non-EU international students, Chinese students must first obtain permission to study in Germany before being able to enroll in a German university. There are two major prerequisites in order to apply for undergraduate study: (1) proof of sufficient German language proficiency and (2) the recognition of equivalence to a native German's university entrance qualification issued by the *Akademische Prüfstelle* (Academic Evaluation Center), or APS (Heublein et al. 2004). On behalf of the Cultural Section of the German Embassy, APS authenticates academic credentials submitted by Chinese students (including primary and secondary school graduation certificates, certified copies of admission to university or *Gaokao*, records of university study, and university degrees) and conducts a validation interview or a Test for Academic Studies with applicants. Those Chinese students who successfully complete the process receive a certificate issued by the APS. It is worth mentioning that except for one student (Interviewee 11) who applied to German universities through *study abroad agents* (留学中介 *liuxue zhongjie*), all interviewees who pursued a degree program in Germany managed the application by themselves.

The duration of the application process varies. Although none of the participants pointed out any particular difficulty in applying, two Chinese students experienced a zigzag path in the application process before being finally being admitted. One student (Interviewee 10) did not receive her result from the APS in time, missed the deadline for application to the university, and had to wait until the following year to apply. Another student (Interviewee 11) failed to register at the university the first time, as she didn't have the visa required by the university, and had to wait one semester to resubmit her application. One interviewee (Interviewee 6) mentioned that many Chinese students she knew had given up their 'German Dream' during the application, as it took too much time. It is important to note here that English language graduate programs and exchange programs have an easier application process (mentioned by Interviewees 4 and 13). Moreover, the process of college admissions is different between China and Germany; as one interviewee (Interviewee 9) mentioned, applying for a master's program abroad, to some extent, is complicated, but the chances of being admitted to a master's program in Germany are bigger than that in China.

In order to increase their chances of being admitted, Chinese students applied to more than one German university, typically between five (mentioned by Interviewee 9) and nine (mentioned by Interviewee 16). In ranking their choices, Chinese students took available majors, prestige, and location into consideration.

For those who chose to study in Germany primarily for academic reasons, availability of a major was the most important factor in choosing a school. One interviewee (Interviewee 16) who received nine letters of admission chose University R because it was very strong in his field—mechanical engineering. Other interviewees similarly pursued particular subjects in making their choices, for example, Interviewee 15 for architecture and Interviewees 18 and 19 for German language and literature.

In choosing their universities, Chinese students and their parents preferred 'famous' or 'well-known' German universities to those they considered 'nameless' or 'unknown'. In Germany, although there are some university-rankings,[1] higher education institutions are not categorized as 'key-universities' or 'non-key-universities', as they are in China. Some Chinese students who knew little about German universities or particular academic programs preferred to focus on a 'famous' university they had heard of. For example, one interviewee (Interviewee 9) mentioned that her relatives had strongly recommended her to study at her current university for its 'big name'.

In addition to the above concerns, other participants cared about the location of the university, particularly in terms of size and cost. Chinese students hold that big cities provide better chances for academic and cultural activities and employment (mentioned by Interviewees 3 and 7); therefore, they preferred to study in larger urban centers. One interviewee (Interviewee 6) applied to all three comprehensive universities in City A, a location also related to concerns about cost of living—City A is much cheaper than other German cities, especially those in southern Germany. Because the majority of Chinese students are self-funded, cost of living is a significant concern. One student (Interviewee 8) received a letter of admission from a university located in Munich in southern Germany, but after considering the relatively high living expenses there, she too chose to study in City A. However, not all Chinese students fancy big German cities. Some Chinese students in Study 2 chose University X, in a smaller city, with the specific intention to avoid meeting too many Chinese students there. One student (Interviewee 18) further explained, 'The city where University X located is really unknown in China. I had expected that there should have been fewer Chinese students here, but obviously this is not the case'.

READINESS: HARD SKILLS AND SOFT SKILLS

Are Chinese students ready for the academic challenge of studying abroad in Germany? Readiness for overseas study is not just a question of German language training. For instance, Taft (1981) proposed that a prospective

---

[1] For instance, CHE (Centrum für Hochschulentwicklung) Ranking, DFG (Deutsche Forschungsgemeinschaft) Funding Ranking, and Humboldt-Ranking are some national university rankings in Germany.

foreign student should have four general capabilities: knowledge of the host society, communication skills, technical skills, and social skills. Inspired by that framework, this book examines pre-departure readiness from both 'hard skills' and 'soft skills' perspectives. The former focuses on Chinese students' previous academic and foreign language background, while the latter refers to their knowledge about Germany and German universities, previous intercultural experience, and psychological readiness (all of which have attracted less attention in prior academic research).

Hard Skills: Academic Readiness, German Language,

Academic Readiness: Transition of Major and Degree

In terms of academic background, Chinese participants can be divided into three categories: the 'graduates' (students who have already received at least one academic degree in China), the 'adventurers' (students who have not achieved any academic degree in China), and the 'relaxed students' (students who are participating in an exchange program in Germany). Table 3.3 indicates the academic backgrounds that students participating in the three studies have achieved in China.

To the 'graduates', studying in Germany is a low-risk decision: even if they should fail to complete an advanced degree in Germany, they have already 'secured at least one academic title in China' (mentioned by Interviewee 20). Most participants belong to this low-risk group.

On the other hand, 'adventurers' have quit their undergraduate study in China to pursue a bachelor's degree in Germany. In Study 1, two respondents (Interviewees 12 and 15) were still registered in their Chinese undergraduate programs while applying to German universities, but would

Table 3.3 Academic degree achieved in China by participants in all three studies

Categories	Degrees	Study 1 (%)	Study 2 (%)	Study 3 (%)
The 'graduates'	Bachelor's	13 (65.0)	4 (80.0)	24 (43.6)
	Master's	0 (0.0)	0 (0.0)	6 (10.9)
	Postgraduate	3 (15.0)	0 (0.0)	1 (1.8)
	Doctoral studies	0 (0.0)	0 (0.0)	3 (5.5)
The 'adventurers'	Undergraduate	2 (10.0)	0 (0.0)	19 (34.5)
The 'relaxed students'	Exchange students	2 (10.0)	1 (20.0)	2 (3.6)
	Total	20 (100.0)	5 (100.0)	55 (100.0)

have had to quit their programs in China to take up study in Germany—a risky decision, as they 'burned their bridges' and no longer had a 'route of retreat' (断后路 *duan houlu*). What motivates those Chinese students to make such a risky decision? One interviewee (Interviewee 12) was not satisfied with the reputation of her home university, not having obtained a good enough score in the National Higher Education Entrance Examination (高考 *Gaokao*) to study at a better university. Another student (Interviewee 15) was not interested in the major chosen for her, despite having been admitted to a prestigious university in Shanghai.

Benefiting from the coordination of partner universities in China and Germany, the 'relaxed students' in academic exchange programs received much more support regarding visa application, attending German language courses, and so on. Some also experienced an easier academic workload and much less academic pressure than other students, whether from shorter time abroad or other kinds of support. In interviews, one undergraduate student (Interviewee 21) only studied one semester in Germany and one master's student (Interviewee 4) spent two semesters. Another student (Interviewee 13) was enrolled in a double-degree program organized by both home and host universities.

Another important aspect contributing to academic readiness is the compatibility of Chinese majors with those in Germany. Participants in all three studies were asked to judge how consistent their majors were between countries (Table 3.4). '(Almost) consistent' indicates that Chinese students' majors in Germany and China were very similar or even exactly the same, 'relevant' means the students' majors in Germany and China were interrelated, and 'inconsistent' means their major in Germany was unrelated to their previous one in China. Study 2 is a special case, as the faculty required participants to have a background in German language and culture studies; the students continued those studies in China.

Table 3.4 Consistency between previous major in China and current major in Germany

	(Almost) consistent	Relevant	Inconsistent	No. of participants
Study 1	57.1 %	14.3 %	28.6 %	14[a]
Study 2	100 %	0.0 %	0.0 %	5
Study 3	29.1 %	47.3 %	23.6 %	55

[a]Among sixteen Chinese students in Study 1, the results of two students who started their first degree in Germany (with no previous major in China) are not included

Consistency between majors helped facilitate Chinese students' academic adjustment in Germany. For instance, one doctoral student (Interviewee 1), whose major in Germany was almost identical with what he had completed in China, reported that it was relatively easy for him to handle the challenges of the new learning environment. German universities often require students applying for master's study to have the same or relevant academic background for their bachelor's study; differences of classifications in academic fields between Germany and China partially explain why some participants (28.6 per cent in Study 1 and 23.6 per cent in Study 3) changed their majors. For example, one interviewee majored in advertising (广告学 *guanggao xue*) in China, did not find an equivalent in Germany, and switched to a relevant topic, media studies, in Germany. Some participants who were able to do so deliberately changed their majors, as they had little interest in their previous one.

German Language
Based on the interviews, the students can be categorized by their German language background into four types: the 'German major', the 'rushers', the 'dumb German learners', and the 'zero-German-speakers'.

The 'German majors' are Chinese students who majored in German language and literature studies back in China. As they are more familiar with German culture and German people (their lecturers), they can be expected to have a relatively good command of the German language. Two students (Interviewees 4 and 10) in Study 1 and all five Chinese participants in Study 2 belong to this category.

The 'rushers' are Chinese students who learned the German language in a rushed, urgent manner; these students account for the majority of Chinese students studying abroad in Germany. As German language proficiency is a prerequisite for applying to German universities, these Chinese students had to learn the German language quickly in order to pass the standardized German language test (TestDaF[2] or DSH[3]) by attending intensive German courses in China or in Germany.

The 'dumb German learners' are those who had some basic German grammar and vocabulary, but were not confident of their German language skills at all. For instance, two interviewees (Interviewees 7 and 9) had minored in German language in China but considered their German

---

[2] TestDaf (*Der Test Deutsch als Fremdsprache*) is an international German language test for foreign students who would like to study at German universities.

[3] DSH (*Deutsche Sprachprüfung für den Hochschulzugang*) is a language proficiency test required for study at German higher education institutions.

studies not to be communication oriented; they regarded their language ability as 'dumb German' or 'mute German' (哑巴德语 *yaba deyu*). As opposed to the 'rushers', the 'dumb German learners' often registered in English-taught master's programs.

The 'zero-German-speakers' are Chinese students who had no German language proficiency at all. Only two Ph.D. students (Interviewees 1 and 2) in Study 1 had no German language training before arrival. These two 'zero-German-speakers' did not appear to be worried, however, rather optimistically expecting that their lack of German language proficiency would cause 'no big problems'. The working language at the lab they would study at was English, and they had been informed that their German colleagues spoke very good English.

Language itself is closely related to the culture and history of a country, so students who studied German also were introduced to important information about German culture, history, and universities. Five out of eighteen interviewees in Study 1 received language training and later passed the standardized German language test in China, while the rest of them attended further training and passed the German language test in Germany. Except for two interviewees (Interviewees 3 and 6), most of the Chinese students were not satisfied with the German courses offered in China. Their reasons included few chances to practice spoken language (mentioned by Interviewee 8) and unsatisfactory quality of teaching (mentioned by Interviewees 5, 12, and 15). In addition, since most participants were full-time students in China, they were only able to attend German language courses part-time, alongside their 'normal' academic workload at the university.

Many Chinese students, then, decided to take their language courses and examinations in Germany. Some (such as Interviewee 5) believed that the ineffective German language learning in China was a 'waste of time' and believed that 'to learn the German language in Germany is better'. The hope of quickly picking up authentic foreign language skills in the country where it is spoken is also found in Chinese students studying in New Zealand, who originally planned to spend as little time studying English in their home country as possible (Zhang and Brunton 2007). Nevertheless, the quality of German language training in Germany also varied. One 'rusher' desired to pass the language test in Germany as soon as possible, but was disappointed with the curriculum she studied.

I went to the 'famous' [German language school located at] theological college in Bonn [...] this college is well known for its high ratio of passing the German language tests. [...] among international students attending the courses, 50 per cent were Korean and 45 per cent were Chinese. [...] given the large percentage of Korean students, some of the German vocabulary was even explained in Korean. In addition, because the language course is established in the theological college, what we had learned in the textbook was about religion and God. It did not relate to my own discipline at all. Anyway, I passed the language test there. (Interviewee 5)

Other students' experiences were much better. Two interviewees (Interviewees 5 and 14) were referred to the *Propädeutikum (prerequisite program)* course at University of T, which offers language training, subject-specific terminologies, and discipline-based knowledge. Both interviewees held a positive opinion about this course.

Subjective Evaluation of German Language Capabilities
Levels of German language proficiency among Chinese students varied greatly. Results of Study 3 indicated that before arrival or shortly after arrival, most participants were not confident of their academic German language ability. Figure 3.2 indicates that the biggest worry for Chinese students was participation in class discussions, as over 61.5 per cent of participants evaluated their German proficiency for participating in class discussions as 'poor or very poor'. In addition, over one-third of participants regarded their ability to understand lecturers (34.2 per cent) and communicate with lecturers and classmates (33.3 per cent) as 'poor' or 'very poor'. Their best confidence in their German ability was in doing homework. Although good foreign language proficiency 'does not necessarily guarantee participation in classroom' (Henderson 2009, p. 404), poor German language skills definitely hindered the Chinese students in participating in class discussions.

It is important to point out that different language skills are closely correlated (Table 3.5). The results of self-evaluation indicated that 'understanding the lecturers' was closely related to both 'participating in the discussions' ($r=0.68$, $p<0.01$) and 'communicating with lecturers/classmates' ($r=0.65$, $p<0.05$). That is, the more Chinese students understood their lecturers, the more confident they were in participating in class discussions and communicating with their lecturers and classmates. In addition, 'reading academic books' and 'homework' were also closely related ($r=.73$, $p<0.01$), two academic tasks that were mainly related to activities outside of class.

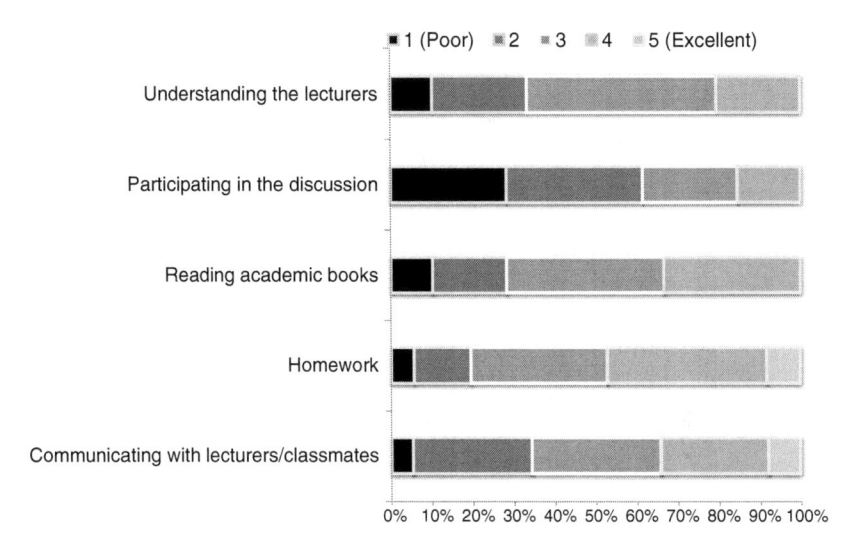

Fig. 3.2 Self-rated academic German language level according to Study 3. Note: Chinese students were asked to assess their academic German language level by using a five-point Likert scale: 1 (Poor) to 5 (Excellent)

Table 3.5 Correlation of self-rated German language level according to Study 3 ($n = 24$)

	(1)	(2)	(3)	(4)	(5)
(1) Listening: Understanding the lecturers	1				
(2) Speaking: Participating in the discussion	0.68[a]	1			
(3) Reading: Reading academic books	0.35[b]	0.38[b]	1		
(4) Writing: Homework or semester paper	0.38[b]	0.45[a]	0.73[a]	1	
(5) Communicating with lecturers/classmates	0.65[a]	0.58[a]	0.37[b]	0.49[a]	1

[a]Correlation is significant at the 0.01 level (2-tailed)
[b]Correlation is significant at the 0.05 level (2-tailed)

Furthermore, Chinese students who registered in English-taught master's programs or Ph.D. programs were more confident of their standard of English (Fig. 3.3). Similar to the results of evaluation of German language skills, only 24.1 per cent of Chinese students regarded their English language skills for 'participating in the discussion' as 'good' or 'excellent'. Based on the results of Study 3, upon arrival, Chinese students generally were worried about their ability to participate in class discussion, regardless of whether the courses were taught in English or in German.

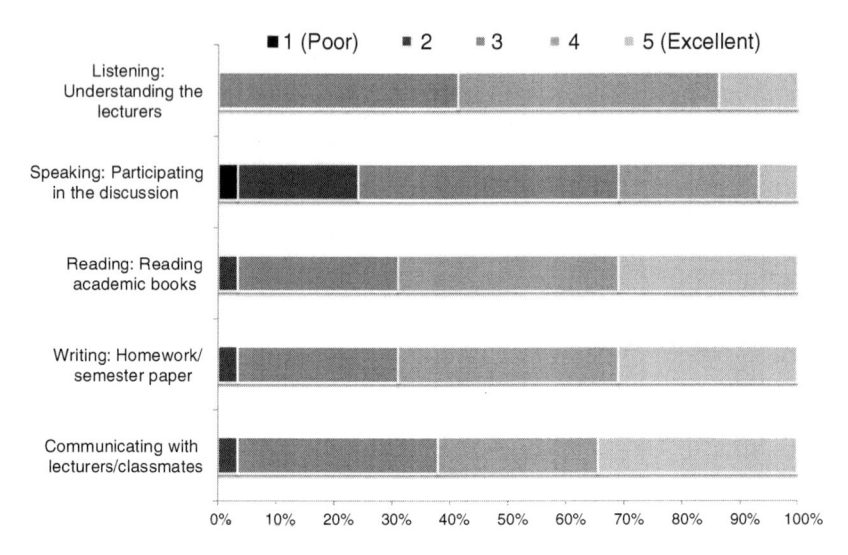

Fig. 3.3 Self-rated academic English language level according to Study 3. Note: Chinese students who did not speak German were asked to assess their academic English language level by using a five-point Likert scale: 1 (Poor) to 5 (Excellent)

Objective Evaluation of German Language Capabilities
Standardized German language tests, such as the *Deutsche Sprachprüfung für den Hochschulzugang* (DSH), *Der Test Deutsch als Fremdsprache* (TestDaF), '*Prüfungsteil Deutsch*' *der Feststellungsprüfung an Studienkollegs*, and *Deutsches Sprachdiplom der KMK-Stufe zwei* (DSD II) *neu* are accepted by most German universities (HRK 2015). Unless they meet exemption requirements, international students have to prove their German language skills through these tests when they apply to German universities. If international students take TestDaF, they are required to obtain a score of 4 (TDN-4)[4] in all four sections of the test (listening, reading, writing, and speaking) by most universities. If they take the DSH, they are expected to achieve a DSH-2[5] or Level-2 DSH.

---

[4] The examination results are assigned to one of three levels: (1) TestDaF-Niveaustufe 5 (TDN 5—TestDaF level 5); (2) TestDaF-Niveaustufe 4 (TDN 4—TestDaF level 4); (3) TestDaF-Niveaustufe 3 (TDN 3—TestDaF level 3). Retrieved from http://www.testdaf.de/fileadmin/Redakteur/PDF/Sprachen/informationen_en.pdf

[5] The DSH certificate documents the candidate's total score as: (1) DSH-3 (100–82%, highest level, suitable for any faculty); (2) DSH-2 (81–67%, generally accepted); or (3)

In Study 1, all interviewees attending German-speaking courses passed their respective standardized German tests, including the exchange students. In Study 3, 54 out of 55 participants answered the questionnaire, half of them passed the standardized test (48.1 per cent), the other half (50 per cent) had not participated in any test yet, and one interviewee (1.9 per cent) attended but failed the test (Fig. 3.4).[6] In total, about two-thirds of the Chinese students enrolled in German-speaking programs passed the German language tests. Half of the participants of the English-taught master's programs passed the language tests as well. For Chinese students pursuing programs in which German language was not a prerequisite for admission, merely 14.2 per cent passed the German language test.

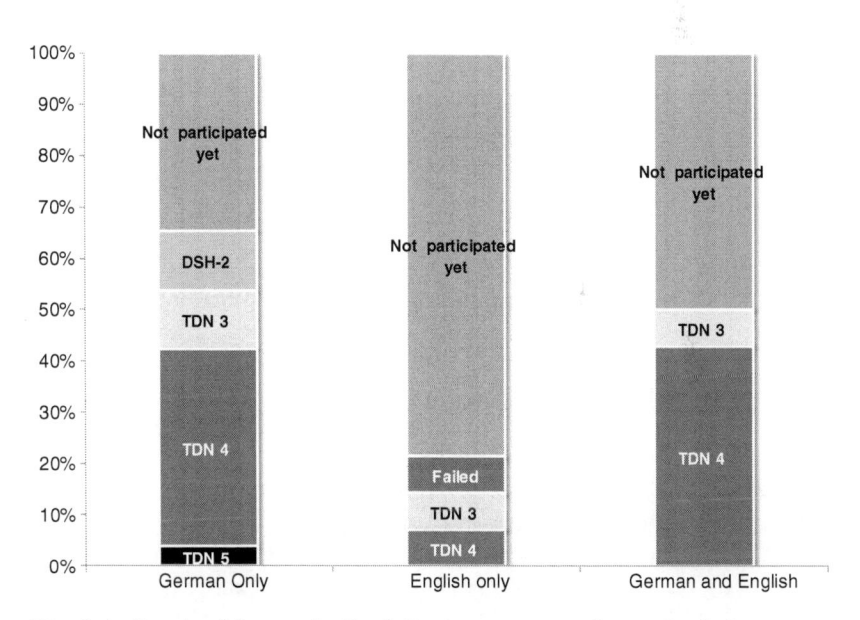

Fig. 3.4 Result of the standardized German tests according to Study 3

DSH-1 (66–57%, lowest possible entrance level, only accepted according to specific university regulations). Retrieved from http://www.isz.uni-heidelberg.de/e_pruef_dsh.html

[6] Some Chinese students in Study 3 participating in exchange programs or cooperative programs between Chinese and German universities are allowed to improve their German language skills after arrival; therefore, for them, the German language test was currently not obligatory.

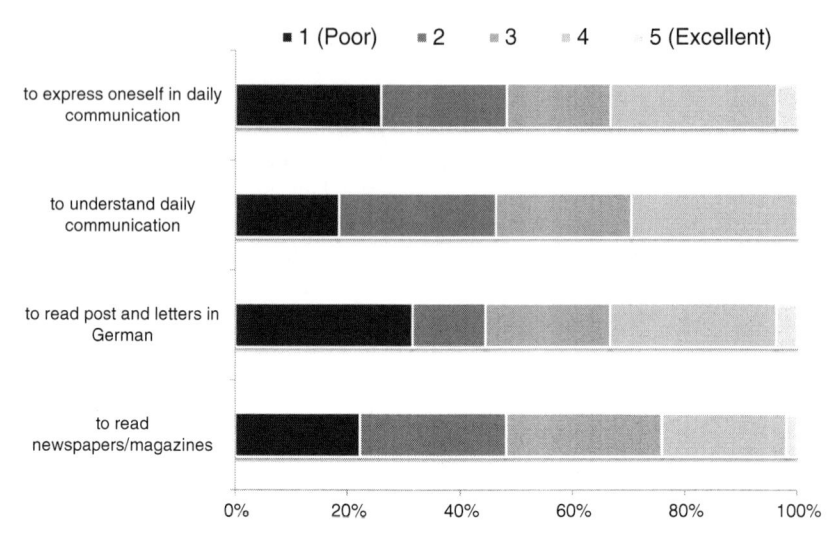

Fig. 3.5 Self-rated daily German language level according to Study 3. Note: Chinese students were asked to rate their daily German language by using a five-point Likert scale: 1 (Poor) to 5 (Excellent)

In addition to their academic language skills, Chinese students' competence at daily navigation was also important. All respondents (including Chinese students in English-taught master's programs) in Study 3 were asked to rate their daily German language level (Fig. 3.5). About half of the Chinese students worried that they would have difficulty in expressing themselves during daily tasks, such as communication or reading newspaper or magazines, rating their everyday German as 'poor' or 'relatively poor'. In addition, they expressed difficulty in daily communication as well as reading posts and letters in German.

On the other hand, non-German-speaking Chinese students for whom English was the working language in their academic programs also faced challenges in navigating daily life in Germany. One interviewee (Interviewee 9) did not bother to open any post at the beginning, as it was all written in German. As a result, she missed many important notifications from the city hall, university, insurance company, bank, and more.

Soft Skills: Knowledge of Germany and German Universities, Intercultural Experience, and Intercultural Training

Chinese students' knowledge of Germany and German universities is an important soft skill, as good knowledge of norms, customs, and values of the host culture facilitates sojourners' adjustment (Church 1982; Pruitt 1978) and can even be considered one of the components of intercultural communication competence (Redmond 2000). However, the results of both interviews and questionnaires indicated that, before beginning study in Germany, only a small number of Chinese students had obtained some knowledge of Germany and German universities, culture, and political issues. Thirty-eight per cent of participants in Study 3 evaluated their knowledge of 'German society', 'cultures and custom' as 'poor' or 'very poor', and 36.4 per cent of them evaluated their knowledge of 'political, economic, and historical information' as 'poor' or 'very poor'.

Despite having researched information about daily life (weather, food, accommodation, traffic, etc.) in Germany during preparation for study abroad, only 30.9 per cent of participants in Study 3 regarded their knowledge of daily life in Germany as 'good or excellent' (Fig. 3.6). Similar results for knowledge of everyday life in Germany were obtained by a questionnaire among Chinese students that found that 49.7 per cent of Chinese students did not prepare or do any research for their stay in Germany (Zhou 2010).

The results of the interviews that inform this book clearly indicated that before going to Germany, very few interviewees had prepared for the

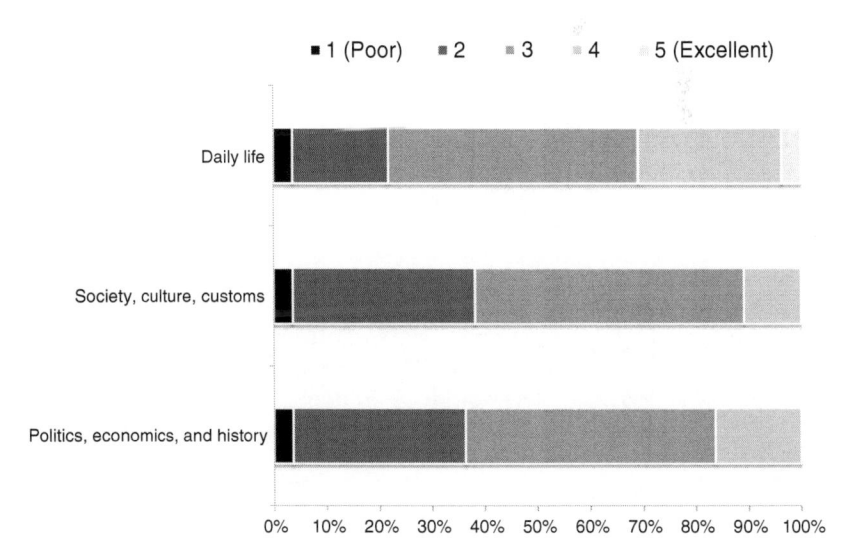

Fig. 3.6 Knowledge of Germany as a country according to Study 3. Note: Chinese students were asked to rate their knowledge of Germany as country by using a five-point Likert scale: 1 (Poor) to 5 (Excellent)

trip by seeking knowledge about Germany or German universities. Only one interviewee (Interviewee 8) read books concerning history, religion, culture, customs, and music in Germany; others admitted that they only had basic knowledge of Germany, obtained through geography or history class in middle school (mentioned by Interviewee 3) or through the media (mentioned by Interviewees 6, 11, and 14).

Perhaps surprisingly, compared to their pre-departure knowledge of Germany and German culture, Chinese students reported having even less knowledge of the learning forms, examinations, homework, or academic resources in place at German universities. Figure 3.7 shows the results of the questionnaires in Study 3. Around 40–45 per cent of participants evaluated their knowledge of 'Homework' (44.4 per cent) and 'Academic resources' (41.2 per cent), 'Lectures and seminars' (40 per cent) and 'Examinations' (40 per cent) as 'poor' or 'very poor'. Although it might be too much to expect Chinese students to know thoroughly how the education system and student life at German universities are conducted before arriving, there is clear room for improving on what they do know.

The group of German majors was an exception to this difficulty. Their previous academic and language background supplied them more concrete information about German universities and culture.

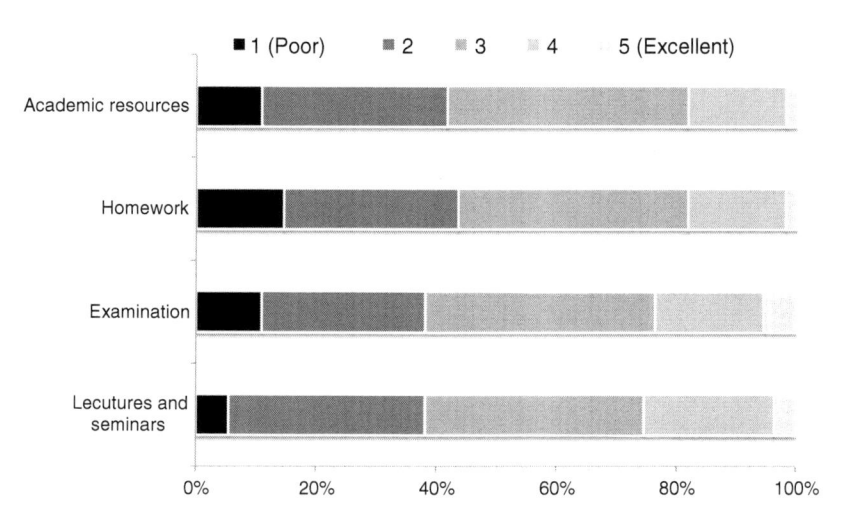

Fig. 3.7 Knowledge of German universities according to Study 3. Note: Chinese students were asked to rate their knowledge of German universities by using a five-point Likert scale: 1 (Poor) to 5 (Excellent)

As German majors, we had the experience of having German lecturers in China; therefore, I've heard about 'Volesung' and 'Seminar.' [...] I met many Germans and had some in-depth communication with them. To be frank, I didn't have too much expectation or worries before coming to Germany. (Interviewee 4)

Moreover, interviewees with German language backgrounds benefited from German teachers in China inviting them to parties and even cooking for them (mentioned by Interviewee 21). Therefore, they were more familiar with what to expect abroad, including some pleasant contrasts: one interviewee (Interviewee 20) mentioned, for example, that the buses in Germany came according to the timetable. This kind of basic knowledge of daily life in Germany fortified Chinese students' understanding of the country as a whole and likely helped them in their initial encounters in Germany.

The Chinese students got their pre-departure knowledge about Germany and German universities primarily second-hand, from Internet forum posts (帖子 *tiezi*) written and shared by other Chinese students studying in Germany (Table 3.6). Detailed original information, such as that found on the home pages of German universities, turned out to be a secondary resource, in part because (as students admitted) their language proficiency was not good enough to understand the more technical information written in German. In Study 3, 51 out of 55 (92.7 per cent) Chinese students obtained information about Germany and German universities by means of reading messages or posts shared on Internet forums as well as by 'consulting Chinese students who studied/were currently studying in Germany' (81.8 per cent). Results from these interviews were

Table 3.6 Sources of obtaining knowledge about Germany and German universities according to Study 3

Source of information	Choice 1	Choice 2	Choice 3	Total
Messages or posts on Internet forums	24	10	17	51
Consulting Chinese students who studied/ are studying in Germany	17	19	9	45
Home page of the German university	3	12	11	26
German course	8	9	8	25
German friends	2	4	9	15
Other	1	0	0	1
Haven't searched yet	0	1	0	1
Total	55	55	54	

consistent with the questionnaire, with interviewees getting information from other exchange students returning from Germany (mentioned by Interviewees 1, 4, and 13). Only one respondent (Interviewee 11) admitted that she had not searched in any fashion for any information concerning German universities.

German universities provide prospective international and native students with considerable information about their schools, programs, courses, and application requirements on their websites. In addition, external organizations such as DAAD and HRK-Hochschulkompass[7] provide a large amount of information about German universities and available programs for prospective students. There are also brochures from universities that provide important information and useful tips. Nevertheless, fewer than half the participants in Study 3 turned to the website of a German university for information.

Previous Intercultural Experience and Intercultural Training
Previous intercultural experience and intercultural training facilitate the sojourners' subsequent adjustment (Church 1982). Given the integration of European Union higher education (e.g. ERASMUS-Programme[8]), many students have ready opportunities to learn abroad and pick up intercultural experience. Nevertheless, only eight students in all three studies had been to Germany before, and for the majority of interviewees, it was their first time abroad. Only those students who had majored in German language and literature had previously accumulated any significant intercultural experience (interactions with native speakers and knowledge of Germany through academic exposure). Two of them (Interviewees 10 and 19) had been to Germany as exchange students, while most participants reported having hardly any intercultural experience.

Not many Chinese students had foreseen or realized the importance of such intercultural training to their study in Germany beforehand. Notwithstanding the increasing number of Chinese graduates going to Germany for advanced study, as well as ever-increasing academic partnerships between Chinese and German universities, there are few institutions offering intercultural training courses university-wide in China and, even

---

[7] HRK-Hochschulkompass (in English: German Rector's Conference-Higher Education Compass) provides information on Germany's higher education institutions, range of studies, and programs.

[8] The Erasmus Programme is a European Union student exchange program established in 1987.

then, the courses may be under-utilized. For instance, the Center for Foreign Language Training at the Tongji University[9] was one of the few schools providing such intercultural training. One interviewee (Interviewee 5) receiving language training at the German Center at Tongji University particularly mentioned the intercultural training program and regretted that she had not attended it. Outside the universities, private or individual organizations in China also provide intercultural training as well, as mentioned by some study participants; nevertheless, the importance of intercultural training has not yet been fully recognized by Chinese students.

Psychological Readiness
Before departure, it is understandable for a student to experience insecurity and worry about the future, but expectation of difficulty is also one of the best predicators for depression among international students (Oei and Notowidjojo 1990). Psychological readiness was therefore an important dimension to explore with interviewees, who were asked about their worries and attitudes leading up to their study abroad.

Before departure, Chinese students worried about daily and academic challenges, as well as possible financial problems. Experiences shared by other Chinese students studying in Germany served as an early warning. One interviewee (Interviewee 13) had expected difficulty in using the German language daily and two students reported concerns that they would be discriminated against (mentioned by Interviewee 13) or attract racist attention in the host country (mentioned by Interviewee 9). Awareness that the duration of study in Germany is much longer than in some English-speaking countries magnified anticipated difficulties (mentioned by Interviewees 5 and 14). One student who had sought out information on life in Germany worried that their current German language level might not be sufficient for study at German universities.

> I had expected that the study in Germany would be very difficult. [...] I've watched some documentary film about Chinese students studying abroad.

---

[9] The Center for Foreign Language Training at the Tongji University, in cooperation with DAAD, developed an intercultural training program for Chinese students aimed at helping those planning to study in Germany to develop intercultural competence for adjustment and improve their written and spoken German language skills at the German universities. The training course offers two moduls: intercultural training (e.g. searching for accommodation, getting registered at the German university, opening a bank account, applying for health insurance, etc.) and discipline-based spoken and written German language at German universities.

> [...] Although my parents support me financially and I don't have to worry about the financing problems, I did expect some difficulty in the study, the language, and the daily life in Germany. I had expected it would be difficult to learn a new subject in a foreign language. (Interviewee 15)

Furthermore, as the majority of Chinese students studying in Germany were financially supported by their parents, they regarded the expenses of studying abroad as a burden to their parents. One self-financed doctoral student (who actually supported by his parents financially) was concerned about disappointing his parents:

> There were too many things to worry about upon departure, but my biggest worry was how to live up to my parents' hope. I feel really guilty to spend their money. (Interviewee 3)

When asked how they dealt with their various concerns, Chinese students responded with two proverbs. One was somewhat pessimistic: 'When the arrow is on the string it must go' (箭在弦上，不得不发 *jian zai xian shang, bu de bu fa*). In most cases, Chinese students and their families had invested much time, energy, and money in preparing for study in Germany; despite many fears or worries, there was, to some extent, no turning back. One interviewee (Interviewee 11) vividly compared her current situation to 'the arrow on the string' and felt she had no other choice but to 'draw the bow and let it go'. The other expression students used was more optimistic: 'Cross that bridge when you come to it' (船到桥头自然直 *chuan dao qiao tou zi ran zhi*). Some Chinese students expressed confidence, saying, 'Even challenged by the difficulties, I think I can manage' (mentioned by Interviewee 13) or 'Even though there are problems, I will solve them. In the end things will mend' (车到山前必有路 *che dao shan qian bi you lu*) (mentioned by Interviewee 1). It is worth mentioning that these more optimistic students were male and believed that they could find solutions to their difficulties.

Goal of Studying in Germany

The most important goal among interviewees was to manage their study successfully and complete their academic degree (学有所成 *xue you suo cheng*) in Germany. Setting specific goals before studying abroad may be especially important, as academic goals set by international students themselves positively relate to their ability for academic adjustment (Gong and Chang 2007).

Frankly, I don't want to just rush for an academic degree in Germany. Some people hinted to me that my major – media science – is easy to get the degree, as some courses just require students to write a semester paper, no written exams. Nevertheless, as long as one has the opportunity to study abroad, he should take it seriously. (Interviewee 53)

In order to achieve their study goals, some students created detailed plans. For example, a law student (Interviewee 3) drew a knowledge-based pyramid: the top was his doctoral thesis, the middle sections were civil law and philosophy of law respectively, and the base was German philosophy and literature, which he regarded as the path to attainment of his knowledge. Another doctoral student (Interviewee 1) specifically planned to publish articles in journals in his research area and to participate in international-level conferences.

However, others had relatively rough plans for what they wanted to achieve in Germany. One Ph.D student had only an elementary plan of what he would do in his research (mentioned by Interviewee 2), and one theology major had a general plan to learn about the history of Christianity (mentioned by Interviewee 10).

References

Apolinarski, B., & Poskowsky, J. (2013). *Ausländische Studierende in Deutschland 2012: Ergebnisse der 20. Sozialerhebung des Deutschen Studentenwerks durchgeführt vom Deutschen Zentrum für Hochschul- und Wissenschaftsforschung (DZHW)*. Retrieved from http://www.studentenwerke.de/sites/default/files/soz20_auslaenderbericht.pdf

Bochner, S. (1972). Problems in culture learning. In S. Bochner & P. Wicks (Eds.), *Overseas students in Australia* (pp. 65–81). Randwick: New South Wales University Press.

Bodycott, P., & Lai, A. (2012). The influence and implications of Chinese culture in the decision to undertake cross-border higher education. *Journal of Studies in International Education, 16*(3), 252–270. doi:10.1177/1028315311418517.

Chirkov, V., Vansteenkiste, M., Tao, R., & Lynch, M. (2007). The role of self-determined motivation and goals for study abroad in the adaptation of international students. *International Journal of Intercultural Relations, 31*(2), 199–222. doi:10.1016/j.ijintrel.2006.03.002.

Church, A. T. (1982). Sojourner adjustment. *Psychological Bulletin, 91*(3), 540–572.

Deutscher Akademischer Austauschdienst (DAAD). (2015). International Programmes in Germany 2015: Retrieved June 30, 2015, from https://www.daad.de/deutschland/studienangebote/international-programs/en/

Deutsches Studentenwerk. (2015). Retrieved June 30, 2015, from http://www.internationale-studierende.de/fragen_zur_vorbereitung/finanzierung/jobben/

Gong, Y., & Chang, S. (2007). The relationships of cross-cultural adjustment with dispositional learning orientation and goal setting: A longitudinal analysis. *Journal of Cross-Cultural Psychology, 38*(1), 19–25. doi:10.1177/0022022106295438.

Han (韩晓蓉), X., & Li(李冰雪), B. (2014, December 27). 全国164.9万人今日参加考研,人数持续第二年下降. *The Paper (澎湃新闻)*. Retrieved from http://www.thepaper.cn/newsDetail_forward_1289246

Henderson, J. (2009). "It's all about give and take," or is it?: Where, when and how do native and non-native uses of English Shape U.K. University students' representations of each other and their learning experience? *Journal of Studies in International Education, 13*(3), 398–409. doi:10.1177/1028315308329788.

Heublein, U., Sommer, D., & Weitz, B. (2004). *Studienverlauf im Ausländerstudium: Eine Untersuchung an vier ausgewählten Hochschulen. Dokumentationen und Materialien* (Vol. 55). Bonn: DAAD.

Hochschulrektorenkonferenz (HRK). (2015). Retrieved July 1, 2015, from http://www.hrk.de/themen/internationales/arbeitsfelder/hochschulzugang-fuer-internationale-studierende/sprachnachweis-deutsch/

Klineberg, O. (1980). Stressful experiences of foreign students at various stages of sojourn: Counseling and policy implications. In G. V. Coelho (Ed.), *Uprooting and development. Dilemmas of coping with modernization* (Current topics in mental health, pp. 271–293). New York: Plenum Press.

Lawrence, R. (2009). *International student perceptions today: Insights derived from a study conducted with over 6,000 prospective, current and recently-graduated international students*. New South Wales: IDP Education Pty Ltd & the International Education Association of Australia (IEAA).

National Bureau of Statistics of China (NBS). (2015b). Retrieved 30 June 2015, from National Bureau of Statistics of China (2014年国民经济在新常态下平稳运行) http://www.stats.gov.cn/tjsj/zxfb/201502/t20150211_682459.html

Oei, T. P. S., & Notowidjojo, F. (1990). Depression and loneliness in overseas students. *International Journal of Social Psychiatry, 36*(2), 121–130. doi:10.1177/002076409003600205.

Pruitt, F. J. (1978). The adaptation of African students to American society. *International Journal of Intercultural Relations, 2*(1), 90–118. doi:10.1016/0147-1767(78)90030-5.

QS. (2015a). QS: Top universities (How much does it cost to study in the UK?). Retrieved June 30, 2015, from http://www.topuniversities.com/student-info/student-finance/how-much-does-it-cost-study-uk

QS. (2015b). QS: Top universities (Undergraduate tuition fees axed at all universities in Germany). Retrieved June 30, 2015, from http://www.topuniversities.com/student-info/university-news/undergraduate-tuition-fees-axed-all-universities-germany

Redmond, M. V. (2000). Cultural distance as a mediating factor between stress and intercultural communication competence. *International Journal of Intercultural Relations, 24*(1), 151–159. doi:10.1016/S0147-1767(99)00028-0.

Snider, S. (2014, October 28). 10 colleges where in-state students pay the most tuition. *U.S. News—Education*. Retrieved from http://www.usnews.com/education/best-colleges/the-short-list-college/articles/2014/10/28/10-colleges-where-in-state-students-pay-the-most-tuition

Taft, R. (1981). The role and personality of the mediator. In S. Bochner (Ed.), *The mediating person. Bridges between cultures* (pp. 53–88). Boston/Cambridge: G.K. Hall; Schenkman Pub. Co.

The College Board. (2015). Retrieved 30 June 2015 from http://www.collegeboard.com/student/pay/add-it-up/4494.html

Zhang, Z., & Brunton, M. (2007). Differences in living and learning: Chinese international students in New Zealand. *Journal of Studies in International Education, 11*(2), 124–140. doi:10.1177/1028315306289834.

Zhou, J. (2010). *Zwischen "Elite von morgen" und "Liu Xue La Ji" ("Müllstudenten")*. Münster: Verl.-Haus Monsenstein und Vannerdat.

CHAPTER 4

A Hard Landing: Beginning the Study Abroad

All things are difficult before they become easy.
万事开头难

— *Chinese proverb*

After arriving at the German universities, the initial period of study abroad was usually the most difficult time for the Chinese students who participated in the interviews. Due to the hustle of the pre-departure period, most Chinese students did not prepare well for the new learning settings of the university, and thus encountered great difficulty shortly after arrival. This book refers to this period as the 'hard landing'. Much like landing an airplane in the middle of a storm, students had no idea that they would experience so many different difficulties so quickly immediately upon entering the country. The following sections will detail how the Chinese students adjusted to their new academic environment cognitively, affectively, and behaviorally.

COGNITIVE DIMENSION ADJUSTMENTS

The challenge of the initial phase for Chinese students is to become familiar with the new learning environment and fulfill its requirements. International students often experience difficulty adjusting to new academic modes and the following are problem areas for them: '(i) being unable to participate fully in seminars, (ii) developing academic self-discipline; (iii) acquiring adequate feedback on performance; (iv) coping with the variety of assignments; (v) understanding examination methods and developing appropriate techniques' (Macrae 1997, p. 139). Yet, how Chinese students conceptualized these new types of courses, academic tasks, and examinations at German universities in order to deal with them varied on an individual level.

Exploring the Modul *System*

In the cognitive dimension, Chinese students quickly realized that their greatest adjustment challenge lay within the organization of the unique *Modul* system at German universities. *Modul*s are the building blocks of the bachelor's and master's programs in Germany. Each *Modul* meets specific objectives for developing competencies, and is composed of complementary courses (e.g. lectures, seminars, exercise classes, or tutorials) that students must organize, and schedule for themselves. Creating a schedule can take a lot of time and effort for students to accomplish each term, depending on how they want to specialize within their major, and what the changing availability of course offerings are. When students finish all courses required by a *Modul*, they attend a *Modul* exam to show they have learned the necessary competencies (in German: *Modulabschlussprüfung*). By finishing all the *Modul*s required by their faculty, students will have completed their bachelor's or master's degree.

However, this *Modul* system is a brand-new concept for Chinese students, and almost the complete opposite of their experience in China in terms of organization and expectations. In China, students immediately declare their major upon officially entering university, and simply receive their prescribed class schedule from the school in the first week of each semester that follows. Excepting a possible exploratory class (选修课 *xuanxiu ke*), the student's entire study plan is usually arranged by the faculty each semester, especially for bachelor's programs. Students do not need to plan their course progression. Instead, they just attend lectures following the predetermined timetable already provided for them.

> However, according to the Studienordnung (in English: study regulation), students in Germany have more autonomy in choosing courses by themselves. In this case, Chinese students first have to understand the Modul concept and the combination of the courses that make a complete Modul (e.g. lecture +

seminar, lecture + exercises, or lecture + seminar + exercise, etc.), before enrolling in classes. Although the Chinese students interviewed had been informed about the *Modul* system before arrival, they merely had a rough idea about it. They were confused by the *Modul* concept, with many describing the experience of the first semester as a "catastrophe." The Chinese students would attend courses, only to find they were outside their required *Modul*s, or out of order, and therefore redundant [...] In retrospect, many felt as though they had wasted their entire first semester, until they finally understood how the *Modul* system worked. One of my Chinese friends attended FOUR courses the first semester. At the end of the semester, he took THREE exams and passed TWO of them. Unfortunately, he eventually found one of the courses that he had passed was redundant. In the end of the first semester, he only achieved the credit point for ONE course. What a mess! (Interviewee 14)

In addition to figuring out how the *Modul* system worked, the students in the study identified difficulties arranging the progress of their coursework. Chinese students had no idea how many courses they should take each semester. Many took either too many courses (consequently, experiencing too much academic stress) or too few (as a result, failing to achieve the goal of obtaining certain credit points as they had planned):

> I was fully aware that my German language was very poor, so I didn't choose many courses the first semester. However, the second semester, I just chose too many courses and was under too much pressure. It was really too difficult for me to manage the balance (between choosing too many and too few). [...] It was a big challenge for me to plan the schedule by myself. (Interviewee 11)

About half of the Chinese students interviewed reported significant difficulties in arranging their study plans in this regard, which is consistent with previous findings (Zhou 2010). It is important to note that the *Modul* system is not just new to Chinese students, but to the German students as well. As such, the academic staff did make efforts to introduce the concepts and fundamental principles of *Modul*s to all freshmen at orientation. Thus, German students also required some time to fully understand the rules for designing an efficient course progression. But unlike their German counterparts, Chinese students often failed to understand these orientation explanations due to language problems. Additionally, since some courses are only available during the winter or summer semester, if students missed a *Modul* course in one semester, then they had to wait another year for a chance to take it. Often, one mistake in how students arranged their coursework resulted in the extension of the student's time abroad.

Attending New Types of Courses

In addition to planning courses, Chinese students were challenged by the new types of courses they took at German universities. There are seven main class types given at German universities: lectures, exercise classes, seminars, introductory seminars, practical courses or laboratory work, field courses, and excursions (Kehm 1999). The required combination of these courses for students varies from discipline to discipline, and university to university.[1] Except for lecture or laboratory work, the majority of these courses, including *Hauptseminar*, *Projektseminar*, and *Forshungseminar*, are relatively new to the majority of Chinese students. Based on their disciplines, interviewees only referred to their experiences with lectures, seminars, and exercise classes, so how students experienced the other four are not discussed in this chapter.

Lectures
Lecture (in German: *Vorlesung*) is one of the key types of courses in which professors and lecturers deliver 'systematic overviews of disciplines' (Peisert and Framhein 1990, p. 57). Students' main academic tasks during lectures are to listen, to take notes, to learn, and to understand. Additional readings are assigned for after class to complement the lecture material (Kehm 1999). In Germany, a lecture is often accompanied by a seminar or exercise classes (in German: *Übung*). Compared to other types of courses, the Chinese students were most familiar with lectures, as it is the standard course format in China. Regardless, they still encountered difficulty in class, which reduced their participation.

First, the Chinese students had great difficulty with listening comprehension during their lectures. International students are expected not only to understand the content of lectures, but also be able to follow the fast and informal language used in class discussion (Cammish 1997). Students overwhelmingly failed to follow lecturers' speed and content. Although they had passed the standardized language tests, their German proficiency was still not good enough to follow the lecturers. One student even expressed frustration: 'I just saw the professor's lips moving, but I could not understand a single word.' This difficulty was not limited to only one discipline. Chinese students from various academic fields experienced difficulty

---

[1] For example, the combination of lecture + seminar or exercises classes is common to humanities, while the academic field of engineering science attaches more importance to lecture + exercise classes and laboratory work.

comprehending the lectures. Even students who had previously majored in German encountered language problems in class at the beginning of the study, making their transition less smooth than they had expected.

The exception to this problem was Chinese students in the English-taught master's programs. In general, Chinese students have much more experience with English language learning and popular culture, as it is introduced and emphasized in Chinese schools from a very early age, unlike German. Although they also met with unknown English terminology during lectures, the language itself did not present a major challenge for them during their studies.

Second, the Chinese students struggled with 'silence' in class, as reported by both Chinese students and lecturers during interviews. Chinese students realized that they were not participating as actively as their German peers, who spoke up frequently to ask questions, engage in discussion, or even rebuke points made by the lecturer. Often, students were silent due to habits and customs that they had developed to succeed in the Chinese learning environment, which treated raising a question or speaking in class as embarrassing.

This cultural conflict also created difficulty for German instructors who often mistook Chinese students' being 'silent' for being 'passive' in class. Because thinking is invisible, Chinese students often leave the impression that they are 'passive' in class, when the reality is they are actively trying to process information. As non-native German speakers, especially at the beginning of their study abroad period, Chinese students need more time to process questions than native students, because the question needs to be translated going in, and the answer translated going out—steps that are bypassed by native speakers. This problem of 'silence' was more common among social science students than it was with engineering students, since engineering courses often involved more lab work and less open discussion.

Seminars

The seminar is one of the features of academic instruction in Germany, in which 'more advanced or more in-depth knowledge (including methodological issues) is conveyed and discussed' (Kehm 1999, p. 107). In seminars, instructors play a less dominant role than in lectures, making students play a more active role by giving presentations, in addition to participating in group discussions.

As participants, the Chinese students had difficulties in understanding and taking part in discussions. Similar to the situation in lectures, Chinese students had difficulty understanding the content presented and discussed in seminars, but were still expected to take part in the discussions. In particular, some participants had difficulties keeping up with the rapid pace of conversation or interaction between students at seminars, and did not always know what the key points to take away from each seminar session were. In this way, they felt left 'outside' of the discussion. One master's student majoring in education shared his frustration with the experience:

> When German students were discussing, I found that I was an 'outsider' on the topic, because I understood and digested the content of the knowledge in another way. The language is one problem; the content of the discussion is another. I didn't understand the text well. [...] Sometimes I thought I had understood tthat I had not really understood it; other times, I expected the lecturer would explain more about the text, as the text was difficult to me; but he just quickly mentioned it and explained other issues. (Interviewee 4)

On the other hand, as presenters, Chinese students did not know the expected method of leading seminars or delivering presentations. This made giving a seminar presentation a surprisingly demanding job for them, as they had no prior experience to draw on. One interviewee explained that in general, students needed to have good comprehensive skills, sufficient knowledge of the discipline, strong presentation skills, and excellent German language proficiency. Furthermore, depending on the number of participants, students were expected to do both solo and group presentations.

In terms of the solo presentations, the student presenting is pushed to the front of the stage, making him or her the sole focus of the seminar. This student is first expected to give a presentation, then answer questions raised by other participants. In some cases, presenting students need to lead the discussion by themselves for the whole class session. Thus, the solo presentation essentially requires the student to role-play as the 'lecturer' or 'topic expert'. As individual presenters, Chinese students felt particularly self-conscious about giving presentations alone in front of other students at the beginning of their first semester.

> I was really nervous in doing the presentation. [...] I had a tremulous voice and even my voice changed. We [Chinese] really think too much about how others see us [...] the seminar is actually a learning form where the presenter introduces and leads the discussion of one topic. But I just managed to 'read' the text I'd written. I guess it must be very boring for others. (Interviewee 5)

For group presentations, everyone within the group is expected to cooperate in deciding the outline of the presentation, exchanging opinions and ideas about the content, and preparing the individual portions of the presentation. While a group presentation does not place all the pressure on a single student, the challenge of cooperating as a team for group presentations still requires more effort from the Chinese students than the Germans. As group presenters, Chinese students also identified differences in the learning styles of other students during the process of cooperating with them. One Chinese student (Interviewee 19) compared her different experiences between working with a Finnish student and working with other international Chinese students. Preparing a presentation with other Chinese students was relatively easier for her, as she and the other Chinese students often generated similar thoughts and ideas, without complicated discussions or arguments. When giving their presentation, they often just recited the prepared presentation notes word for word, as she felt she could not express herself freely in German. However, her experience working with the Finnish girl was quite different.

> The presentation with the Finnish girl turned out to be a new learning experience for me [...] The Finnish student spoke excellent German, and during the presentation, she sometimes didn't follow the 'rules' that we had discussed. For example, she sometimes spoke my part or chimed in [while I was speaking]. Although it was a little bit annoying, the cooperation with her was overall good. (Interviewee 19)

On the other hand, rather than feeling less pressure, some Chinese students often had no confidence as group presenters, and were concerned that their performance would destroy the overall group presentation. As all students in the same group shared the presentation grade, these Chinese students worried that their participation would actually hinder the group. Sometimes, they also felt hurt when their group members lost patience with their lack of ability to communicate during the planning process. One Chinese female recounted an unpleasant experience that occurred while preparing for one group discussion. She had joined a group presentation with two other female Germans, and they were preparing for their presentation at one of the German students' apartment. During the group discussion, she could not follow the tempo of the conversation and was unable to express her thoughts to them clearly. Feeling awkward, she did not stay any longer and told the two German students, 'Sorry, just tell me which part I should do, I will prepare it alone at home' (Interviewee 5), before quickly running away from the apartment. Feeling she could not find a better way to solve the problem, she escaped so as to avoid any further embarrassment.

Exercises
Exercise classes (in German: *Übung*) differ from lectures and seminars in that they provide more practical application of material, rather than just introduction to it. Additionally, these classes are often monitored by junior academic staff members or senior students, commonly called 'tutors', rather than lecturers or full professors. These senior students have typically attended similar lectures or exercise classes previously in this discipline themselves. This was very different compared to the standard Chinese lectures, which rarely do more than introduce concepts and ideas.

> One difference I've noticed between the learning form at Chinese and German universities is that the exercise class is given much attention. What the professor refers to at lectures will be discussed at the exercise class. (Interviewee 4)

Because of their student status, tutors were more accessible to the Chinese students, as the relationship between them was less unequal. Therefore, Chinese students often turned to tutors for help, rather than lecturers or professors. This was especially true for Chinese students studying in the fields of engineering and natural sciences. Since there were more occasions for students to have contact with tutors at exercise classes, they went to meet the tutors regularly during consultation hours when doing projects. In contrast, one Chinese student majoring in media science reported that, instead of face-to-face contact, she only had contact with her tutor through emails. However, this tutor was still more accessible than her lecturers and professors, whom she emailed very seldom.

Completing Academic Tasks

Reading
Academic reading constitutes an important method of input for students to obtain knowledge about a discipline. Chinese students experienced a variety of difficulties when reading depending on the different requirements of their majors. For instance, students majoring in engineering and

the natural sciences did not specify any difficulty in reading. In addition to textbooks, these students often obtained and understood technical knowledge through other forms, such as conducting experiments or engaging with universal formulas and symbols. Meanwhile, the Chinese students majoring in social sciences indicated that reading became a big challenge for them, as discussion in seminars was mainly based on the materials assigned for reading outside of class. In particular, these Chinese students encountered two main problems: lack of reading skills and difficulty in understanding the textual content.

In terms of the first problem, Chinese students were not equipped with efficient reading skills, and felt frustrated and miserable when completing their reading tasks. Insufficient German language capabilities aside, they did not know more efficient reading techniques, such as scanning or skimming the text. Many interviewees often read very slowly, far below the average speed of German students, and had to invest more time to the task. Thus, they were unable to finish many of the reading tasks required by the lecturers. This was a major contributing factor to the previously mentioned low Chinese student participation in class discussions.

As a result, one German lecturer noticed that Chinese students often depended too much on their electronic dictionary. These students probably were not aware of their own reading habits and just how much they depended on their electronic dictionary, as no other Chinese mentioned this point. This is a common compensation technique where hardworking international students read, by, '[plodding] doggedly through complete books, carefully looking up every unknown word in a dictionary' (Cammish 1997, p. 153).

In terms of the second problem, the Chinese students had difficulty trying to understand the discipline knowledge of the text due to differences and changes in educational backgrounds. As each faculty expected students to have a broader interdisciplinary knowledge base surrounding their discipline, Chinese participants found significant disconnects between the expected educational background required to understand the reading material and the actual educational background gained through the Chinese education system. One Chinese majoring in media science was confounded as to why some of her courses required general knowledge of Western philosophy. Another Chinese student majoring in German language and literature was similarly confused as to why she had to read materials from anthropology, philosophy, and culture.

Lecturers also pointed out that Chinese students had difficulty in understanding the text in a deeper way.

> Chinese students, sometimes German students as well, seem to be very satisfied with themselves, as long as they are able to understand the text. However, they cannot further discuss about the reading materials. This is related to the conceptualization. Let me cite an example, if I show you a table, on which lie the bread, coffee, jams, cheese, and so on. Then, I will ask, what is it? Chinese students probably will repeat the items on the table (bread, coffee, jams, cheese, etc.), while German students might say breakfast. German students have already learned such conceptualization at schools. (Lecturer 1)

Having little to no previous intercultural experience in Germany, Chinese students had difficulty forming and adopting such culture-based conceptualizations, as their cultural background and training did not prepare them for processing and recognizing these new ideas. Chinese students were still struggling to develop the expected interdisciplinary knowledge base, while German students were already connecting dots between these bases. However, this does not mean that Chinese students did not have the capability to connect the dots as many German lecturers perceived. Rather, this scenario highlights that Chinese and German students start at different conceptual points when beginning their majors in Germany. In contrast, if Chinese students were to see a steamed stuffed bun (包子 *baozi*), twisted cruller (油条 *youtiao*), and porridge (粥 *zhou*) on the table, they would immediately say 'breakfast', while German students would probably have no idea what the items were.

Writing

While reading provides input of information, academic writing provides the output for evaluation in order to demonstrate a student's academic opinion or understanding of the content. Writing difficulties for Chinese students tie into academic writing skill, German language proficiency, and academic rules for writing.

For academic writing skills, Chinese students lacked the ability to synthesize the information they had collected, and draw connections between different ideas to accomplish the written task. Additionally, Chinese students often did not know how to cite others' thoughts correctly in their papers. This was especially frustrating for lecturers, who acknowledged that Chinese students were very good at finding information, but also often categorized their work as plagiarism:

Chinese students pull the information [directly] from the internet, without clearly stating the source. It is not wrong to search for information in the internet, but it is wrong if students do not provide the source of the information found in the internet. This [rule of academic writing] is something that Chinese students need to be clear and accept. (Lecturer 2)

As a result, students often felt misunderstood in their intentions. Western rules for academic writing and proper citation are not commonly taught or followed in the Chinese education system. Understandably, Chinese students are taught different rules for organizing their essays in Chinese. For instance, in China, copying or quoting the masterpiece (without particularly noting the source) is a pedagogical practice to show respect for traditional wisdom. However, these rules for Chinese academic writing do not translate over into the German writing context. Low German language proficiency and limited knowledge of conventional rules for academic writing often caused unintended plagiarism. Though there certainly are instances of Chinese students committing intentional plagiarism, there are also many instances where it is unintentional among Chinese students when writing academic papers.

Finally, Chinese students were confused about what kind of academic writing style was expected of them in their new context. To this end, one German lecturer shared his own sympathetic overseas experience in this regard.

When I was young, I was always a straight-A student in Germany. After finishing my Magister degree at a German university, I went to the U.S. to pursue a Master's degree. To my great surprise, the first semester in the USA I got two 'Cs' for two of the semester papers. All of a sudden, I realized, 'Somehow, things are different here.' I had been always proud of my penetrating analysis in these two semester papers, while my American supervisor seemed to be just annoyed at it. He questioned me, 'Why haven't you written the paper concerning the theme? Why do you necessarily have to clarify the author's concept of language?' Obviously, this was uninteresting to him at all. I realized the 'correct' American expression and argumentation is culture-specific and sometimes discipline-specific. The second astonishing experience happened in France, when I was doing my 'Habilitation' [2] there. I wrote the text in French. The comment I got from the first version was 'You can't write it in this way. This is absolutely the "Teutonic Wagner-style". One cannot read and digest the text.' In terms

---

[2] Habilitation is a 'postdoctoral qualification showing ability to lecture and do research at professorial level' (Quinlivan 2009, p. 76). It is a qualification at a higher level than a doctorate in Germany and other European countries.

of the academic writing, the French 'Esprit' style is highly valued. Until then, I was unaware of the different style in these three countries: in the USA one's strength is based on reading a large amount of articles; in Germany, the ability of arguing the basis of knowledge or theory in a penetrating way is appreciated; while in France, the elegant expression is highly valued. (Lecturer 1)

The above experience shared by the German lecturer makes an interesting point about writing academic papers. Writing an academic paper well is more than simply the application of translating an idea word for word and writing about it in a foreign language. It requires an understanding of the cultural expectations for the academic discipline at a higher education institutional level. In addition to a good command of German language, Chinese students also have to be familiar with the valued traits and characteristics of academic writing at German universities.

Attending Academic Assessments

On the surface, exams are a universal assessment used around the world to measure students' knowledge. However, the form of this academic assessment is not identical in China and Germany. In China, a proctored written exam is the main form of final assessment for each course. Exam times are scheduled by the school for students to attend at the end of the semester.

However, in Germany, students register for an appointed time to take their final examinations, once they feel ready. Moreover, the form of the final examination is often either composed of both written (in German: *schriftliche Prüfung*) and oral parts (in German: *mündliche Prüfung*) or a term paper (in German: *Hausarbeit*), if in the social sciences.

Because of these differences, Chinese students often felt that the examinations in Germany were more demanding. In China, if students stayed up late cramming, they might still get a good grade, because tests only required memorizing information. However, this strategy would not work in Germany, because tests required a deeper understanding of content in order to analyze and apply information. Moreover, as oral exams required spontaneous answers and good German language proficiency, interviewees were good at written exams but experienced more difficulty during oral exams. Thus, students who wanted to earn a good grade had to work much harder in German universities than they had in Chinese universities.

Affective-Dimension Adjustments

In the affective dimension, many interviewees complained, 'Nobody takes care of me here' (in Germany) at the beginning of their studies. In general, students had not taken organizational differences into account, and had expected a similarly structured learning experience in Germany as they had had in China. Initially, Chinese students were not able to identify the support systems or resources available at the university, and felt miserable when lecturers showed no sympathy for the difficulties they faced as international students.

'No One Takes Care of Me'

When initially facing all the new requirements of the German learning environment, Chinese students often felt at a loss, or that they had lost their orientation, because they did not know how to navigate the German university system.

The first challenge to make them feel at a loss was designing their own syllabus. Students would read through the available course catalog to figure out what and how many courses to take, but still did not understand exactly what they were supposed to do, due to their lack of experience. One important impression frequently mentioned by Chinese students at the very beginning of their study was, 'No one monitors me' (没人管我 *meiren guan wo*). Some students compared the universities in China to kindergartens where everything has been organized for students in advance. All the student needs to do is follow the course schedule and attend the prescribed classes. If students ever skip class, the class teacher will call them in to deliver a scolding.

Such a sense of loss is due to the different conceptualizations of 'freedom' versus 'care' behind student relationships and student supervision systems at Chinese and German universities. The relationships and oversight present at Chinese universities is a way of caring for Chinese students, and ensuring that they develop into good moral citizens. However, when these Chinese students 'landed' in German universities, their expectations of a similarly supervised system were not fulfilled, giving them the impression that no one at the university cared about their wellbeing. Rather, they had to face everything by themselves, because they did not know how to turn to others for help. They thought they had to rely on their own efforts to solve the problems by spending more time previewing and reviewing the lecture materials after class.

Feeling Misunderstood

Constantly frustrated and stressed by the new challenges they faced in the initial period of their study, many of the Chinese expected their lecturers to show sympathy and understanding toward the problems they encountered. However, as was more often the case, their lecturers simply did not. As a result, many students felt that all their hard work were greatly misunderstood (委屈 *weiqu*). Following are some key anecdotes to highlight this sentiment.

Episode 1: 'Why Didn't You Participate in the Discussion as Other Students Did?'

Chinese students are more likely to encounter frustrating experiences if their lecturers have had little or no experience with Chinese students before (Zhu 2007). In the interviews, the impression that some lecturers did not show understanding and sympathy to their situations as international students facing difficulties adapting to a new culture also frustrated Chinese students.

> At class, if we failed to answer one question raised by the lecturer, the lecturer would question us unsatisfactorily: 'Why don't you participate in the discussion as other students?' I felt misunderstood, as the lecturer could not understand: we actually did participate in the discussion, but we need more time to understand the question and think about how to answer it in German language. But some lecturers just could not understand us. (Interviewee 18)

Episode 2: Unexpected Consultation Hours

One interviewee shared her experience of a conflict she had at a lecturer's office, as the lecturer pointed that the student should have come for a discussion during consultation hours before giving a class presentation.

> I was also impetuous at that moment and shouted at him, 'I SIMPLY had no idea what the concept of "consultation hour" in Germany is. We SIMPLY don't have it in China and this is SIMPLY new to me. You can't expect us to know everything as German students do, because they know the system ever since their childhood. That's not fair.' […] If I have been informed what consultation hour looks like or how it functions, I will also try my best to follow the suggestion of the lecturers. […] But I didn't know these stuff before studying here. I just feel rather hard done by the German lecturer. (Interviewee 20)

Another Chinese student also shared a very pertinent story about consultation hours. She went to one professor's office to talk with him, but had mistaken his schedule. The assistant told her that the professor was at a meeting, and that he had no consultation hours that day. In response, the Chinese student told the assistant that she had something urgent to discuss, and asked when the meeting would end. The assistant then became angry, insisting, 'You don't have any appointment with the professor and it is impolite of you to ask his agenda'. Upon hearing this, the Chinese student was shocked:

> All of a sudden, I realized that this was totally a new academic system. I had the feeling that I was an unexpected guest. [...] At that moment, I really felt guilty. Since then, I have become careful in dealing with consultation hours to make sure that I didn't interrupt anyone. This experience left me with a deep impression. (Interviewee 10)

It often takes Chinese students some time to grasp the German concept of *consultation hours* (in German: *Sprechstunden*). In China, lecturers are expected to be at their offices if they are not in class. This means, they are essentially expected to have 'consultation hours' all day long. It is common for students to find staff available for discussion without the need to schedule an appointment (Wong et al. 2015). In Germany, however, professors and lecturers are expected to conduct their own academic work, or prepare for their teaching without interruption. Hence, they are only available to students outside of class at certain times for a specific period of time—often only about one to two hours each week. Other professors even require students to make an appointment first via email, instead of freely visiting during consultation hours.

Episode 3: Are Excursions an Off-Class Academic Exercise or a Sight-Seeing Trip?
Both a German lecturer and a Chinese student recalled experiencing a cultural misunderstanding during an excursion. The department once organized an excursion to the Czech Republic to explore the theme of fashion there. Considering the large number of Chinese students attending the excursion, teachers deliberately assigned them to different groups, so that no single group was only Chinese. Obviously, the purpose was to encourage intercultural communication among group members. To the lecturers' great surprise and disappointment, Chinese students automatically broke

from their assigned groups, and stayed with only other international Chinese throughout the excursion. Upon return to Germany, one lecturer flew into a rage, demanding angrily, 'Why did you just stay only with Chinese students? I am really sad.' However, the Chinese students did not understand why he was so upset. One of the Chinese students (Interviewee 20) who was present at this excursion said, 'I just don't understand why our lecturer was so sad, when we Chinese students stayed together'.

Obviously, for German lecturers, it was frustrating to see their good intentions of promoting intercultural communication between Chinese and other students turn out to be in vain, as Chinese students automatically banded together during the excursion. One of the lecturers clearly reported his disappointment about this experience in his interview. However, the Chinese students had not been well informed of the meaning behind such an excursion. Rather, they regarded it more or less as a trip or tour. They felt misunderstood when the lecturer was angry about their performance during the excursion:

> It is because I didn't know the aim and rules [of the excursion] before, and most of the Chinese students regarded the excursion as a trip. If I had been informed of it earlier, I wouldn't have stayed only with the fellow Chinese students. […] In the meantime, our lecturer just took it for granted that we Chinese students should have known the concept of 'excursion' as well. […] Unfortunately, we just didn't know what excursion meant (like the German students do). […] No one had explicitly informed us that we should always stay with our mixed group. (Interviewee 20)

This episode is a good example showcasing Chinese students' lack of knowledge of German courses and their low willingness to communicate with German counterparts. Chinese students regarded the excursion as an informal academic trip. When they were assigned other German or international students with whom they were supposed to stay group mates, they instead talked exclusively with other Chinese students during the trip. In this instance, the German students actually felt marginalized as the 'minority' student group during this trip, since the percentage of German students was smaller than that of the international students. Seeing that Chinese students only stayed with other co-national students and talked in Chinese, German students had no motivation to approach their Chinese peers, resulting in ineffective intercultural communication between Chinese and non-Chinese students (i.e. German and other international students).

Stress

Stress is typically at its height at the beginning of an academic sojourn (Brown and Holloway 2008). Cultural and educational disparities between China and the host country, foreign language deficiencies, ineffective interactions with faculty members of the host country, and high motivations to achieve cause Chinese students stress when studying in a foreign country (Yan and Berliner 2009). The heavy academic workload and personal concerns were the two main stressors for Chinese students during their study in Germany.

Heavy Academic Workload

The introduction of the Bachelor-Master-System in Germany encourages students to manage and complete their course of study in a relatively short period of time—theoretically, six semesters for a bachelor's and four semesters for a master's. Within this context, students in Germany are expected to finish their studies quickly and efficiently, which places a lot of pressure on students in general, not to mention the international students. Sometimes, students even overloaded on too many classes in order to complete their coursework more efficiently. Encountering this pressure, some students kept an open mind and positive attitude toward their stress, using it instead as motivation.

> To study in Germany is my own decision, after careful consideration. I like my current subject, and I am not forced by anyone else to learn hard. I do find the subject interesting. (Interviewee 18)

> Since my motivation of studying in Germany is to find the difference of education system between China and Germany, the challenge, to some extent, is exciting to me. If everything is same here in Germany as in China, or I encounter no challenges, why bother I come to Germany? (Interviewee 6)

However, not every Chinese student shared the same experience. One exchange student mentioned that she did not have to take many courses and reported less stress.

Personal Concerns

In addition to academic pressure, the hopes and expectations of parents and friends in China exerts tremendous pressure on Chinese students during their study in Germany. The academic success of a child relates to the reputation or 'face' (面子 *mianzi*) of the parents. Anyone who fails in school is a shame to the whole family. Such family pressure was typical among interviewees, and in some cases, caused more stress to the students than their actual study program.

Compared with the length of study in the USA, the UK, or Australia, it takes longer to complete an academic degree in Germany. However, the students' parents and friends in China are often not well informed about the education system and organization in Germany, and its differences. They often compared the length of study in Germany with that in Anglo-Saxon countries and wondered why it takes students so much longer to finish their degrees. Several interviewees were constantly asked by their relatives or friends in China why it had taken them so long to finish the programs in Germany. Interviewees admitted that these questions made them upset and nervous. Only one Chinese student mentioned that she did not experience much pressure from her parents, as her father had been to Germany several times for business trips, and was already familiar with the length of study in Germany.

According to one Chinese proverb, 'Among all kinds of kindness, filial piety goes first' (百善孝为先 *bai shan xiao wei xian*). In Confucian philosophy, filial piety (孝 *xiao*) is a core virtue of traditional Chinese culture. Good children are expected to respect, follow, and take care of their parents. In China, a typical expectation for children to exercise filial piety (尽孝 *jinxiao*) is to find a job after graduation, become financially independent, and later take care of their parents. However, since the majority of Chinese students interviewed were funded by their parents, they felt their studies were a burden on their family. One student felt guilty, because at age 26, he still depended on his parents financially as an adult, rather than working to earn money for himself, and later, to take care of his parents.

Behavioral-Dimension Adjustments

Yet, in spite of all these challenges, in the behavioral dimension, most Chinese students did not give up easily. Instead, they made efforts to adjust to their new environment through a variety of ways. Some spent more time previewing or reviewing the textbooks and reading materials. Others consulted students or teachers for doing homework after class. Still others took German language courses to improve their German language skills. Many did all of the above.

After encountering problems and feeling 'at a loss' in the initial phase of their study abroad program, some of the participants realized that they could not simply wait for others to help them. Instead, they needed to take the initiative to make efforts themselves to change their situations. One student (Interviewee 11) mentioned: 'The lecturer and the tutor can only help you to explain the question, but it is YOU who has to understand the knowledge. Nobody else can do that.'

Trying to Keep Up with the Pace

Figuring Out How the Modul Works

In Germany, all course information details are available in the course catalog (in German: *Vorlesungsverzeichnis*) each semester. Students are expected to read through the introduction to courses and decide which ones they would like to take in the coming semester. Courses are introduced according to their corresponding *Moduls* (lectures + seminar/+exercises, etc.). In learning how to deal with the *Modul*, the Chinese students either studied the course catalog alone or asked tutors for help.

> I printed the catalog, marked all the introductory courses, and read the course introduction thoroughly. As I still could not figure out the content of the courses, I finally went to the tutor for help. At the beginning of the first semester, I went to her consultation hour every week, and she introduced the courses to me. Finally, I began to understand the rule in choosing the courses here. (Interviewee 10)

Most interviewees spent a lot of time studying the course catalog on their own. In some departments with a large number of Chinese students, interviewees would try to figure out the art of choosing courses together. However, students quickly realized this method of coping was ineffective, as apparently no one understood the rules thoroughly.

Taking Notes in Class

For engineering and natural science majors, taking notes is an especially useful method to supplement their knowledge if they fail to understand the content given in class immediately. The formulas or figures written by lecturers on the blackboard often later proved to be important resources for learning.

> In the beginning, I could not understand the lecturer. I just took down the notes, which helped me to understand what the lecturer said in class. [...] Lecturers often write down a lot of formulas on blackboard. If one doesn't understand what the lecturer said in words, it is important for him to understand the formula. Later he can try to figure it out by himself at home. (Interviewee 11)

However, this same strategy did not work as well for students majoring in social science or humanities, as lecturers did not write every main point on the blackboard or include them in their PowerPoint (PPT) slides. For these students, the note-taking strategy only worked well when they had the learning materials (e.g. PPT slides and referred reading materials) also provided in class. In some cases, the lecturers did not even prepare any PPT slides at all.

> I have tried recording the lecture, but the quality of the recording was not so good. In the meantime, I didn't have so much time to listen to all the contents again. So the only way to deal with the problem (not understanding the content) is to read more books concerning the topic after class. (Interviewee 10)

Sometimes, lecturers who understood the situation did try to help by sharing their teaching materials and PPT slides from class online, so that students could later review them after class.

Raising Questions After Class
Another strategy adopted by Chinese students to better understand the lectures was asking the lecturer questions immediately after class. Although lecturers leave some time for answering student questions shortly before the end of class, the Chinese students preferred to raise questions after lectures. This strategy was a more 'comfortable' method for Chinese students to deal with the difficulty of information they did not understand during lectures. A couple of participants mentioned that asking questions after class with other students was also a common practice in China, so it was not so strange for them to adopt it in the German context. This method solved many of their difficulties immediately after class, while also avoiding the trouble of waiting in line or the 'embarrassment' of an individual 'face-to-face' situation when going during consultation hours. In this way, the student had 'less risk of loss of face' (Cortazzi and Jin 1996), while also striking a compromise between the German expectation of asking questions in class, and the Chinese expectation of asking none.

> I never raise any question at class or go to the consultation hour. Instead, I ask lecturers questions after class. [...] Although I have to admit that I could not immediately understand the lecturer's explanation, his answer still helped me a lot: as it provides me with some clues so that I can go over the note after class. (Interviewee 11)

Searching for Secondary Literature
While some Chinese students invested more time in reading the original materials, some turned to secondary literature for supplementary help, such as Chinese versions of the German textbooks. They hoped that the content written in their mother tongue would help them to understand the content better.

In the short term, this strategy of reading secondary literature did help the Chinese students to understand the original text better. Nevertheless, dependence on secondary sources did not solve their main problem of lecture comprehension in the long run. They might have obtained the general idea of the text, but their knowledge and reading skills, such as skimming and scanning, did not improve. Similarly, the effect of reading course textbooks in Chinese varied. Some participants regarded the books or learning materials in Chinese as very helpful. Others reported that they were disappointed, as the content in the Chinese version was just as difficult to conceptualize and understand as the German version.

Persevering in German Language Learning

As mentioned earlier, German language became a big challenge for the Chinese students, who were fully aware of its importance with regard to understanding lectures and participating in seminars. Each student adopted different ways to improve their language proficiency, including attending language courses, finding a language partner to practice the language with, or learning the language by themselves.

Language Problems
Because of their insufficient German language capabilities, students were unable to understand the content when attending courses. When asked about the kind of difficulties they encountered in the initial phase, language difficulty was typically the first answer from Chinese students, especially in terms of pace. One student expanded on her frustration:

> At lectures, the professor kept on talking. I was still thinking about his words in the first part and he already moved to the second part. There were no PowerPoint slides at all and I had nothing to refer. (Interviewee 5)

Even though the information written or shared by lecturers in class contained the most important information they needed to learn in the course,

Chinese students, as well as other international students in Germany, had difficulty immediately understanding and digesting the knowledge delivered by lecturers.

Language Courses
Language courses were one of the default ways students tried to improve their German proficiency, as they provided students with professional and systemic language instruction. Currently, both on-campus and off-campus German courses are available for all students.

Overall, more than half the Chinese students (55.8 per cent) of all three studies in this book were 'often' or 'sometimes' learning German in addition to their studies at German universities (Fig. 4.1).

In Study 1, thirteen out of sixteen interviewees (81.3 per cent) 'often' or 'sometimes' attended German courses during their study abroad period. Even Chinese students attending international master's and doctoral programs attended German language courses. For instance, the 'zero-German-speakers,' two doctoral students who had not learned any German before arriving at their universities, also attended German courses during their first semester. Although the working language of their international

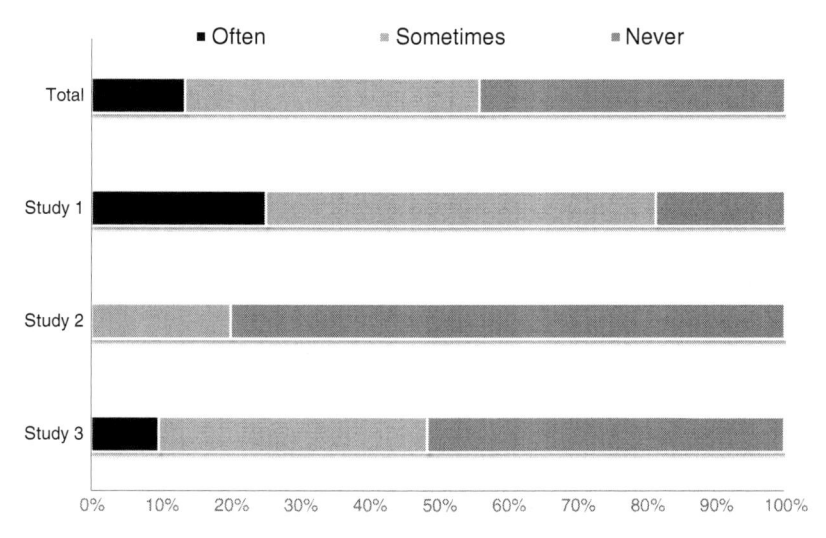

Fig. 4.1 Frequency of attending further German language training in Germany

degree program was English, they gradually found it necessary to learn German to communicate with colleagues and navigate daily life.

The 'German majors' were a special case. In Study 2, 80 per cent of these participants did not enroll or participate in any German course, and only one student out of five 'sometimes' took German as an official language course. Because of their previous language proficiency background, most did not feel the need to 'waste time' attending extra German courses that would not count toward their *Moduls*.

More than half (51.6 per cent) the participants in Study 3 did not attend any language courses in their first academic year in Germany, as many were also German majors. Among 31 students, 12 were German language and literature studies majors (57.1 per cent), and only one of them reported attending German courses regularly. Thirty-nine per cent of these students chose to improve their current German language by 'occasionally' attending German language courses, while only 9.7 per cent 'often' attended German courses.

A substantial number of German universities have established language centers (in German: *Sprachenzentren*), which provide both German courses for international students and other foreign language courses for all students. Furthermore, private language schools or further-/adult- education institutions also offer German courses. Many of the international Chinese students had been informed of the different opportunities to take German courses provided by the language center, during orientation at the start of their first semester. Compared with the courses provided by private language schools, those offered by universities are relatively cheap, and focus on specific learning skills for university study, such as academic writing and oral communication.

Only a couple of Chinese students (Interviewees 7 and 11) indicated that they did not attend the course because of the fees.

However, not every participant was satisfied with the language courses offered by the university, or found them helpful for their individual needs. One student (Interviewee 6) registered for a course with the intention of practicing her spoken German. However, she was disappointed, as the lecturer simply asked course participants to prepare general presentations, instead of teaching specific spoken language skills. Another student (Interviewee 10) took two German language courses, one comprehensive and one grammar-based, but was not satisfied with the pace of the courses. The teacher often spent a lot of time using in-class games so as to motivate students. She later withdrew from the course.

Finding a Language Partner
Everyone has his or her own method of learning a foreign language, and what works for one student may not work for or be available to another. Thus, in addition to attending German language courses, students sought many other outside options to improve their German language skills. One interactive way Chinese students used was to find a language partner. Compared with language courses, learning German through face-to-face communication with a peer is more informal and relaxed. The student can play the role of both 'learner of German language' and 'teacher of Chinese language'. This method was also helpful because not only could students learn the German language, but they could also learn German culture, customs, and conventions that they would not have learned in a standard language class.

Learning Alone
The Chinese students who did not attend language courses, or had no language partner sometimes chose to learn and practice German by themselves. They would read novels (mentioned by Interviewee 11), watch films or TV (mentioned by Interviewee 5), or talk with their flat mates (Interviewee 17) in German to improve their language skills. Nevertheless, while this kind of self-learning initially seemed more comfortable in terms of 'saving face,' it was not very efficient or systematic, and they had no real chance to practice their spoken language. Thus, they did not make much progress in trying to learn German on their own.

References

Brown, L., & Holloway, I. (2008). The adjustment journey of international postgraduate students at an English university: An ethnographic study. *Journal of Research in International Education, 7*(2), 232–249. doi:10.1177/1475240908091306.

Cammish, N. K. (1997). Through a glass darkly: Problems of studying at advanced level through the medium of English. In D. McNamara & R. Harris (Eds.), *Overseas students in higher education. Issues in teaching and learning* (pp. 143–155). London: Routledge.

Cortazzi, M., & Jin, L. (1996). Cultures of learning: Language classrooms in China. In H. Coleman (Ed.), *Society and the language classroom* (pp. 169–206). Cambridge: Cambridge University Press.

Kehm, B. M. (1999). *Higher education in Germany: Developments, problems, and perspectives.* Wittenberg: Inst. for Higher Education Research.

Macrae, M. (1997). The induction of international students to academic life in the United Kingdom. In D. McNamara & R. Harris (Eds.), *Overseas students in higher education. Issues in teaching and learning* (pp. 125–142). London: Routledge.

Peisert, H., & Framhein, G. (1990). *Higher education in the Federal Republic of Germany*. Bucharest: CEPES.

Wong, G., Cooper, B. J., & Dellaportas, S. (2015). Chinese students' perceptions of the teaching in an Australian accounting programme—An exploratory study. *Accounting Education, 24*(4), 318–340. doi:10.1080/09639284.2015.1050678.

Yan, K., & Berliner, D. C. (2009). Chinese international students' academic stressors in the United States. *College Student Journal, 43*(4), 939–960.

Zhou, J. (2010). *Zwischen "Elite von morgen" und "Liu Xue La Ji" ("Müllstudenten")*. Münster: Verl.-Haus Monsenstein und Vannerdat.

Zhu, J. (2007). *A cross-cultural learning case study: Comprehending Chinese international students' adapting and learning strategies at Canadian universities*. Master thesis. Halifax, Nova Scotia, Canada, Halifax, Nova Scotia, Canada. Retrieved from http://dc.msvu.ca:8080/xmlui/bitstream/handle/10587/282/JiaZhu-MAED-2007.pdf?sequence=3&isAllowed=y

CHAPTER 5

The Battle Continues: Negotiating with the Differences

Any circumstance hitting a limit will begin to change. Change will in turn lead to an unimpeded state, and then lead to continuity.
穷则变,变则通,通则久

— *Books of Changes (易经 yijing)*

After experiencing a 'hard landing' in the initial phase, 'the battle continues' for Chinese students in the developing phase as they gradually become more familiar with the learning expectations at German universities. Student progress in German language was a key factor facilitating the adjustment. In the developing phase, the international Chinese students often struggled to balance German academic expectations and maintain their Chinese learning habits and traditions. 'Each person comes to the intercultural experience with former critical events in his or her life, personal goals, varying amounts of intercultural training, and previous intercultural experience that influence the learning process (Taylor 1994, p. 160).' Thus, students in this phase 'live[d] an academic life filled with paradoxes' (Campbell and Li 2007, p. 389) and were challenged with mediating the differences between learning in China and being a student in Germany.

Preconditions for Adjustment

Two important preconditions for the students' further adjustment in the developing phase were the improvement of their German language skills, and increased knowledge of German universities.

Making Progress in German

Progress made in German proficiency facilitates Chinese students' academic adjustment. Overall, Chinese students showed great improvement of their German language skills after two semesters (Table 5.1). In particular, they reported general progress in writing (t = −2.12, $p < 0.05$), reading (t = −2.25, $p < 0.05$), and listening (t = −2.82, $p < 0.05$).

Additionally, Chinese students' academic communication ability with German lecturers and students was closely related to their German listening (r = 0.50, $p < 0.05$) and speaking (r = 0.51, $p < 0.05$) skills. Chinese learners with lower German skills generally had lower participation in tutorial discussions. Although they reported some progress in speaking and communicating with lecturers and classmates, they did not feel that they achieved much progress in terms of class discussions and participation.

The Chinese students achieved progress in daily, non-academic German language, as well (Table 5.2). Again, except for 'speaking,' Chinese students made progress in reading newspapers and magazines (t = −2.44, $p < 0.05$), writing daily posts and documents (t = −3.18, $p < 0.01$), and understanding daily communication (t = −2.45, $p < 0.05$).

Table 5.1 Progress of academic German language skill according to Study 3

Academic German language	Round 1 Mean	SD	Round 2 Mean	SD	N	t
Listening: understanding the lectures	2.73	0.88	3.36	0.85	22	−2.85[a]
Speaking: participating in class discussions	2.27	1.08	2.50	1.01	22	−0.89
Reading: academic reading	3.27	0.77	3.68	0.95	22	−2.25[a]
Writing: homework	3.43	0.87	3.86	1.06	21	−2.12[a]
Communicating with lecturers/students	3.05	0.92	3.19	0.75	21	−0.68

Note: Chinese students were asked to rate their academic German language level by using a five-point Likert scale: 1 (Poor) to 5 (Excellent)

[a]Correlation is significant at the 0.05 level (2-tailed)

Table 5.2 Progress of daily German language skill according to Study 3

Daily German language	Round 1 Mean	SD	Round 2 Mean	SD	N	t
Listening: understanding daily communication	2.73	1.05	3.20	0.93	30	−2.45[a]
Speaking: expressing oneself in daily communication	2.77	1.25	3.07	1.02	30	−1.51
Reading: reading newspapers and magazines	2.63	1.00	3.07	0.91	30	−2.44[a]
Writing: writing post and documents	2.80	1.30	3.30	1.24	30	−3.18[b]

Note: Chinese students were asked to rate their everyday German language level by using a five-point Likert scale: 1 (Poor) to 5 (Excellent)
[a] Correlation is significant at the 0.05 level (2-tailed)
[b] Correlation is significant at the 0.01 level (2-tailed)

Table 5.3 Progress of knowledge about German universities according to Study 3

Knowledge about German universities	Round 1 Mean	SD	Round 2 Mean	SD	N	t
Types of courses	2.71	0.94	3.52	0.926	31	−4.05[a]
Examinations	2.68	0.95	3.52	1.03	31	−4.25[a]
Academic tasks	2.39	0.92	3.87	0.99	31	−8.92[a]
Academic resources	2.55	0.96	3.58	0.77	31	−4.69[a]

Note: Chinese students were asked to assess their knowledge of German universities using a five-point Likert scale: 1 (Poor) to 5 (Excellent)
[a] Correlation is significant at the 0.001 level (2-tailed)

Becoming Familiar with German Universities

Another important step the Chinese students took in their adjustment process was becoming more familiar with the German university system. Compared with what and how much they knew about German universities at the beginning of their first semester, Chinese students had learned a lot more about the academic activities at German universities by the end of their second semester (Table 5.3). After two semesters, about half the Chinese students in Study 3 regarded their knowledge of German universities as 'good' or 'excellent'.

The results of the paired samples *T*-Test between Round 1 and Round 2 indicate that, after two semesters,[1] the Chinese students had acquired more knowledge about academic tasks than at the beginning of their first semester (t = 8.92, $p < 0.001$). Similarly, their knowledge of examinations (t = 4.25, $p < 0.001$), academic resources (t = 4.69, $p < 0.001$), and types of courses (t = 4.05, $p < 0.001$) had increased.

The Chinese students in Study 1 also indicated that after two semesters, not only did they understand how the system at German universities worked, but they also had more confidence in the whole process of arranging their studies independently.

> Until the second semester, I finally had the feeling that I was 'on the right track' and knew the 'pattern' of learning—when should I exert more effort for preparing the exam and when can I take a short break and relax during the semester. (Interviewee 14)

At the same time, there were still noticeable differences among Chinese students in how they adjusted:

> It takes some Chinese students only one month to get to know the pattern; but some need much longer time. Some Chinese students are extroverted and get the information immediately by asking others for help; while others are introverted and shy; they are hesitant to ask others for help. (Interviewee 14)

Cognitive-Dimension Adjustments: 'Studying in China' Versus 'Studying in Germany'

In the developing phase, one difficulty Chinese students encounter at German universities is how to negotiate between their former educational experiences in China and their current expectations in Germany. Chinese students often struggled with the conundrum of being 'thick-skinned' (脸皮厚 *lianpi hou*) versus 'thin-skinned' (爱面子 *ai mianzi*) in tackling their new academic challenges. Here, four episodes demonstrate the different ways this dilemma manifested in students' lives.

---

[1] Since thirty-one students of the fifty-five students (who attended the first round of the questionnaire) continued into the second round of the longitudinal research phase, the results of pairs-comparison are based on the 31 students who answered both rounds of questionnaires.

Episode 1: To Reserve or Raise One's Opinion in Class?

Chinese participants often attributed their silence in class to the learning traditions they acquired in China. Traditionally, especially in primary and secondary schools, Chinese students are expected to either answer teachers' questions or otherwise keep quiet during class. Growing up in this type of learning environment, Chinese students come to believe that spontaneously asking questions or raising their own unsolicited opinions is an interruption in class which will 'waste other students' time or sidetrack teacher talk' (Cortazzi and Jin 1996, p. 197). Reserving their opinions in class was a 'habit', 'tradition', 'custom', or 'pattern' (习惯 *xiguan*) that interviewees had picked up in China. Although they realized that this custom was neither favored nor encouraged at German universities, they still felt embarrassed, shy, or uncomfortable to break from this norm to interrupt the teacher in class.

> In China, we regard interrupting lecturers at class as impolite, thus we seldom ask questions at class [...] unless I was asked to raise my opinion by the lecturer, I won't disrupt him (by raising any question). (Interviewee 7)
>
> The active class atmosphere [in Germany] has much to do with the democracy as well. For example, the communication between lecturers and students in Germany is very relaxed, and one doesn't have to worry about 'respecting the teacher and his teachings', and you can 'interrupt' the lecturer if it is necessary. (Interviewee 6)

Unlike many Western contexts which encourage spontaneous, impromptu student participation, many Chinese students do not believe in speaking simply for the sake of speaking. 'Asking questions is one thing [...] and asking high-quality questions is another' (Liu 2002, p. 41). Rather, they prefer to practice 'treasuring one's words' (惜字如金 *xi zi ru jin*) or 'silence is golden' (沉默是金 *chen mo shi jin*) in class. If students speak, it should be after 'deliberate thinking' (深思熟虑 *shen si shu lü*), and should 'amaze the world with a single brilliant feat' (一鸣惊人 *yi min jing ren*). Those who frequently present their own opinions are culturally regarded as 'show-offs' or inconveniences in China. One participant (Interviewee 9) actually expressed annoyance at international students from other countries who often gave 'simple answers' in class, which to her were not worth mentioning at all.

Table 5.4 Hesitation to voice opinions in class

Perception	Reserving one's opinion in class		Voicing one's opinion in class
In China	☺ Shows respect when others talk; deliberate and careful thinking is expected	⟷	☹ Shows off; interrupts the lecturer and other students
In Germany	☹ Shows passivity, silence, low engagement	⟷	☺ Shows active participation

However, not every participant regarded such active participation as negative. Some interviewees (e.g. Interviewee 4, 7, and 8) had a more neutral attitude toward class engagement, simply accepting such active participation as the normal learning tradition for most students growing up in Western countries.

However, while Chinese students struggled with the issue of whether or not to voice their own opinions in class, German lecturers typically expected the active involvement of all students, and were often disappointed with the silence of their Chinese students (Table 5.4).

Episode 2: To Respect Authority or Express One's Opinion in Class?

In China, students are expected to respect teachers and value their instruction absolutely. A 'good student' will fulfill required academic tasks like presentations exactly according to the lecturer's advice, and respect the authority figure's ideas. Students who finish their work without first consulting the lecturers might actually be regarded by others as self-centered (自以为是 *zi yi wei shi*). However, in Germany, students are encouraged to do the exact opposite: form their own opinions, try to do the work first without help, and approach all ideas critically. One interviewee shared how different his experiences in China and Germany were:

> In China, before doing a presentation, we will first ask lecturers for their advice. By doing so, we can be sure that we are on the right track. If we don't ask the lecturers, they will probably think that we don't respect them. [...] The situation is totally different in Germany. If one asks the lecturers' opinion at the consultation hour without having his own idea in mind, the lecturer would feel strange. 'Why this student comes to me with an empty mind?' Look, there is a big difference in thinking between China and Germany. (Interviewee 20)

One German lecturer similarly observed how firmly Chinese students believed in teacher authority. They rarely questioned sources designated as authorities, and took it for granted that the information presented was

Table 5.5 Unquestioning respect for authority

Perception	Respecting authority		Expressing one's opinion
In China	☺ Means asking lecturers for advice outside of class, then following it	⟷	☹ Appears opinionated, self-centered
In Germany	☹ Shows dependence, or has no definite views of one's own	⟷	☺ Shows critical and independent thinking

Table 5.6 To ask questions or not?

Perception	Not asking questions		Asking questions
In China	☺ Shows understanding of what the lecturer says in class or the ability to figure out the problem alone	⟷	☹ Shows stupidity and inability to understand lecturer immediately
In Germany	☹ Shows student does not think much about knowledge content	⟷	☺ Shows learning progress and enthusiasm through asking and discussing

true. Chinese students believe their teachers are 'a model of authoritative learning, expert knowledge and skills, and moral behaviour, and should have an answer to learners' questions' (Jin and Cortazzi 2006, p. 10); therefore, they express deferential respect to authority. In contrast, German students typically show respect to lecturers by being critical, and engaging in the class as a way of showing interest in what the lecturers say. In this context, such 'unquestioning obedience' may actually be perceived by the German lecturer as lack of interest (Table 5.5).

Episode 3: To Ask or Not to Ask?

In the developing phase, the Chinese students were still shy about directly asking lecturers questions. In their eyes, asking lecturers questions meant they were not as smart as other students, or failed to understand the knowledge taught in class. Therefore, they perceived the action as a public show of weakness, which they did not want to do (Table 5.6).

The students also brought this thinking with them when they came to Germany. Interviewees explained that they preferred investing more time to solve homework problems alone, or asking their peers to ask lecturers questions on their behalf. Similarly, Chinese students tended to ask the lecturer questions during consultation hours as a last resort (Cortazzi and Jin 1996), which is in direct contrast to lecturers in Western countries who regarded raising questions as primary 'discussion-promoting devices' (p. 196).

Chinese students who preferred informally asking lecturers questions directly after class in order to avoid face-to-face situations at consultation hours later realized the disadvantages of this strategy. Many lecturers did not have much time in the short break after class, so they could not provide sufficient answers for students (mentioned by Interviewee 7). Other lecturers became impatient (mentioned by Interviewee 19) when asked questions after class, because they wanted to leave or go home immediately.

Based on these reactions, the students realized that the better option was to attend consultation hours, even if the situation was more uncomfortable for them. Asking lecturers was more effective than asking fellow students, as lecturers were more familiar with certain themes, and would offer more professional suggestions and advice (mentioned by Interviewee 10). However, the participants also realized that in Germany, their lecturers would never approach them first to answer questions. Students had to take the initiative themselves.

> German lecturers welcome those students who 'have plenty of cheek' (indicating students who continually ask lecturers questions, without worry about showing their weaknesses). Lecturers will give good advice and suggestions, only when students come to them and ask. If one waits for lecturers to come to him and offer help like the situation in China, he will probably get disappointed—really, this (that lecturers come to students first) will never happen in Germany, especially at the doctoral-level study. (Interviewee 3)

As a result, Chinese students gradually transitioned from the attitude of 'nobody takes care of me' to 'the lecturers are available but we have to take the initiative to ask'. By actively asking questions, they realized that they would not 'lose face' for taking the initiative, but instead 'gain face' in the long run. As long as they approached the lecturers with questions first, they would often receive helpful feedback from them.

Episode 4: To Learn Individually or With a Group?

In Germany, peer learning in the form of group work is both valued and commonplace in the school system. Teamwork emphasizes in-depth communication and discussion among members of the group. Each member is expected to contribute ideas and time to the assigned work. In China, students also learn and study with each other, but not usually in the form of group work or group projects—especially at the bachelor's level. Because some Chinese students are not very familiar with this concept, group work becomes a complicated task, incorporating the application of German language skills, intercultural communication skills, and discipline-based knowledge. Based on these reasons, a previous study found that only one-third of Chinese students regarded group work as 'good or very good' (Zhou 2010).

During the developing phase, Chinese students noticed that they had little academic communication with fellow classmates. For example, one student recognized the importance of communicating with peer students. Lack of academic communication with peer students was the biggest problem for her, because one interviewee indicated that 'Learning knowledge is based on academic communication, which expands my horizons of knowledge'. By limiting her communication, she was unintentionally inhibiting the capacity of her learning. However, there were pros and cons to individual and group work:

> If one does the project alone, on the one side, he can implement his own idea and obtain more experience; on the other side, he has to deal with a great amount of work by himself. That is tiring and he often worries about whether he manages the work on time. [...] Nevertheless, when one works with others, he will get feedback and obtain support from his team members. For example, the team member will point out the mistake which he can't identify by himself. One learns new things and makes progress by learning with others. However, one might sometimes have an unreliable or irresponsible teammate, who will definitely make the preparation more complicated. [...] Every coin has two sides. (Interviewee 15)

Some Chinese students worried that their poor spoken German skills would drag the group down (拖累 *tuolei*), and would negatively affect the group's shared grade. Other Chinese students were sometimes too sensitive to outside suggestions and regarded help from other non-Chinese students as 'sympathy' (同情 *tongqing*), which hurt their self-esteem and pride (自尊心 *zizunxin*).

> When working together with German students, it is better to say that they 'mentor' or 'coach' me than to say that we cooperate with each other. I don't want to drag others down with me. If German students want to work together with you, they won't bother to lead you. And neither do I want to beg them to let me join them, even though I have to make more effort when working alone. (Interviewee 15)

Affective-Dimension Adjustments: Feeling Confused and Frustrated

The Chinese students were often confused by the conflicting paradigms of what made a 'good student' in China versus Germany, and often went back and forth between these learning norms. The conflict between these two learning cultures is a big challenge for international students (Lin and Yi 1997). Chinese students were stressed and discouraged by the need to leave their 'cultural comfort zone' (Kingston and Forland 2008, p. 211) when facing the requirements of the new learning environment.

Feeling Frustrated in Dealing with the Difference

Chinese students felt frustrated in dealing with the different expectations between their old and new learning environments. Specifically, they were quite frustrated to find that what they had always regarded as 'correct' in the Chinese learning environment became 'wrong' in the German. Similar experiences have been recorded among Chinese students studying in the USA: 'I found my low-profile personality and humble attitude, which is so valued in the Chinese classroom, has been taken by American professors as a lack of talent and an inability in many cases. This makes me feel frustrated, depressed, and stressed' (Yan and Berliner 2009, p. 953).

The Chinese students also felt frustrated, and even miserable, when their lecturers did not show any empathy about their situation as international students. In some cases, the initial difficulty in adapting to the new educational settings gave instructors or tutors the impression that an international student was 'a poor candidate for the program that he or she has selected' (Westwood and Barker 1990, p. 253). Chinese students in other countries also have faced professors in the host country asking 'How come you keep extremely silent in the seminar and never raise questions? Are you not interested in my topic or does my class bore you?' (Yan and Berliner 2009, p. 954).

However, such differences did not always cause frustration. Some of the Chinese students reported a positive and open attitude toward these differences, which was important for their further development in the coming phase of adjustment. They embraced the differences as an exciting challenge that stimulated communication with others and also stimulated personal growth.

Feeling Hesitant to Show Weakness

Chinese students often hesitated about what steps to take in negotiating these differences, because they had many fears and worries about 'losing face'. These fears hindered them from turning to their lecturers for help. The Chinese students believed that if they do not raise a 'silly' question, the lecturers would not find that they have not understood the knowledge.

> Many of us [Chinese students] think: If I ask the lecturer a 'silly' question, will he think that I am foolish? [...] Chinese students are shy, but this is absolutely wrong in Germany. [...] I should have had 'thick skin', had been more bravely, and had displayed great initiatives to discuss research question with my supervisor. (Interviewee 3)

Although Chinese students did realize that their 'thin-skinned' attitude would not solve their problems at all, they were still not confident enough to take the first step and ask lecturers specific questions about the majors or disciplines. In this way, the traditional Chinese learning method becomes a millstone around many of the Chinese students' necks, which slowed or prohibited their academic adjustment in Germany.

BEHAVIORAL-DIMENSION ADJUSTMENTS: USING DIFFERENT STRATEGIES TO DEAL WITH THE CONFUSION

The results of Chinese students' negotiations between Chinese and German learning traditions varied. Some of the participants went to lecturers' offices to ask questions. Some invested more time in their studies so as to figure out solutions to the problems alone (mentioned by Interviewee 15) and avoid discouraging situations when working with other German students. Others turned to fellow international Chinese students for help (mentioned by Interviewees 12 and 14), or asked their German peers (mentioned by Interviewee 13). Still others tried to adopt new habits, and learn to express their opinions in a familiar and friendly atmosphere, especially in small groups.

Asking German Lecturers and Students for Help

During interviews, Chinese students agreed that German students were helpful in the course of their daily interactions. Compared with their initial period in Germany, the Chinese participants were much more willing to ask German students questions. One interviewee majoring in German language and literature studies explained that she would often turn to German peers attending the same course for help because of their familiarity with the context. In answering her questions, they not only explained the basic content, but their thinking and logic behind it, as well as the skills to understand and interpret it.

Overall, interviewees who asked German students for help reported that their counterparts were supportive and their responses were useful.

For discipline-specific questions, asking lecturers for help either after class or during office hours was also effective, as they could solve most questions. However, sometimes office hours were too short or infrequent to meet the needs of students. Regardless, sometimes students' progress in their academic adjustment was less about which option interviewees used to solve the problems or even if they solved the problem at all. Sometimes, the most important step in the process was simply making any efforts at all to solve it (mentioned by Interviewee 3).

Joining a 'Friendly' Learning Group

Another strategy that the more 'shy' Chinese students used in their adjustment process was to work in a small group or with 'friendly' fellow students. Sometimes, Chinese students participated in group discussions more actively if they were in small groups, rather than in large groups (Zhu 2007). These small groups were effective in taking the spotlight off individual students and also not overwhelming them in a crowd. Students may get lost in a large group, and have difficulty keeping pace with so many different participating speakers. However, one drawback is that small groups can also exacerbate individual characteristics, as there are fewer people to balance out more aggressive speakers. The roles that the Chinese students played within their work groups also differed, depending on students' personal traits. Some Chinese students drew back or followed other German students' instructions passively when working on a project together, especially during the first or the second semester. They were not yet equipped or comfortable with the necessary language skills to argue or raise their opinions in German. Other Chinese students became more confident over time and later actively participated in group discussions, but with mixed results. Just because the Chinese students expressed their opinions did not mean the German students in the group would automatically agree. Often, their cultural backgrounds would lead to different thinking processes that sometimes conflicted during group work.

As a consequence of losing these 'battles', students sometimes had to carry out German students' instructions, but felt reluctant to 'work for them'. In this situation, the German students dominated the group work. Based on this kind of scenario, some Chinese students were full of misgivings about cooperation and communication with German students, because they were not always treated as equals.

> At the very beginning, I didn't want to leave others with the impression that 'she's a very quiet Chinese'. […] It is true that I am a foreigner here, but as other students, I have done the homework and formed my own opinion as well, why should I be a small potato in the group? […] I want to be the player as well, instead of just a participant of the game. (Interviewee 6)

Modifying Learning Habits

In order to meet the challenges in learning their discipline, many Chinese students began to preview and prepare for lectures well in advance of the actual class sessions. This was a much more proactive approach to learning, compared to when they were in China and only expending efforts to study for exams. Actively previewing the materials not only facilitated increased class participation by helping prepare students to answer lecturers' questions, but also gave them more time to digest the material so they could develop and ask more pertinent questions during class discussions.

Likewise, international Chinese students also began to prepare for their exams earlier. Having experienced the more rigorous nature of the preliminary exams at German universities, Chinese students would begin learning about and studying for the specific requirements of their general class exams in Germany, and accumulate the necessary practical experience to understand and pass them. Hence, preparing for the exam earlier became an important priority, rather than a last-minute activity.

One major shift was the move for students from extrinsic to intrinsic motivation to study abroad. In China, motivation is extrinsic; students are pushed by parents and teachers, and 'expected to study' (要我学 *yao wo xue*). In Germany, motivation is expected to be intrinsic; studying is the Chinese students' own decision, and they should 'be motivated to learn by themselves' (我要学 *wo yao xue*). Motivation moved from extrinsic to intrinsic, and student participation moved from passive to active. One

Chinese student (Interviewee 10) reflected on this experience, saying, 'I notice that I have made progress and I enjoy the process of learning. I learn more actively and earnestly'.

Having Patience for the 'Long-Term Battle'

Chinese students participating in the interviews realized that adjusting to German universities was a long-term battle, which could not be won immediately. By and large, most of the participants accepted this idea, and were not overly anxious or upset by it. When asked about their attitude toward this difficulty, they often replied that they just needed to 'take time' or accepted it as just a process where 'things will be much easier someday'. Often, they were very self-reflective and introspective during this process, analyzing their own strengths and weaknesses in order to develop step-by-step strategies to help themselves adjust. Sometimes even simple steps could be a daunting task.

> We [Chinese students] do realize that we are very shy, but from being aware of the problem to taking actions is a long process. For instance, I realize that I seldom raised opinions at the seminar. Ever since the first semester, I have been thinking about how to adjust to the learning environment here better and I set a step-by-step goal: I first 'forced' myself to speak up at least once at each group discussion, and then I upgraded the goal and 'forced' myself to speak up twice at other situations. (Interviewee 6)

Reflecting on Progress in the Developing Phase

By and large, after two semesters' study in Germany, 70 per cent of the participants were satisfied with the progress they had made (Fig. 5.1). For instance, many students were particularly proud of progress in their ability to solve problems by themselves (80 per cent reported 'some' to 'much' progress), and in their ability to understand specialized academic knowledge (76.7 per cent reported 'some' to 'much' progress). Although Chinese students also made a lot of progress in their German proficiency, they were not content with their progress in overall German language skills and progress in communication with lecturers and peers compared to their other skills.

Not surprisingly, Chinese students' progress in German language was closely related to their achievement in communication ability. Based on Chinese students' self-assessment, Table 5.7 indicates that the correlation

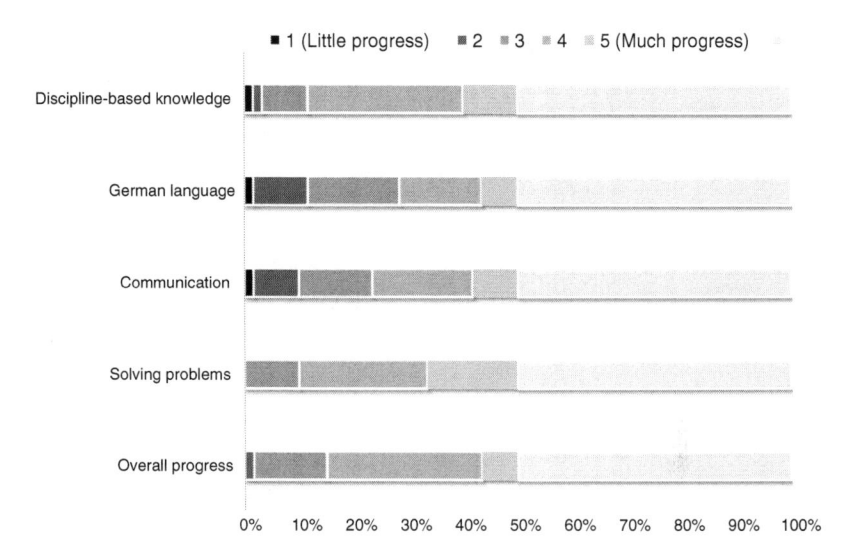

Fig. 5.1 Satisfaction toward the progress according to Study 3. Note: Chinese students were asked to rate satisfaction toward the progress by using a 5-point Likert scale: 1 (Little progress) to 5 (Much progress)

Table 5.7 Correlation of items of achievement according to Study 3 ($n=30$)

	(1)	(2)	(3)	(4)	(5)
(1) Discipline-based knowledge	1				
(2) German language	0.08	1			
(3) Communication	0.32	0.45[a]	1		
(4) Problem-solving	0.34	0.22	0.53[b]	1	
(5) Overall progress	0.39[a]	0.59[b]	0.62[b]	0.58[b]	1

[a]Correlation is significant at the 0.05 level (2-tailed)
[b]Correlation is significant at the 0.01 level (2-tailed)

between their German language and their communication ability was significant ($r=0.45$, $p<0.05$). In essence, those who reported bigger gains in language proficiency probably also gained more confidence in communicative ability.

Likewise, overall progress is correlated to individual items of progress such as subject knowledge, German language, communication, and problem-solving, as overall progress is closely related to the progress of communication (r = 0.62, $p < 0.01$), German language (r = 0.59, $p < 0.01$), problem-solving ability (r = 0.58, $p < 0.01$), and discipline-based knowledge (r = 0.39, $p < 0.05$). Chinese students regard studying abroad as an opportunity that provides them with a chance for personal growth (Skyrme and White 2011). As time passes, international students 'become more organized in managing their time for studies, committed to the course of the study, confident of using a greater range of study skills, comfortable in small-group discussion, (and) confident of managing independent studies' (Gu et al. 2010, p. 18).

References

Campbell, J., & Li, M. (2007). Asian students' voices: An empirical study of Asian students' learning experiences at a New Zealand University. *Journal of Studies in International Education, 12*(4), 375–396. doi:10.1177/1028315307299422.

Cortazzi, M., & Jin, L. (1996). Cultures of learning: Language classrooms in China. In H. Coleman (Ed.), *Society and the language classroom* (pp. 169–206). Cambridge: Cambridge University Press.

Gu, Q., Schweisfurth, M., & Day, C. (2010). Learning and growing in a 'foreign' context: Intercultural experiences of international students. *Compare: A Journal of Comparative and International Education, 40*(1), 7–23. Retrieved from http://dx.doi.org/10.1080/03057920903115983

Jin, L., & Cortazzi, M. (2006). Changing practices in Chinese cultures of learning. *Language, Culture and Curriculum, 19*(1), 5–20. doi:10.1080/07908310608668751.

Kingston, E., & Forland, H. (2008). Bridging the gap in expectations between international students and academic staff. *Journal of Studies in International Education, 12*(2), 204–221. doi:10.1177/1028315307307654.

Lin, J.-C. G., & Yi, J. K. (1997). Asian international students' adjustment: Issues and program suggestions. *College Student Journal, 31*(4), 473–479.

Liu, J. (2002). Negotiating silence in American classrooms: Three Chinese cases. *Language and Intercultural Communication, 2*(1), 37–54. doi:10.1080/14708470208668074.

Skyrme, G., & White, C. (2011). Getting the big picture: A longitudinal study of adaptation and identity in a New Zealand university. In L. Jin & M. Cortazzi (Eds.), *Researching Chinese learners. Skills, perceptions and intercultural adaptations* (pp. 188–211). Basingstoke/New York: Palgrave Macmillan.

Taylor, E. W. (1994). Intercultural Competency: A Transformative Learning Process. *Adult Education Quarterly, 44*(3), 154–174. doi:10.1177/074171369404400303.

Westwood, M. J., & Barker, M. (1990). Academic achievement and social adaptation among international students: A comparison groups study of the peer-pairing program. *International Journal of Intercultural Relations, 14*(2), 251–263. doi:10.1016/0147-1767(90)90008-K.

Yan, K., & Berliner, D. C. (2009). Chinese international students' academic stressors in the United States. *College Student Journal, 43*(4), 939–960.

Zhou, J. (2010). *Zwischen "Elite von morgen" und "Liu Xue La Ji" ("Müllstudenten")*. Münster: Verl.-Haus Monsenstein und Vannerdat.

Zhu, J. (2007). *A cross-cultural learning case study: Comprehending Chinese international students' adapting and learning strategies at Canadian universities*. Master thesis. Halifax, Nova Scotia, Canada, Halifax, Nova Scotia, Canada. http://dc.msvu.ca:8080/xmlui/bitstream/handle/10587/282/JiaZhu-MAED-2007.pdf?sequence=3&isAllowed=y

CHAPTER 6

Approaching the End: Appreciating the German Learning Environment

Acknowledging, understanding, and then appreciating.
了解, 理解, 谅解

— *Anonymous*

When approaching the end of their study in Germany, the Chinese students achieved a relatively good command of the German language, showed more understanding about features of the German university system, and learned to reflect on their time and experiences during their study abroad.

German Language and Its Role in Academic Adjustment

Compared with the previous developing phase, the majority of the Chinese participants became more confident in their German language and no longer regarded it as their biggest difficulty in the final phase of their academic adjustment. Several students stated that they no longer had any problem understanding the lecturers during class. In looking back, what had been very difficult and painful for them in the first semester, was now very easy. Many Chinese students reported having a 'Eureka' moment in their German language studies.

© The Editor(s) (if applicable) and The Author(s) 2016
J. Zhu, *Chinese Overseas Students and Intercultural Learning Environments*, Palgrave Studies on Chinese Education in a Global Perspective, DOI 10.1057/978-1-137-53393-7_6

> Since the fifth semester, I have made progress in German language as well. One turning point was a project with another international student who speaks German well. After intense communication with him, I felt that I made great progress in listening and speaking. (Interviewee 15)

This 'Eureka' moment was actually the result of students' accumulated German learning over the course of several semesters. Many Chinese students were not fully aware of their progress until that one moment. This 'sudden' discovery of improvement made them feel more confident about their learning experience, as language difficulty was no longer a barrier to learning in an intercultural environment.

Cognitive-Dimension Adjustments: Appreciating the German University System

At German universities, students are provided with a higher degree of freedom compared to Chinese universities. They have the freedom to choose the institution, discipline, classes, and concentrations within the discipline, and to fulfill many of the requirements at their own pace (Peisert and Framhein 1990). Chinese students' initial impressions of being 'left alone', having 'no supervision', or 'nobody takes care of me', have now changed to 'academic freedom' (学术自由 *xueshu ziyou*). The students gradually realized that they could take the exams according to their own readiness, rather than the school's schedule. In this last phase of academic adjustment, a large number of interviewees understood and appreciated this academic freedom in Germany, and how everything related to their education now depended on their own initiative. In particular, doctoral students were also provided with greater research freedom in Germany by their supervisors.

> He (the supervisor) never specifies what I should do, although he has a clear research plan for supervising me. At the first semester, he suggested a book list to me as he thought it was important to have 'common sense' but he did not specify what I should read. [...] It all depends on me. He encouraged me to do the research according to my interests. (Interviewee 2)

In this phase, the Chinese students also showed appreciation for the diversity of courses available. The *Modul* system, which had been a brand new, yet troublesome, concept for them in the beginning, turned out to be meaningful and helpful for them in the end. As interviewees were familiar with all types of courses under the *Modul* framework, they regarded the *Modul* as a good form of course structure. As a result, they were more critically able to compare and contrast shortcomings of the system in China.

Chinese students expressed that over time they had become particularly fond of the seminar as a prevailing form of university teaching and learning. Although they had encountered substantial problems participating in discussions and giving presentations in seminars initially, eventually, many master's students indicated that they enjoyed the seminar form and regarded it as a special course with German characteristics, which stimulated deep and creative thinking.

> Seminar, especially the Hauptseminar (in English: advanced seminar), is the best and most meaningful learning form in Germany […] it is a training of thinking. […] The purpose of the lecturer was to teach us a learning method: learning how to do research through demonstrating research work of others. […] It was a great deal of work and it was really exhausting […] But after this, one learns not only how to build the structure of his own thesis, but also how to process the data. (Interviewee 9)

Affective-Dimension Adjustments: Accomplishments and Self-Confidence

In the affective dimension, the Chinese students felt satisfied with their learning experience in Germany. By dealing with their difficulties, they became more confident about themselves and their abilities in the final phase of their academic adjustment.

Feeling Accomplished

Interviewees who finished or were about to finish their study programs in Germany were very satisfied with their academic performance. One interviewee (Interviewee 13) achieved a very high score of 1.0 on his master's thesis. Others reported an average score of 1.5 or 1.6 (Interviewees 12 and 16). Furthermore, Chinese students reported that their study in Germany enabled them to broaden their horizons and obtain knowledge of an advanced field of study. They also gained a great sense of accomplishment in how they were able to learn and apply information more in-depth than in Chinese universities. One student (Interviewee 16) accomplished his *Diplom* degree faster than other students in his department did. According to him, the average length of study of his department was 16.8 semesters. As he had already learned the basics with a four-year bachelor's study in China, he only needed ten semesters.

Chinese students, in spite of all the difficulties and hardships they faced, were proud of the adequate research and writing skills they had acquired during their studies (Campbell and Li 2007). However, many Chinese students still felt that they could have done better or worked harder, so as to finish their studies more quickly. One Chinese student (Interviewee 12) felt that she was relatively slow in finishing her degree and that she had wasted some time during her studies. Given another chance, she would work harder to finish and graduate earlier. Such 'guilty' feelings might also be related to cultural logics carried over by the students from their traditional Chinese learning environment. This sentiment is less common among students from other countries.

Becoming More Self-Confident

Similar to other international students, who reported 'a growth in intercultural competence that carried implications for their future professional and interpersonal relationships' (Brown and Holloway 2008, p. 242), Chinese students obtained a sense of achievement by completing various academic tasks, which made them feel more confident about their ability to manage their future studies.

> At the very beginning, I had the feeling 'I cannot manage studying in Germany'. But after passing the most difficult course, I gained self-confidence. Now when meeting a challenge, I will first look back: I passed the most difficult course, so I should solve the problem this time as well. Now I hold the attitude: one should not first make the judgment 'I can't manage it'. Instead, he should just have a try. Then he will see whether he can manage it or not. (Interviewee 11)

BEHAVIORAL-DIMENSION ADJUSTMENTS: PARTICIPATING IN ACADEMIC ACTIVITIES

In the final phase of academic adjustment, based on their understanding and appreciation of the learning traditions in Germany, Chinese students became more active participants in class discussions and consultation hours. They viewed their experience in Germany through a different lens, and no longer simply judged the learning environment from the one-sided perspective of their previous experience in China.

First, having realized that their previous learning customs were inappropriate for current academic expectations, Chinese students now made efforts to change their thought processes behind learning.

> Previously, I just noticed that the professor had a wide theme and talked about everything under the sun. I thought that I would learn nothing from him. But gradually, I realized that if I follow his thought, think together with him, and gather the courage to share my own view point... I will benefit tremendously from the course. (Interviewee 18)

Second, some Chinese students, who had previously worried that their poor German language skills would disadvantage everyone in a group work setting, later consciously and actively tried to work together with German peers in group projects. One interviewee (Interviewee 6) previously felt embarrassed to ask for help from her peers; she felt reluctant to show others that she did not comprehend an idea or needed extra help. However, based on her observation and understanding of the learning custom at German universities, she changed her stance on this and learned to ask for help.

> My previous working experience teaches me, [...] it is important to know how to solve the problem especially when the opinion within the team varies. [...] I have been making progress in cooperating with other team members. [...] I learned to listen to others' suggestions and realized that no one is perfect and everyone needs help and support from others. (Interviewee 6)

As a result, she grew to appreciate the importance of group work and regarded it as a good opportunity for students to learn from each other. She became less sensitive and more willing to accept help, which she regarded as a supplement to her own understanding, not as 'awkward' or 'embarrassing'. Over time, East Asian students participating often come to '[enjoy] and [feel] comfortable with group work, as this gave them the opportunity to share ideas and develop personal ideas in a supportive environment' (Kingston and Forland 2008, p. 215).

Third, Chinese students no longer feared asking lecturers questions during their consultation hours. Visiting the lecturers during consultation hours was a significant psychological challenge for many Chinese students.

However, after several semesters, some of them began to take advantage of this important source of academic help. One student mentioned that while some lecturers would not provide specific solutions, they did give her some suggestions for making decisions regarding her master's thesis, which was more important.

The Chinese students adopted new strategies and learned how to take better advantage of consultation hours. For instance, many realized that they should prepare topics and questions in advance to discuss with the lecturer during consultation hours. They learned how to communicate with the German lecturer in a more efficient way so as to benefit from the instruction.

> I remembered I once was at a professor's consultation hour and asked for his advice. During the conversation, he kept asking me, 'If you want to write the term paper, what kind of preparation have you done?' 'What kind of materials have you already read?' and 'What do you think about this' Then he shared his opinions concerning that theme. [...] I realized what really mattered was one's own point of view. But I could not reply to these questions at that moment [...] From then on, I first did my homework before going to the consultation hour. I first read the materials and formed my own opinions. [...] One should never visit the lecturer in the consultation hour with an empty mind, as this is not appreciated in Germany at all. (Interviewee 6)

Visiting the lecturers during consultation hours was an important opportunity for Chinese students to obtain help, as German lecturers were more than willing to help students. Nevertheless, it took the Chinese students to learn how to ask for and accept that help.

> I didn't visit consultation hours the first semester, as I asked questions after class. [...] The second semester, as a group, we first did our homework, visited him in the consultation hour, and introduced our theme before the presentation. [...] The third semester, I knew how to take advantage of consultation hours and was brave enough to go to the consultation hour alone. (Interviewee 6)

One Chinese student even 'dared' to argue with her lecturer, as she had read the materials required in advance and had confidence in her replies to her lecturer's questions. She found that the lecturer offered useful instruction, especially when he noticed that she had been well prepared for this discussion.

> This time, when I just sat down, Prof. K came straight to the point. 'What have you done so far? Please let me see your work.' He thought I had done

nothing. [...] To his surprise, this time I clearly told him, 'I have read theory of X, Y and Z, but I am sorry that I just cannot understand it. I have even searched this theory in Chinese, trying to understand it in my mother tongue, nevertheless I failed.' After hearing that, Prof. K moderated his temper. Realizing that I had tried my best to understand the reading materials, he replied gently, 'What you are reading now won't contribute much to your presentation, [...] actually you should read the article of this author...' Although I was on the wrong track in preparing for the presentation, I won his understanding. This experience was encouraging. (Interviewee 20)

Fourth, Chinese students reported that they also learned to reflect on the state and progress of their studies in Germany. Phrases often referred to by participants were 'to think or reflect' (思考 *sikao*), and 'to use one's brain' (动脑筋 *dong naojin*). This self-reflection allowed students to identify and compare the strengths and advantages of their education in Germany, and make up for their prior deficiencies or lack of understanding.

Reflection and Outlook: Satisfaction, Self-Assessment, Future Plan, and Recommendation

Approaching the end of their studies in Germany, Chinese students reflected on their academic achievement, personal development, and growth in general, and made plans for future career development.

Satisfaction with the Education in Germany

International student satisfaction in Germany depends on two factors: (1) international students' expectations and what the university can offer to meet their expectations; and (2) international students' abilities in relation to the academic requirements of the German universities (Ro 2006). Results from questionnaires and interviews indicated that Chinese students were generally satisfied with their learning experience, lecturers, and academic resources.

General Learning Experience in Germany

Chinese students participating in this research generally reported satisfaction with their learning experience at German universities. In spite of the difficulties and challenges they encountered, they still firmly believed that Germany was a good choice for their overseas study.

182　J. ZHU

> Germany is an ideal destination for an overseas study. The situation here is different from that in the USA The academic atmosphere in Germany is more relaxed, while competition plays a more important role in the USA and researchers are under more stress. In Germany, (even without such big pressure,) one does excellent research as well. In addition, students here enjoy good service. (Interviewee 13)

International students put a premium on the quality of lectures, programs, academic environments, and academic resources available in the host country (Campbell and Li 2007; Chan and Drover 1997). Among thirty-one participants, about 70 per cent of them were satisfied with their learning experience at German universities in general, according to the results of Study 3 (Round 2) (Fig. 6.1). Seventy-four per cent of the Chinese participants reported that they were 'satisfied' or 'very satisfied' with the academic resources they had available at German universities, and over 66 per cent were 'satisfied' or 'very satisfied' with the teaching and research quality, lecturers, and institution.

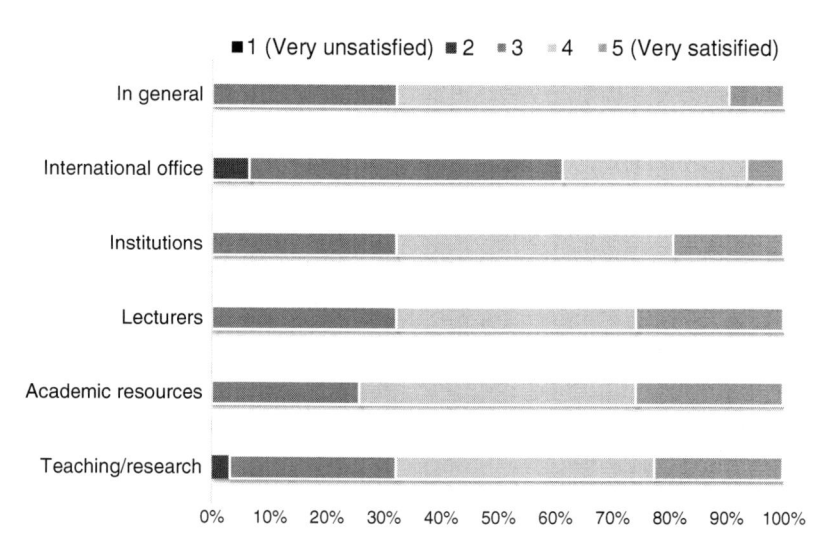

Fig. 6.1 Satisfaction with the learning experience at German universities according to Study 3. Note: Chinese students were asked to report their satisfaction with the learning experience at German universities by using a 5-point Likert scale: 1 (Very unsatisfied) to 5 (Very satisfied)

In comparison, the students were less satisfied with the service provided by the international student office, as 61 per cent of Chinese students rated their opinion of its services either as 'unsatisfied' or 'very unsatisfied'. This does not necessarily mean that the international student office provides poor service. One possible reason for the dissatisfaction is that the Chinese students may have expected too much from the international office, in terms of academic and daily help. Additionally, they themselves did not take proper advantage of the services actually provided by it, such as study guidance and support for prospective students before and during the application stage. One interviewee mentioned, 'I know that the international office of our university has organized many activities, I have been just too busy, or sometimes too lazy, to join' (Interviewee 7).

Chinese students were particularly satisfied with their lecturers and the teaching quality in Germany, as well as the academic resources in Germany. Seventy-four per cent of the interviewees (twenty-three students out of thirty-one) were 'very satisfied' or 'satisfied' with their academic resources. Similarly, Chinese students also spoke highly of the infrastructure and easy access to academic resources. Information in class and the textbooks was always kept up to date, and students were kept informed of academic and work opportunities that could help build their career.

One doctoral student in the natural sciences (Interviewee 2) was extremely impressed with both the software and the hardware available to help conduct research in the laboratory environment.

> The administration and organization of the laboratory is in good order. [...] first, the registration and use of the experimental facilities or equipment is well organized. [...] second, the cooperation among different departments is quite good. [...] third, the technicians at the laboratory are professional and helpful. They have a profound understanding of my research area. I learned a lot by talking with them. (Interviewee 2)

Self-Assessment

Chinese students were proud of how their experience dealing with difficulty helped them develop persistence, and the ability to 'survive the battle'.

Furthermore, they became open to new experiences in an intercultural learning environment. The learning experience in Germany also provides contact with German and international students from other countries. They learned specific 'German ways', like how to study in a more serious, earnest, and accurate way.

As long as one is in Germany, he should learn to be a man 'with his feet on the ground,' instead of using his wits or tricks. Tricks seldom work in Germany, as the academic criteria are settled (one has no choice but to fulfill it). (Interviewee 2)

It is important to mention, higher education in China is 'hard to enter, but easy to leave' (严进宽出 *yan jin kuan chu*). Therefore, after years of hard work preparing for the intimidating *Gaokao*, some Chinese students do not work as hard in university as they did in middle and high school.

This situation is reversed in Germany. Except for some restricted disciplines, such as dentistry and psychology, German universities have open doors for high school (or equivalent) graduates, who can apply for enrollment. However, after admission, students must work hard to earn their degrees.

In general, Chinese students were very pleased with their changes and improvements regarding their overall academic achievement and personal growth at the end of their overseas studies. After conquering their academic difficulties and enduring the stress of a new life and academic setting, international students often achieved 'personal development and growth,' and '(inter)cultural experience,' increasing their independence, confidence and coping abilities (Brown and Holloway 2008; Ehrenreich 2006).

Career Plan

Students' future career plans were tied to the decision of staying in Germany or returning to China after graduation. In most cases, the decision was consistent with Chinese students' original motivation for studying in Germany. Those who came to Germany for an overseas degree (e.g. Interviewee 11, 14, and 17) with the goal of having more opportunities in the Chinese job market would return as soon as they received their degrees or certificates.

However, with rising numbers of Chinese students returning with overseas certifications, the job market in China is increasingly competitive. Given that, after graduation some interviewees (mentioned by Interviewees 9 and 19) planned to work in Germany for maybe two to three years (mentioned by Interviewees 7 and 12) to gain some practical working experience overseas first, in order to further increase their competitiveness in the Chinese job market. Students' personal situation also influenced their decisions of whether to stay or go. For instance, scholarship recipients (e.g. Interviewee 1) or exchange students (e.g. Interviewees 13 and 21) were expected to return immediately after completing their study abroad programs. Meanwhile, self-funded students had more freedom in choosing whether to stay or return. Sometimes, the experience of living and studying in Germany changed Chinese students' minds about returning to China. One Chinese student (Interviewee 9), who had originally planned on returning, decided to work in Germany instead after having a positive internship work experience.

Advising Prospective Students

Students who enjoyed or benefitted from the overseas academic and life experience often recommend this path to others as well. If the Chinese students recommend Germany as a study abroad destination to other Chinese students, this means they discovered more advantages than disadvantages to studying there. According to the results of the interviews, the majority of the participants would recommend Germany to prospective Chinese students, although a few would still first recommend the USA. (e.g. Interviewees 2 and 7). In addition, nobody would dissuade others from studying in Germany.

> I will recommend Germany—to study here is not that expensive and the teaching quality here is really high. Compared with those countries which have a reputation for 'buying a degree', an academic degree from Germany is highly valued. (Interviewee 5)

REFERENCES

Brown, L., & Holloway, I. (2008). The adjustment journey of international postgraduate students at an English university: An ethnographic study. *Journal of Research in International Education, 7*(2), 232–249. doi:10.1177/1475240908091306.

Campbell, J., & Li, M. (2007). Asian students' voices: An empirical study of Asian students' learning experiences at a New Zealand University. *Journal of Studies in International Education, 12*(4), 375–396. doi:10.1177/1028315307299422.

Chan, D., & Drover, G. (1997). Teaching and learning for overseas students: The Hong Kong connection. In D. McNamara & R. Harris (Eds.), *Overseas students in higher education. Issues in teaching and learning* (pp. 46–61). London: Routledge.

Ehrenreich, S. (2006). The assistant experience in retrospect and its educational and professional significance in teachers' biographies. In M. Byram & A. Feng (Eds.), *Living and studying abroad. Research and practice* (Languages for intercultural communication and education, Vol. 12, pp. 186–209). Clevedon/ Buffalo: Multilingual Matters Ltd.

Kingston, E., & Forland, H. (2008). Bridging the gap in expectations between international students and academic staff. *Journal of Studies in International Education, 12*(2), 204–221. doi:10.1177/1028315307307654.

Peisert, H., & Framhein, G. (1990). *Higher education in the Federal Republic of Germany.* Bucharest: CEPES.

Ro, H.-K. (2006). *Zufriedenheit ausländischer Studierender an deutschen Hochschulen: Eine empirische Untersuchung am Beispiel ostasiatischer Studierender. Schriften zur Arbeits-, Betriebs- und Organisationspsychologie* (Vol. 23). Hamburg: Kovač.

CHAPTER 7

Key Factors Influencing Chinese Students' Academic Adjustment

The previous discussion indicates that the Chinese students involved in this study demonstrated different degrees of academic adjustment at German universities. Based on the interviews, some Chinese participants demonstrated better adjustment to the German learning environment than others did. In order to understand why, this chapter explores key factors and examines how they interact with Chinese students' academic adjustment.

BACKGROUND FACTORS AND THEIR INTERPLAY

Is It Only German Language?

When the Chinese students were asked about difficulties they had encountered in Germany, without any hesitation they immediately referred to the German language. Insufficient German language capability may result in difficulty in completing their studies on time, difficulty in communication and social adjustment, difficulty in understanding the terminology, and difficulty in relating the discipline's knowledge to previous knowledge learned in China (Danckwortt 1984). At their peak at the beginning, problems caused by inadequate German proficiency accompanied the Chinese students like an 'invisible ghost' throughout the entire duration of their stay in Germany. But is the German language to blame for all adjustment difficulties to the new learning environment?

© The Editor(s) (if applicable) and The Author(s) 2016
J. Zhu, *Chinese Overseas Students and Intercultural Learning Environments*, Palgrave Studies on Chinese Education in a Global Perspective, DOI 10.1057/978-1-137-53393-7_7

Often, academic subject terminology, theories and practices, and social-cultural knowledge of the target culture (Zhao and Bourne 2011) are regarded by international students as a 'language problem'. However, it is important to differentiate difficulties caused by standard foreign language skills from difficulties caused by specialized terminologies. Even native speakers can have difficulties with the latter. Actually, the impression students have of having difficulty with German fluency is often intermixed with major subject knowledge, specialized terminology, and knowledge of other academic subjects (Fig. 7.1). Chinese students need a good command of all three areas in order to understand the content of lectures, seminars, and other courses. In addition, fixed expressions regarding campus life and academia, such as 'attending courses', 'doing a presentation', and 'visiting consultation hours' also require specific language knowledge related to German cultural norms and patterns of communication. Given that, when students talk about 'difficulty with the German language', they are actually conflating it with several problems related to German language proficiency that are not themselves foreign language proficiency problems.

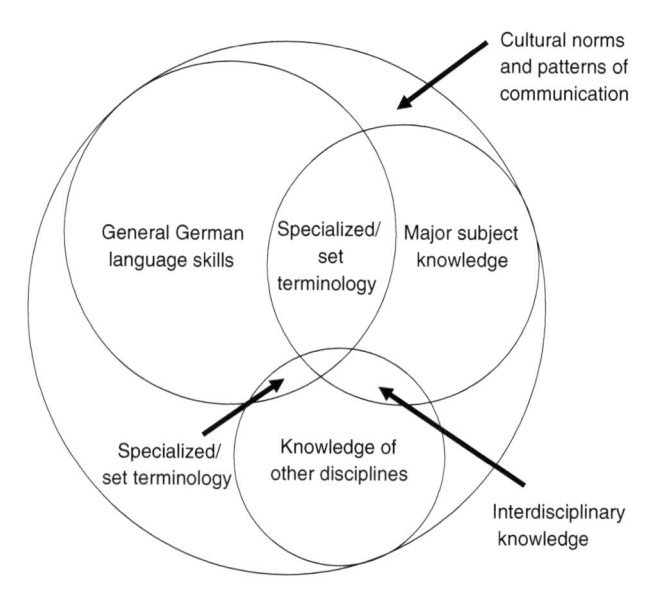

Fig. 7.1 The use of academic German language at university

Major Subject Knowledge

What major a Chinese student chooses when studying abroad in Germany has a huge impact on their academic adjustment. The standardized German language examinations assess international students' general German language skills. However, these proficiency exams do not focus on or measure students' prior knowledge of the majors they choose when enrolling at German universities. Therefore, passing the standardized language tests for admission does not guarantee that international students will understand the lectures or be able to communicate with German instructors or students. Many of the Chinese students realized that their previous academic knowledge learned at Chinese universities was not sufficient or the right kind to match the academic requirements in German universities.

> Some subject reading materials are difficult to understand. Sometimes after reading one academic article three times, I still fail to figure out the meaning. [...] There are many metaphors in the reading materials: one needs to have prior knowledge to understand it. (Interviewee 17)

Without the proper subject knowledge base, the Chinese students did not understand the content discussed in class. Without previous preparation and relevant study of the subject, students still would have had difficulty understanding the content even in Chinese. In particular, two Chinese students who switched majors for study in Germany reported more difficulties adjusting academically than those who stayed in the same or related discipline.

Specialized or Set Terminology

The content conveyed at lectures is based on the subject knowledge of a specific academic field. Chinese students met with the challenge of not only German language, but also set terminologies from specific disciplines. Here, *terminology* refers to words and phrases used in the contexts of subject knowledge and general German language. The Chinese students were not familiar with specific and set terminologies in German used in their fields of study, which became obstacles to understanding the lectures, expressing their opinions, and joining the seminar discussions. In interviews, both law students (Interviewees 3 and 8) participating in this study mentioned that the terminology was a big challenge to them. For instance, much of the specialized legal terminology they had to master was in Latin—something they had not prepared for when studying for the standard German language exam. Although new terminology can be a challenge for anyone, Chinese students need more time than their German counterparts to familiarize themselves with these specialized words and concepts.

Considering this challenge, German universities provide preparatory courses specifically targeting international students. For example, *Propädeutikum* or *Studienkolleg* offer international students opportunities to learn necessary subject terminologies. *Propädeutikum* is a 'preparatory tutorial' or 'prerequisite program' (Quinlivan 2009, p. 119) for international students, while *Studienkolleg* is 'preparatory college' meant only for students from abroad (Quinlivan 2009). However, except for one participant, the Chinese students did not attend any of these preparatory courses. Consequently, many participants reported trouble with terminologies.

Interdisciplinary Knowledge and Knowledge of Related Disciplines

Chinese students often lack the necessary interdisciplinary or academic knowledge from other fields. Both the subject matter and the set terminologies constituting the interdisciplinary knowledge present a big challenge for them. For instance, students majoring in social sciences mentioned that their current studies involved a great deal of knowledge from other disciplines. The subject of economics required students to have a good foundation in mathematics. One student majoring in Media Science had to read books concerning linguistics. Another student majoring in German language studies was required to have previous knowledge of philosophy. Yet, Chinese students seemed unaware of the true nature of this challenge. Lacking prior knowledge in other disciplines to provide a sufficient interdisciplinary knowledge base, they still reported all this difficulty as a problem with their German language.

Cultural Norms and Patterns of Communication

In addition to *what* subjects to learn in German, the competence, knowledge, or skills concerning *how* to use German appropriately to communicate with German lecturers and students on campus also played an important role in academic adjustment. For Chinese students, to know *what* the words mean is necessary, but *how* and *when* to use them is more important. Without the knowledge and skills of how to use the German they learned properly, the students could not communicate or participate academically in the university. Often, Chinese students lacked the German language pattern or paradigm to participate in lectures, give presentations, or ask questions during consultation hours appropriately and efficiently. What came naturally to the German students did not for the Chinese students. Inefficient intercultural communication in the academic setting might lead to misunderstanding (Schumann 2008), as illustrated by difficulties surrounding consultation hours discussed in the Chap. 4.

University Environment Factors

The academic support system is composed of support at multiple levels. University-level support provides services such as orientation and language courses. Department[1]-level support provides services such as academic consultation on how to organize *Moduls*, class schedules, and examinations. Meanwhile, peer-level support is a bit more informally organized, and available simply through befriending and communicating with lecturers, tutors, and students attending the same courses. Each level offers different benefits in terms of how they assist Chinese students.

Academic Support

Support Provided at the University Level: Orientation Courses
At German universities, there are typically two types of orientation courses (in German: *Einführungskurs*) available, which are sometimes also called 'orientation activities' (in German: *Einführungsveranstaltung*). There are some offered by the university and some offered by individual institutions or departments (Table 7.1).

First, orientation courses offered by the university provide general information to all newcomers, which is an important chance for incoming freshman to acquaint themselves with the overall university system and facilities, advisory services, and university life. In addition to general information, universities also offer campus tours and organize meet-and-greet

---

[1] Here, *department* stands for a division of a university devoted to a particular academic discipline.

Table 7.1 Academic support at German universities

Support providers	Items
University	Delivering information about academic and campus life, language center, library, and dining hall
	Orientation for freshmen (university-wide)
	Orientation for international freshmen (university-wide)
International student office	Various activities
	Intercultural training course
Language center	General language course
	Academic reading and writing
Institutions and departments	Introduction to the department, course (learning plan, participation), and the examination
	Orientation for freshmen (institution/department-wide)
	Orientation for foreign freshmen (institution/department-wide)
Lecturers, tutors, and mentors	Offering support for academic activities
Fellow students/colleagues	Note-taking
	Learning together with other Chinese students

events for all the new students to welcome them. Some universities, like Albert-Ludwigs-Universität Freiburg and Universität Heidelberg, also offer special orientation courses specifically for international students, which covers information such as German health insurance, visas, and so on. The length of these orientation courses varies from university to university. Some universities offer an orientation week; some provide several organized orientation days; and others offer only a single-day orientation.

Second, orientation courses organized at the department level deliver more information concerning the specific academic programs students will be studying. Freshmen have a chance to get to know 'Who is who' among the administrative and academic faculty staff. Possibly the most important feature of the institution or department orientations is the chance to learn about the *Modul* system. Much like the university-level orientations, the content and length of time for department-level orientations varied from department to department as well. For example, some departments organized preparatory courses, such as mathematics for economics students. Some prepared an entire 'orientation week' (in German: *Orientierungswoche*) of courses to help acclimate students to their new learning environments. Others only speedily offered half a day of courses. One Chinese participant (Interviewee 9) majoring in economics reported that her department organized a two-day preparative course of mathematics for them, which she found very helpful for understanding coursework in her major later on.

In addition to offering formal orientation courses, some institutions or departments organized more informal mixer events to encourage newcomers to get to know each other, and help them integrate into the new learning environment. Departments hosted events such as a day trip to a nearby city (in German: *Erstsemesterfahrt*), 'Freshman Breakfast' (in German: *Erstsemester-Frühstück*), a 'Welcome Breakfast' (in German: *Begrüßungsfrühstück*), or 'Meet Your Neighbors'. Some departments also organized thirty-minute 'orientation talks', where each newcomer had an opportunity to talk with professors or lecturers face to face. During the course of orientation or mixer events, some departments also arranged for senior students from the same country to attend the orientation courses and meet with the newcomers. Their presence helped avoid the language problem many new students encountered at orientation. At other times, departments provided courses specifically for facilitating adjustment to the German culture.

In spite of the importance of these orientation courses, attendance among the Chinese students was low. None of the interviewees attended both university and department orientations. Many missed their appointments for university orientations, because they either did not know when the orientation took place or underestimated its importance. Two students mentioned that they had heard orientation was only about touring around the library, classroom building, and dining hall.

Even for those participating in orientation courses, Chinese students encountered several problems concerning the information they were provided. For many, their insufficient German language proficiency impeded them from fully catching or understanding the important information to take away from the orientation courses. One German major student (Interviewee 4) reported difficulty in understanding the detailed nature of the information presented. Another interviewee (Interviewee 9) complained that it took her some time to 'digest' such a large amount of information, but it was presented too quickly.

> The [department] orientation course lasted about one hour, in which we are introduced to the Modul system and the rules on how to organize the learning plan and choose the courses. We did not receive any handout. [...] To be frank, after attending this course, I was still very confused. Although I got a general idea of the Modul system, I did not figure out how it works. (Interviewee 10)

Attendance at these events generated mixed feelings. Some Chinese students mentioned that they enjoyed the first opportunity to meet their peers. Others felt uncomfortable and nervous, as they had very little intercultural experience and did not know how to behave or what to say.

Support Offered by Lecturers
Lecturers played an important role in facilitating the academic adjustment of Chinese students. Some lecturers provided academic support by modifying their teaching methods. Others showed understanding toward the language difficulties and cultural differences Chinese students faced.

Involving Chinese students in class While many German lecturers were unsympathetic to the challenges Chinese students faced in trying to adjust, some lecturers were more considerate of Chinese students in the class and tried to supplement class content with topics that were more familiar to them. They hoped this would encourage them to participate more in class discussions.

> I noticed that our lecturers have made some modifications in class. The first semester, all examples that lecturers cited in class were Europe-centered. For instance, the lecture used a TV advertisement as an example in class. But we Chinese students had not seen the advertisement, therefore we could not say anything in the discussion. One Chinese student among us complained about this to the lecturer after class, and since this (the second) semester, in class, in addition to the regular questions, the lecturer often asks us 'what is the situation in China?' [...] Obviously, lecturers are making efforts to encourage us to raise our opinions and participate in the discussion. (Interviewee 17)

Such initiatives from the lecturers were helpful to the Chinese students studying in the social sciences and humanities, as many examples discussed in class were culture-specific. As Chinese students had little prior knowledge of German culture, they often felt excluded from conversations and discussions in class (Wong et al. 2015). Not all lecturers were as culturally aware, and unfortunately in most cases, lecturers assumed Chinese students already knew the background context and culture of the information being taught in class. In general, some lecturers do not realize the importance of explaining acronyms, cultural-specific terminology, and sociocultural background knowledge in class (Zhao 2007).

Encouraging Chinese students to ask questions It is important for lecturers to encourage students to ask questions. To Chinese students, this simple action was a form of emotional support. With lecturers' encouragement, students were more likely to take risks in raising questions or expressing their thoughts in class, rather than staying silent.

At the same time, Chinese students were not the only ones to undergo adjustment. Lecturers also experienced an adaptation process to Chinese students in their classroom. Lecturers in the host country, similar to Chinese students, also experience different stages of adaptation in both classroom and group communication contexts (Zhao 2007). First, they experience frustration at the initial unfamiliarity of Chinese students in their classrooms, but gradually learn to integrate their presence and communication into intercultural academic identity of the environment. Thus, intercultural adaptation in classroom and group communication is a two-way process.

At the same time, some lecturers showed understanding for international students who often had difficulties answering questions in German. Many of the Chinese students mentioned that during written exams, they were allowed to use dictionaries. During oral exams, some lecturers even offered students the opportunity to choose German or English to answer their questions (mentioned by Interviewee 11).

Academic support also turned out to serve an emotional function for Chinese students. Lecturers' encouragement, praise, tolerance, understanding, and sympathy provided emotional support for Chinese students.

> After the first lecture, our lecturer came to me after class and said 'I once had some Chinese student in my class as well. Do not worry about the German language; it is normal that one has difficulty at the very beginning. According to my experience with Chinese students, they all wrote excellent semester papers at the end.' (Interviewee 4)

The lecturer's reference to success of other Chinese students comforted this student, made him feel less worried about his current difficulty and more capable of overcoming it.

Support Provided by Faculty Staff
In some departments, there is a coordinator in charge of the international students, providing suggestions for how to plan their studies. Support from the coordinator at the department level is an important resource to Chinese students. The Chinese students reported that talking with these coordinators was especially helpful with regard to handling the *Moduls* and examinations. One international Chinese student had a coordinator

in charge of her master's program who knew the structure of the program very well. If students ever had any difficulty, the coordinator was available and willing to help.

In addition to coordinators, tutors were also a valuable resource in helping Chinese students. Tutors were especially helpful to students with poor German language skills.

However, the extent to which tutors helped Chinese student's adjustment varied. Sometimes this support was limited and hard to access, as tutors themselves were also students with their own academic tasks. Some advisors could be very strict in their attention and requirements to monitor the progress of Chinese students. Others barely showed any concern, at all.

Compared with other international students in Germany, Chinese students also seldom seek help from the Student Advisory Service (in German: *Studienberatung*). Only two Chinese students turned to the *Studienberatung* for help during the course of their studies. In comparison, about 60 per cent of other international students at German universities have turned to the *Studienberatung* for help at some point (Peroz 2008).

Support Provided by Fellow Students
Fellow classmates enrolled in the same courses provide essential help to Chinese students, as well. As 'mentoring facilities' (Kingston and Forland 2008, p. 214), local classmates play a role in the academic support system. Well-adjusted students establish higher levels of social companionship support than the less-adjusted ones (Ramsay et al. 2007). One common way the Chinese students received help from fellow students was in terms of doing group work. Group work provided an opportunity for Chinese students to socialize and make friends with other German students, helping them connect better with their learning environment and gain additional emotional support. Group work also allowed Chinese students to receive collaborative help to catch up in class and complete their academic tasks.

However, this support depended heavily on individual temperaments and whether or not native German or other non-Chinese international students had the patience or understanding to work with Chinese students. Some German students showed no motivation to learn together with foreign students or offer any necessary help (Heublein et al. 2007). An open attitude and willingness to help on the part of German students were necessary for successful cooperation with Chinese students.

Support Provided by Supervisors and Research Groups
For doctoral students in the natural sciences and engineering, supervisors and research teams at their labs became a significant source of support. Compared with their counterparts in the social sciences and humanities, these Chinese students often worked with their supervisors at the same laboratory, thus meeting with their supervisors more often. By working more closely with their supervisors, these doctoral students had better working relationships, and sometimes even had the opportunity to participate in projects led by them.

Research groups also provided academic support for these Chinese students. Colleagues contributed to the research progress of Chinese students by communicating and collaborating with them frequently. Many Chinese students and their German colleagues also spent time together at more relaxing social events, such as barbecue parties. This fostered an emotionally supportive environment that also indirectly provided academic support for all students in the lab.

Unlike doctoral students majoring in the natural sciences or engineering, doctoral students majoring in humanities often work individually, rather than in a team. Because of the different structures of the disciplines, it is not as common for humanities students to work in teams and obtain help from their colleagues. Science and engineering students who played active roles as researchers or teaching assistants for their supervisors had more opportunities to communicate with their supervisors than humanities students who typically wrote their theses in the library or at home alone. Thus, humanities students received relatively less help from colleagues compared to natural science and engineering students. Although humanities students did have some chances to communicate with each other and discuss their research progress at colloquia, they still had much fewer chances overall.

Department Culture and Lecturers' Own Intercultural Experience Matters
In addressing the needs of Chinese students, the department's culture matters. Each discipline has its own 'study climate, the structure of demands, and the intensity of the work expected of students' (Peisert and Framhein 1990, p. 62). In addition to different departments requiring different degrees of individual and group work among students, how the faculty conceives of supervising and supporting international students also differs. One Chinese student (Interviewee 5) mentioned that some departments

organized better orientation courses than hers did. She felt that the orientation course provided by her department was too simple and too short. Professors only spoke briefly to introduce themselves and inform students of their consultation hours, while the department did not provide the newcomers with any instructive handouts or write anything on the blackboard. However, she heard from a Chinese friend that her orientation course in the Education department was much more detailed. Freshmen students were instructed the first day on how to choose the *Modul* using a PowerPoint presentation.

Second, lecturers' own intercultural experience also played a role in their sensitivity and attitude toward helping Chinese students. 'Many lecturers in our department have overseas academic experience themselves. They understand us better and were ready to help us' (mentioned by Interviewee 17). German professors and lecturers who had studied abroad previously shared experiences similar to those currently challenging the international Chinese students. Therefore, they could empathize with many of the problems that international students encountered in Germany, as well as offer helpful advice and assistance.

Support Provided for Exchange Students
In recent years, with the ever-increasing cooperation between German and Chinese universities, more students on both sides are able to obtain overseas study opportunities. Study abroad groups in these scenarios are often composed of exchange students or students from partner universities.

A typical exchange program to Germany normally employs a coordinator to take care of the exchange students. Chinese participants who were exchange students benefited substantially from additional support and privileges offered by their programs, which were not available to Chinese students in regular degree programs. Before departure, they had access to pre-departure training and orientation, including a basic introduction to the German language and general information about Germany and German universities. Upon arrival to the country, the German program coordinator even picked them up at the airport, helped them to find their accommodations, and registered them at city hall. The coordinator also organized special orientations for them. From the beginning, their adjustment experience in Germany was relatively easier than it was for other Chinese students.

Chinese students who arrive in groups demonstrate different patterns of specific academic adaptation from those who arrive individually (Zhou and Todman 2009). Coordinators from both the host and home universities contacted the exchange students regularly and were more available to lend a hand when dealing with academic and daily problems. In addition, exchange students had the opportunity to attend free German language training specially organized for them. These students greatly appreciated the substantial academic support provided for them by their program.

Intercultural Communication with Peer Students

Cultural Composition of Friend Circles

Lacking German language proficiency, intercultural skills, or common topics of interest made communication with acquaintances from other nations more difficult for Chinese students. As a result, Chinese students' friend circles were overwhelmingly dominated by other international Chinese students in Germany. Among thirty-one questionnaire participants in Study 3, 81 per cent indicated that they had 'more Chinese friends'; while only 6 per cent reported that they had 'more German friends'. Surprisingly, 13 per cent of participants mentioned that they had 'no friends at all' (Fig. 7.2). It is worth noting that participants who answered questionnaires were Chinese students who either had already spent two semesters in Germany, or were exchange students. No one reported that they had 'more friends from other nationalities (i.e. non-Chinese or non-German)' or mixed circle

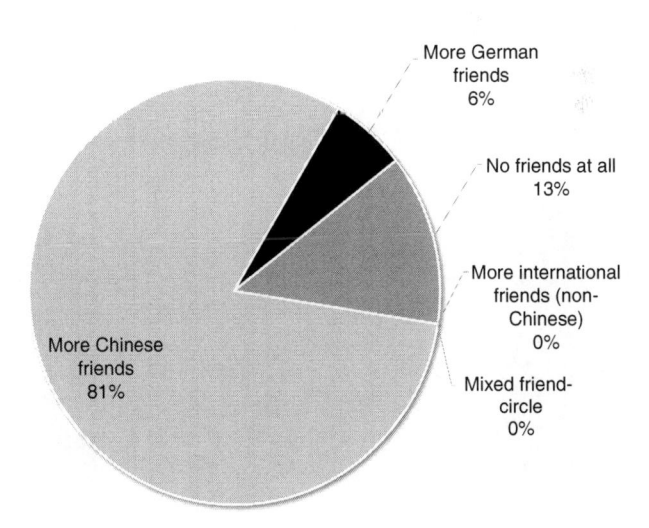

Fig. 7.2 Composition of friend circles in Germany according to Study 3

of friends (friends from various nationalities, but no specific nationality of friends is dominant).

Chinese students not only had more co-national Chinese friends in their friend circles, but also more frequent contact with co-nationals in general. In terms of the frequency of contact with different national groups, 77.4 per cent of participants in Study 3 often had contact with Chinese friend groups, while only 19.4 per cent had frequent contact with German friend groups. The frequency of contact was even lower with other nationalities (Fig. 7.3). This is surprising, given the fact that in 2014, only 8.4 per cent of the entire student population in Germany was composed of international students. Chinese students accounted for 13.0 per cent of this total (Wissenschaft weltoffen 2014). In general, Chinese participants maintained relatively poor contact, in both frequency and intensity, with German or other international students.

There were a few Chinese students who had some international friends they referred to as 'fellow sufferers' (同病相怜 *tong bing xiang lian*). In this case, their similar student identities as 'foreign students' provided a common ground for empathy and communication, prompting these Chinese students to become friends with them more easily than with other German students.

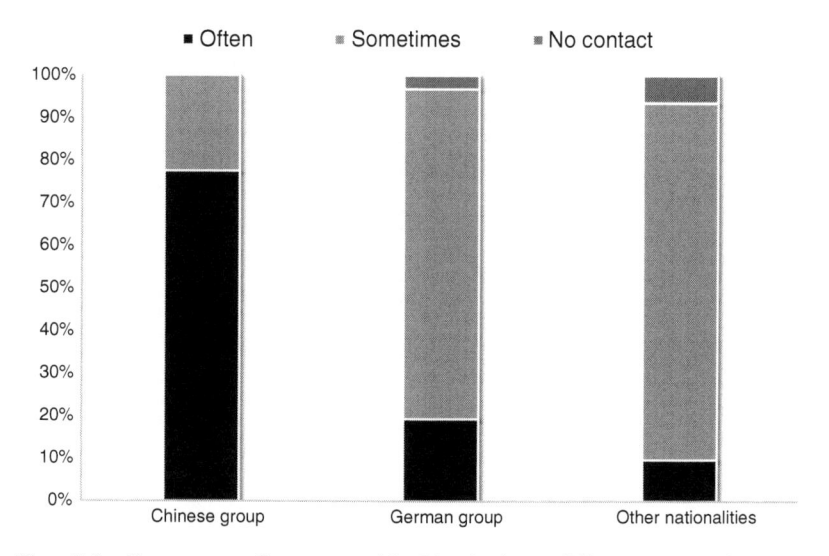

Fig. 7.3 Frequency of contact with friends from different national groups according to Study 3

In particular, one Chinese student (Interviewee 15) had a very good relationship with Chinese and Korean students, because 'We all come from Asia and I feel genial in talking with them. [...] I regard [this communication] as an important emotional support.'

Reasons for Chinese students' Patterns of Friend Making
Several factors contributed to the composition of Chinese students' friend circles in Germany. First, the percentage of international students in departments varied. Some departments like engineering and economics had a large number of Chinese and international students, and thus had easier access to co-national friends. Since co-national communication was easier and involved no language difficulty, many of the Chinese students preferred to turn to other Chinese students for help, instead of approaching German lecturers or students.

One lecturer described what he perceived as an intercultural communication problem typical to departments with a large number of Chinese students.

> I see the difference between Chinese students and other international students in our department. It is true the Ukrainian students have close contacts with other Ukrainian students, but they also often talk with Italian, Arabic, and Czech students. [And] they talk with each other in German [...] Nevertheless, the Chinese students in our department only have contact other Chinese students; they do not have Korean or Japanese friends at all. The problem result from the fact that they have little contact with German society, but also they fail to improve their German language. (Lecturer 1)

However, not every participant regarded such large percentages of co-national Chinese students as positive. Unlike those majoring in engineering, Chinese students in German language and literature studies regarded the large number of Chinese students in their department as a downside. They noticed that their German counterparts had less motivation to communicate with them, as Chinese students always stayed together. 'When two Chinese students meet, automatically, we will talk in Chinese. However, if a German student also happens to be there, he will feel excluded from the conversation (mentioned by Interviewee 17).'

By contrast, in some departments with a very small number of international students, the Chinese students could not rely on other co-nationals, and either asked their lecturers for help or solved the problems alone. In these departments with fewer Chinese or international students, German students showed greater concern for the international students and were more willing to offer help from the very beginning.

The second factor influencing friend circles involved difficulty keeping and maintaining friendships on campus. The structure of the student-student relationship itself is different between China and Germany. At Chinese universities, especially at the bachelor's level, students in the same cohorts (班 *ban*) attend all the same lectures together as an organized class for the entire duration of their degree program until graduation. Thus, a 'classmate' (同学 *tongxue*) refers specifically to a fellow student who is assigned the same prescribed schedule of lectures, classes, and teachers. As a student will have the same syllabus as his or her classmates, classmates play an important role in providing constant academic support.

However, at German universities, the concept of a 'classmate' is very different, as each student has his or her own individually chosen curriculum. This means that the original peer-support system Chinese students relied on is gone and they need to search for a new one. Often, participants searched for other students who attended the same courses, as this provided an opportunity for them to make German friends at the university level, especially through group work. At the same time, while it was not necessarily difficult to make friends in Germany, it turned out to be surprisingly difficult to achieve and maintain 'in-depth' friendships. Two interviewees mentioned that they used to have good relationships with other German students, but because they later chose different courses, they did not manage to keep in contact. This relationship between Chinese and their peer German students resembled more of a 'hi-bye friends' type (Sovic 2009). Especially in the initial phase, there was no deep communication between Chinese students and their peer German students.

> I do not understand German students' jokes and I don't know about the politician, the film, or the songs they are talking about. I feel it's difficult to join their topics. […] The culture is different and we do not share the same topic. When we meet, we just greet each other by asking 'how are doing?' and that is all. (Interviewee 21)

Students attending English-taught master's programs or studying at a university of applied sciences tended to have better friendships with peer students, as all students had more courses in common. Furthermore, because these programs were smaller in scale, relationships among students were closer.

Third, the Chinese students did not attend off-campus activities often, and thus had fewer chances to get to know and integrate with peers in the host country. On the one hand, Chinese students often complained that they had few chances to get to know other peer students in Germany. On the other hand, when presented with opportunities to attend on- and off-campus activities to meet German students, few Chinese students went. As these activities were not directly related to their academic fields, they regarded such activities as a waste of time, and preferred to spend the time studying alone. The overwhelming majority of Chinese students in Study 3—90 per cent—'sometimes' attended sport activities on campus or social activities off-campus in Germany (Fig. 7.4). While there were many off-campus activities available, only 7 per cent of Chinese students reported that they 'often' took part in the cultural events available.

In Germany, participating in various off-campus gatherings and parties is one of the main opportunities to get to know new friends. Nevertheless, the Chinese participants did not attend social activities as often as their local counterparts did. Staying in their dormitories and seldom taking part

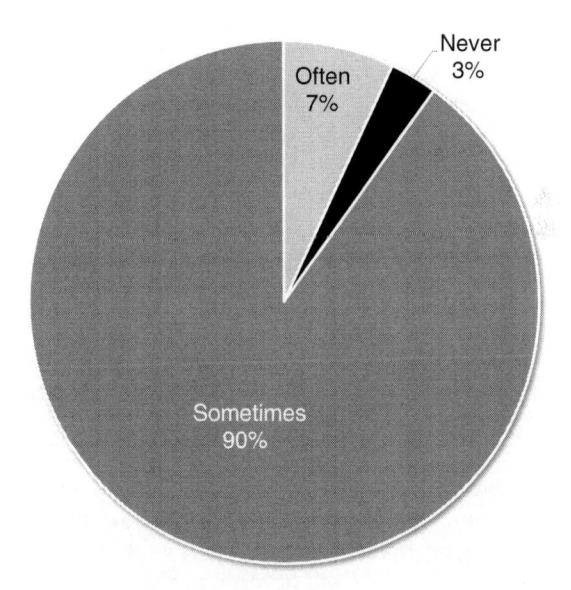

Fig. 7.4 Frequency of attending local activities/events in Germany according to Study 3

in university- or department-sponsored activities naturally limited their chances to meet German or other international students. As a result, they felt lonely and had few topics in common with their German counterparts. Unlike some German students who enjoyed the 'night life' or were 'party-animals', a lot of Chinese students did not like the party culture, and were accustomed to more conservative daily life habits, like going to bed early. In addition, many of the Chinese students in the study also did not approve of the 'drinking culture' at many German parties. Some interviewees (e.g. Interviewees 12 and 16) clearly stated that they did not like drinking alcohol and found these types of parties in Germany a little bit boring. This became a vicious cycle: Chinese students would not participate in activities with other Germans, as they did not have topics in common. But the less they talked with their German counterparts, the fewer common topics they could share with the peer students. After persevering over a period of time, some students managed to adjust to this situation and learned to find common ground with other Germans. However, many did not bother to take the initiative to invite German students to any activities.

Instead of going to German 'drinking and talking' parties, the participants enjoyed cooking with other Chinese students. Participants often had easier access to other co-national Chinese students when building their friend circles. Their similar language, national and ethnic backgrounds, and shared difficulties while studying in Germany provided common ground that easily linked them together. When talking about familiar topics—like Chinese news, politics, and movies—in their mother tongue while cooking food from home, participants felt safe in this 'comfort zone'. The significance of 'cooking' is more than just the activity of cooking the food itself. When Chinese students get together and cook, they are also exchanging information and their experiences at the university, seeking sympathy and emotional support from people in the same situation or giving advice for overcoming challenges encountered by others.

In the short term, all of this beats homesickness and loneliness. It is good that Chinese students have co-national friends in Germany who are an important source of support while studying and living abroad. However, in the long term, if Chinese students limit their circles of friends to only co-nationals, then they will never have the chance of leaving their co-national 'friend nest' and become more independent.

The fourth factor contributing to patterns in friend making consisted of the motivation and initiative of both Chinese and German students to engage in intercultural communication. Some Chinese students had little interest in building intercultural contacts, because their motivation was primarily to complete their degree or study program as soon as possible. For instance, as German majors already had some knowledge of Germany beforehand, they did not have much motivation to get to know German students. Some just wanted to get in, get their degree, and then get out. Although many of the Chinese students complained about difficulty in making friends with peer German students, only a few took the initiative to communicate with them by inviting German students over to cook together or participate in other social activities on or off campus.

> I have invited one German student to eat 'hot pot' (火锅 huoguo) at my apartment, and the experience was quite successful. He enjoyed the time very much. [...] I think it is important to make friends with those Germans, who are interested in Chinese culture, have been to China [as they also have motivation to communicate with us], as it is important for both sides to have a topic to talk with. (Interviewee 21)

Surprisingly, many Germans were not as outgoing as Chinese students had thought. Some Chinese students indicated German students were 'shy' or did not show much initiative. This resulted in a metaphorical 'stand-off' where Germans and Chinese students were waiting for the other side to initiate communication.

Fifth, the type of housing and accommodations available played a role in the availability and type of intercultural communication for Chinese students. A majority of students lived with mixed nationalities by default of their living arrangements. Fourteen of the Chinese participants in Studies 1 and 2 lived in student dormitories (66.7 per cent); four of them lived alone or with their partners in an apartment (19.0 per cent); and, three Chinese students lived in a shared apartment (in German: *Wohngemeinschaft*) with various other nationalities (14.3 per cent). Study 3 indicated similar arrangements, where of the thirty-one participants, fourteen (45 per cent) lived in an environment with different nationalities; ten (32 per cent) reported their flatmates were mainly Germans; and four (13 per cent) lived alone or with their partners (Fig. 7.5).

A *Wohngemeinschaft* (or WG) is a shared apartment and a common form of accommodation for German students. A WG often has a kitchen and living room for cooking and entertaining, creating an environment more conducive for flatmates to talk with each other. Most Chinese

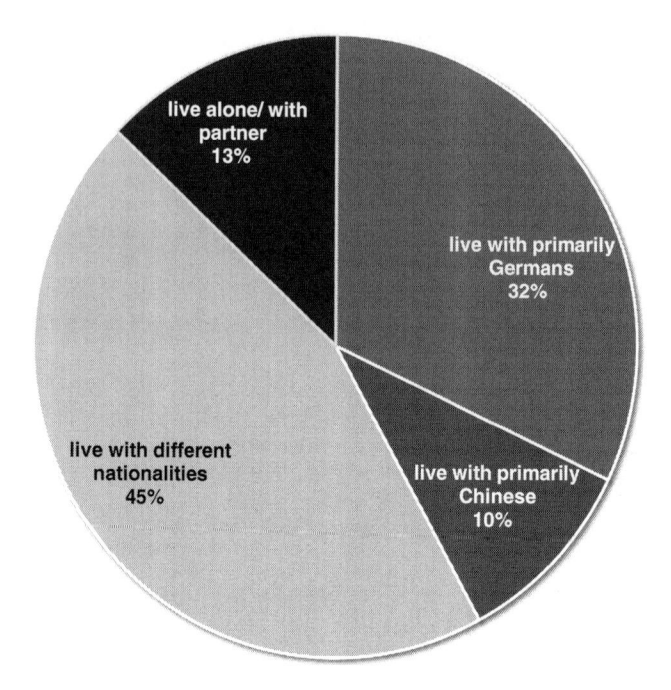

Fig. 7.5 Situation of accommodation according to Study 3

students living in a WG had a positive opinion of this form of living. They regarded the WG as an important way to meet and communicate with native German students, and changed their accommodations from dormitories to WGs in order to obtain more opportunities to communicate with local people. In spite of the advantages and opportunities for increased communication when living in a WG, only a small number of the Chinese students (Interviewee 1, 17, and 18) chose to live in one. Since the rent for student dormitories is relatively low, Chinese students often chose this form of accommodation to save on finances. They had a choice of single-room or double-room student dormitories. Furthermore, 'homestays' where international students could live with a local family were not very common among Chinese students in Germany. Only one interviewee (Interviewee 9) reported that she lived with a German family.

Personal Factors

In addition to the background and university environment factors key to academic adjustment, personal factors also played an important role for Chinese students. The types and extent of personal factors present for Chinese students in the German learning context may be different from those present for Chinese students in other intercultural contexts.

Part-Time Jobs

During the adjustment process, many students took on part-time jobs to help relieve the financial burden their study abroad caused their parents. Just because the Chinese economy has grown to the point where a majority of participants are self-funded does not mean that study abroad no longer poses a significant financial investment or sacrifice for many Chinese families. While study expenses in Germany were much cheaper than in many other Western countries, their daily living expenses were often still higher than if they had stayed in China to continue their studies. However, some Chinese students also regarded working on a part-time job as an important part of the study abroad experience, instead of simply a way to make money (mentioned by Interviewee 20). While some looked for part-time jobs purely out of curiosity, and the opportunity to gain a new experience, others regarded part-time jobs as an integral way to exert their independence and status as a contributing adult. One Chinese student felt that having a part-time job provided her with an opportunity to contribute to and have a link with German society, instead of merely 'being a guest':

> When doing a part-time job, one achieves the feeling that he has a closer relationship with Germany, as one is no longer a guest (here). Instead, he or she [actively] participates in the production of Germany. (Interviewee 20)

In most cases, shortly after arrival, Chinese students were usually only able to find manual labor jobs in Germany, as their German language proficiency was not good enough for higher-level jobs. Chinese students found employment in a variety of services, such as waiters in Chinese restaurants (Interviewee 5), shop assistants in Asian markets (Interviewees 7 and 14), housekeepers in hotels (Interviewees 12 and 13), tour guides for travel agencies (Interviewee 3), or workers in factories (Interviewees 7 and 12)—all of which are typical for Chinese students doing part-time work in Germany. Later, as they acquired better German language proficiency, some students found jobs as translators (Interviewee 3) or research assistants at universities or research institutions (Interviewees 13 and 16). Some of the interviewees had clear career goals in mind concerning the purpose of their part-time jobs. While some were content working purely manual jobs, others searched for part-time jobs related to their academic disciplines.

> At the very beginning, I did some manual work, but I understood very clearly that making money is not the only aim of a part-time job. One should do something which promotes his academic development as well. I know that every self-funded student needs money, but one should always keep in mind their purpose of coming to Germany. If necessary, one should still turn to parents for help (instead of investing too much time on a part-time job). (Interviewee 3)

Most Chinese students admitted that their part-time jobs did have a negative effect on their study. One interviewee (Interviewee 14) pointed out that 'there are only 24 hours per day. If [I] spend more time working a part-time job, [I] will have less time in resting and studying. Because of this, I gave up my part-time job'.

Personality: Being Brave and Open

Positive sojourner adjustment is related to less authoritarianism, increased personal flexibility, and increased modernism, sociability, and assertiveness (Church 1982). To this end, Chinese students emphasized the importance of having an open attitude or extroverted personality. A few participants in the studies described not only their personalities, but sometimes their entire culture group, as 'shy' or 'introverted', which they regarded as a big obstacle in communication.

> The problems lie in the personality or character of us Chinese. Students from South America or Africa will not have such problems. Only we Chinese students or Asian students are shy and timid. (Interviewee 12)

For instance, three interviewees emphasized that they would not encourage 'little girls' (小女生 *xiao nüsheng*)—who embody the traditional and gentle female ideal in China—to study in Germany. They worried that these students would be 'too vulnerable', 'not tough', or 'too young and too weak' to deal with the academic difficulties in Germany. The above assertions do not suggest that students who are shy or introverted should never go abroad. Rather, it highlights how Chinese students are very conscious of the role a strong personality can play in academic adjustment to Germany when studying abroad.

REFERENCES

Church, A. T. (1982). Sojourner adjustment. *Psychological Bulletin, 91*(3), 540–572.
Danckwortt, D. (Ed.). (1984). *Werkstattberichte: Vol. 11. Auslandsstudium als Gegenstand der Forschung: Eine Literaturübersicht*. Kassel: Gesamthochschule, Wiss. Zentrum f. Berufs- u. Hochschulforschung.
Heublein, U., Özkilic, M., & Sommer, D. (2007). *Aspekte der Internationalität deutscher Hochschulen: Internationale Erfahrungen deutscher Studierender an ihren heimischen Hochschulen* (Vol. 63). Bonn: Hrsg. der Reihe Dok & Mat, Dokumentationen & Materialien: DAAD, Deutscher Akademischer Austausch Dienst.
Kingston, E., & Forland, H. (2008). Bridging the gap in expectations between international students and academic staff. *Journal of Studies in International Education, 12*(2), 204–221. doi:10.1177/1028315307307654.
Peisert, H., & Framhein, G. (1990). *Higher education in the Federal Republic of Germany*. Bucharest: CEPES.
Peroz, N. (2008). *Auswertung der Fragebogen für ausländische Studierende an der Fakultät IV*. Retrieved from http://www.flp.tu-berlin.de/fileadmin/fg53/ZiiK/ZiiK_Reports/Report_Nr9.pdf
Quinlivan, G. (2009). *Wörterbuch des Hochschulwesens: Deutsch-Englisch* (2nd ed.). Stuttgart [u.a.]: Raabe.
Ramsay, S., Jones, E., & Barker, M. (2007). Relationship between adjustment and support types: Young and mature-aged local and international first year university students. *Higher Education Research & Development, 54*(2), 247–265.
Schumann, A. (2008). Interkulturelle Fremdheitserfahrungen ausländischer Studierender an deutschen Universitäten. In A. Knapp-Potthoff & A. Schumann (Eds.), *Mehrsprachigkeit und Multikulturalität im Studium* (pp. 29–50). Frankfurt am Main: Peter Lang.
Sovic, S. (2009). Hi-bye friends and the herd instinct: International and home students in the creative arts. *Higher Education, 58*(6), 747–761. doi:10.1007/s10734-009-9223-z.
Wissenschaft weltoffen. (2014). Retrieved from http://www.wissenschaftweltoffen.de/daten
Wong, G., Cooper, B. J., & Dellaportas, S. (2015). Chinese students' perceptions of the teaching in an Australian accounting programme—An exploratory study. *Accounting Education, 24*(4), 318–340. doi:10.1080/09639284.2015.1050678.

Zhao, T. (2007). *An ethnographic study of the intercultural adaption process between Chinese students and their British lecturers and fellow students in the UK*. Doctoral thesis. University of Southampton, Southampton.

Zhao, T., & Bourne, J. (2011). Intercultural adaptation—It is a two-way process: Examples from a British MBA programme. In L. Jin & M. Cortazzi (Eds.), *Researching Chinese learners. Skills, perceptions and intercultural adaptations* (pp. 250–273). Basingstoke/New York: Palgrave MacMillan.

Zhou, Y., & Todman, J. (2009). Patterns of adaptation of Chinese postgraduate students in the United Kingdom. *Journal of Studies in International Education*, *13*(4), 467–486. doi:10.1177/1028315308317937.

CHAPTER 8

Reflections and Implications

The journey is the reward.

— *Chinese proverb*

Summary

This research explored Chinese students' academic adjustment to an intercultural environment. The three dimensions of Anderson's 'Affective, Cognitive, and Behavioral' model were applied to Chinese students' learning experiences in Germany when analyzing the pre-departure, initial, developing, and ending periods of students' sojourn (Table 8.1).

Before departure, Chinese participants only left themselves a short period of time to prepare for study abroad in Germany. As a result, the majority of them only managed to pass the standardized German language exam required by the German universities for application and prepare some general 'survival' or daily life information in Germany before leaving China. For the future academic challenges they would face overseas, the majority of the participants had poor preparation. Most students had relatively little knowledge of Germany, in terms of its culture, history, customs, or universities.

Table 8.1 Summary of challenges mapped to an 'affective, cognitive, and behavioral dimensions' model

Phases	Tasks/challenges	Cognitive, affective, and behavioral dimensions

Initial phase	Planning and organizing university study
	Attending new types of courses
	Completing academic tasks: reading and writing
	Attending academic assessments
		Cognitive dimension:
		  Initial learning experience
		Affective dimension:
		  Feeling at a loss and misunderstood
		Behavioral dimension:
		  Making efforts

Developing phase	Negotiation
	  Reserving opinions in class
	  Respecting authority
	  Asking questions
	  Group learning
		Cognitive dimension:
		  Negotiating between 'studying in China' and 'studying in Germany'
		Affective dimension:
		  Feeling confused and frustrated
		Behavioral dimension:
		  Using different strategies to deal with confusion

Final phase	Reflection
	  Satisfaction
	  Self-assessment
	  Career plan
	  Recommend study to prospective students
		Cognitive dimension:
		  Showing appreciation for the German university system
		Affective dimension:
		  Feeling accomplishment and confidence
		Behavioral dimension:
		  Participating in academic activities

Such an underprepared state led directly to the 'hard landing' of the initial phase, as Chinese students encountered many difficulties upon arrival in Germany. The first semester was perceived by many interviewees as 'a catastrophe' or 'chaos', as they were not at all familiar with much of the specific academic information in Germany. Facing such difficulty, they felt 'at a loss', and misunderstood when lecturers showed little understanding toward their situation and background as international students. Furthermore, as newcomers, Chinese students were not familiar with the on-campus academic support system. As a result, they overwhelmingly relied only on themselves or co-national Chinese friends to deal with the problems. This initial process of adjustment often lasts one to two semesters and depends heavily on students' own attempts and personal factors to fit into the rhythm of the new learning environment.

In the developing phase, Chinese students reported progress in their proficiency of German language and knowledge of German universities. This phase usually occurs after two semesters of study. Both of these factors facilitated the further development of students in their academic adjustment. One of the challenges in this phase was negotiating the difference between their previous Chinese educational traditions and the current German academic expectations. Chinese students were frustrated to find that what they had regarded as correct in the Chinese learning environment was 'wrong' or unappreciated in the German one. In this phase of adjustment, they became more familiar with the academic support system at German universities, and began asking lecturers, tutors, and fellow students for help in solving their difficulties.

In the final phase, Chinese students showed appreciation toward the different academic expectations at German universities. This phase occurs during the last one or two semesters. Students no longer felt 'left alone at the German universities', but began to regard the learning experience as 'academic freedom'. Most students successfully modified or developed strategies to deal with their challenges. Chinese students' understanding of academic expectations and appreciation of features unique to German universities encouraged them to participate in classroom discussions and approach lecturers or tutors directly during consultation hours. Furthermore, since they were now familiar with their institutions, students made better use of available resources to deal with an array of difficulties. More students interacted and communicated with faculty and fellow students during this stage. During the process of academic adjustment Chinese students identified, understood, and later appreciated the differences present in this intercultural learning environment.

This research study also probed the factors that influenced Chinese students' learning experience in Germany. Factors such as German language competence in academic fields, academic support, and intercultural communication with peer students, personality, and part-time jobs together exerted influence on the Chinese students' academic adjustment at German universities.

Reflections

Academic Adjustment as a Dynamic Process

The process of international students' adjustment can be viewed as an 'academic journey' (Stier 2003), as such an experience crosses not only national boundaries, but also social, cultural, intellectual, and emotional ones (Stier 2003). Similarly, in what can also be regarded as a dynamic process, Chinese students also experienced ups and downs while learning in their intercultural environment.

First, Chinese students' academic adjustment in Germany was a cyclical, recursive, and dynamic process. Adjustment is a process with vicissitudes, where difficulties will be a given, regardless of anything else. In different phases of academic adjustment, Chinese students met different challenges. However, Chinese students, like international students from other countries, made consistent, gradual progress, adjusted to the new academic environment, and finally achieved educational growth and personal development.

Second, each Chinese student had his or her own pace for the process of academic adjustment. Individuals are heterogeneous. It is impossible to depict the paradigm of academic adjustment for Chinese students in Germany, as such a process varies from student to student according to an individual's background, university environment, and personal factors. Sojourners demonstrate different degrees, modes, and levels of adaptation (Anderson 1994), and 'not all individuals are equally successful in making transitions toward adaptation' (Kim 1988, p. 58). Some Chinese students quickly identified and understood that German universities have different expectations from those in China, and accordingly made modifications to meet them; others needed more time to figure out their problems for academic adjustment.

Academic Adjustment as an Ability to Learn in an Intercultural Environment

Growing up in any given educational system, students take its rules, relationships, and evaluation methods for granted. But when suddenly transferring to the learning environment of another culture, students quickly learn how firmly their educational beliefs and habits are anchored in the context and practices of their home culture. To study in an intercultural milieu is 'more complex and stressful than learning in one's home culture' (Hughes-Wiener 1986, p. 493). The most difficult issue for Chinese students to adjust to in an intercultural learning environment is not how to pick up new learning styles in the host universities, but how to integrate their original educational beliefs with their new findings in the host country. Students are confused and frustrated to see that what they once valued highly when in the home country is now unappreciated or criticized in the host university. Most Chinese participants in the interviews tried very hard to negotiate with such confusion and frustration.

However, as their knowledge of the university system in the host country increases, students better understand its expectations. These processes of confusion and negotiation, to some extent, stimulated Chinese students to mediate the differences, and try to reflect and better understand the differences between their home and host countries. Stimulating 'personal expansion' or 'an opening of one's potential universe' (Murphy-Lejeune 2003, p. 113) is an important experience. For instance, some international students learn how to be 'critical but respectful of other academic cultures and opinions' (Ehlers and Hemmingsen 2011, p. 39). The experience of adaptation and learning abroad can also be depicted as 'a maturing process' (Murphy-Lejeune 2003, p. 113). In the process of academic adjustment, Chinese students are 'pushed' to the development of a broadened perspective on learning. In general, most international students have 'realistic self-perceptions' (Kaczmarek et al. 1994, p. 246) about their capability to adjust to the intercultural learning environment.

Adjusting to German universities does not mean that Chinese students have to abolish their original learning traditions and become 'German students'. Instead, through supplementing and improving their learning skills, they obtain another perspective by which to view and judge their prior learning experience in China, and enrich their overall intercultural learning experience. Academic adjustment is the ability to 'fit or not fit' but not be 'better or worse'. The academic adjustment process stimulates Chinese students to 'learn how to learn' (Hughes-Wiener 1986, p. 485) in an intercultural academic milieu. Instead of sticking to the original learning tradition in China or switching to the new German style, Chinese students develop a new strategy to fulfill the academic tasks according to their discipline-based requirements. This process of combining one's 'first' academic culture with his 'second' develops a 'third' 'transnational academic culture' (Ehlers and Hemmingsen 2011, p. 39).

Adapting the Learning Environment

As 'guests' in the host universities, international students have long been regarded as the ones who should make more effort to fit into the intercultural learning environment. However, this type of thinking means universities '[run] the danger of being new colonialists' (Smith and Smith 1999, p. 77). As long as Germany continues increasing the internationalization of its higher education system and recruiting more international students, its universities also share the responsibility of facilitating international students' academic adjustment. Whether or not German universities will create an open learning environment depends largely on its attitude regarding the presence of international students on campus as a challenge versus a burden or as a change versus an opportunity. The former dichotomy favors a 'monocultural, monodisciplinary, and monolingual' (Otten 2003, p. 14) learning environment and regards the recruitment of international students as trouble. As a result of incorporating international students, lecturers will have an extra workload in trying to integrate international students into their class activities. The latter attaches great importance to building an intercultural learning environment and enhancing the cultural diversity at German universities.

The university's philosophy of encouraging and facilitating an open and culturally diverse environment contributes to Chinese students' academic adjustment. German lecturers' and students' assistance played a role in supporting Chinese students' academic adjustment at the German universities. For instance, the Chinese participants emphasized that lecturers worked to involve Chinese students by introducing topics with which they were familiar. As many courses require teamwork, in terms of peer students' support, Chinese students felt more at ease working with German students who were open-minded and willing to listen to their opinions. However, they preferred to keep silent or act passively when teammates ignored their opinions or were not friendly.

SUGGESTIONS FOR BETTER ACADEMIC ADJUSTMENT: INDIVIDUAL AND INSTITUTIONAL

In order to facilitate the process of academic adjustment, at the individual level, Chinese students should make efforts to deal with the challenges. At the same time, according to the difficulties that Chinese students encounter, host universities should provide a facilitative environment for adjustment at the institutional level. Having a good understanding of international students' needs is essential to ensure both their academic success and that domestic students benefit from an internationalized classroom experience.

In order to promote the adjustment of international students to the intercultural learning environment, universities should provide international students with help before the students arrive and continue to assist them until their graduation (Lin and Yi 1997). Because adjustment is a continuing process, international students have different academic demands at different periods of time while studying abroad, and hosting countries and universities should make efforts to satisfy their unique and varied needs (Mahr and Peroz 2001). Accordingly, this section provides recommendations both to Chinese students and German universities for each stage of students' academic adjustment.

In the Preparation Phase

To Chinese Students: Prepare Well Beforehand
In Chinese, there is a proverb—'half the work, twice the effort' (事半功倍 *shi ban gong bei*). Although adequately preparing for the future academic journey takes time, the effort will quickly pay off when Chinese students start their programs in the host university. In the pre-departure period, international students form a general picture of the host country (Klein et al. 1971). Based on this empirical research study, students planning to study abroad should never underestimate the importance of becoming familiar with the overseas study program, university, and country beforehand. Preparation for the new educational system and cultures of learning before students' departure is important for Chinese students to obtain an accomplished academic experience overseas (Wang 2012), so they should be mentally, culturally, and linguistically prepared (Henderson et al. 1993). While sojourners cannot be completely prepared for every eventuality in another culture (Hughes-Wiener 1986), it is important for them to be psychologically 'ready' and familiar with the host culture in order to facilitate their adaptive potential (Kim 1988, p. 135).

Focus on the German language It is significant for Chinese students to fully realize the importance of German language preparation ahead of their departure. Most interviewees, before leaving China, believed that they could only truly learn a foreign language in the host country, and did not take their German language learning seriously prior to departure. However, interestingly enough, when they were asked to make suggestions for prospective Chinese students, they would always emphasize good preparation of German language learning before departure. In interviews, almost every interviewee suggested that prospective Chinese students should pay more attention to and spend more time learning German before beginning their study abroad. The better their German language skills beforehand, the fewer problems they will meet after arrival in Germany. One German lecturer pointed out 'The better Chinese students' German language is, the better they can adjust to the class interaction and campus life'. Good knowledge of a foreign language reduces failures and feelings of helplessness in the foreign context (Henderson et al. 1993). Furthermore, compared with engineering or natural science students, students majoring in social science and humanities are expected to have a better command of German language, as the reading, writing, and speaking skills play a very decisive role in their academic success. Engineering or natural science majors can often depend on the symbols or formulas of their fields as a main tool to understand and communicate academic knowledge. However, social science and humanities majors have to depend more on German language in terms of preparing for and doing presentations, participating in class discussions, defending their view points, and writing essays.

Learning about Germany and German universities It is necessary for Chinese students to gain some basic knowledge about Germany and German culture during the preparation phase. Students' lack of cultural knowledge or understanding particularly challenged Chinese students in social sciences (Lin 2002). In contrast, international students who had done preparatory reading about life in the host country before arrival did not report 'feeling lost' in the new culture (Brown and Holloway 2008). Specifically, students should learn 'knowledge about the host communication systems, particularly language, and about relevant norms, rules, customs, history and art as well as economic, social, and political institutions' (Kim 1988, p. 135).

Some might argue that with the impact of globalization, mass media, and the internet, Chinese students are already familiar with western societies before going overseas. However, a lot of the information available in the media is not accurate or portrays a stereotyped image of the host country. For instance, many international students realized they had false conceptions about Germany before arriving in the country (Aich 1963). In spite of the importance of having basic knowledge of the host country beforehand, very few interviewees from this study knew Germany well before arrival. The short period of preparation only allowed Chinese students to collect daily life information about things such as accommodation and transportation. Thus, it is strongly recommended that before departure, Chinese students should take time and learn more about the host country, as a good knowledge of the host country will, in general, lay the foundation for understanding people in the host country and avoiding potential misunderstanding.

Having realistic expectations and readiness for study Good knowledge of German universities helps Chinese students to build realistic expectations. For instance, unlike in China where universities automatically provide and arrange living accommodations for every student, students at German universities have to make these arrangements by themselves. However, some newcomers will first go to the international office (in German: *Akademisches Auslandsamt*) to find a room. At some universities with a relatively small number of international students, the international office is able to arrange a room for the newcomers in the student dormitory. However, not every international office can guarantee this service. Chinese students who expect to find accommodations from the international office would probably be frustrated. As one interviewee suggested, 'Prospective students should not expect that everything will get better when they arrive in Germany [...] To those who have little self-confidence, such sense of disappointment is risky and dangerous' (Interviewee 14).

Furthermore, international Chinese students must familiarize themselves with the learning environment in advance. Some participants struggled at the beginning of their academic journey because they had not known exactly what was expected of them before going to Germany. When possible, Chinese students should consider arriving in the host country a few weeks earlier, so as to orient themselves in the host country before the new semester begins. Before suddenly plunging into the new learning environment, they can first take time to explore the campus and local living environment. Such exploration avoids encountering the challenges in both the new academic and daily environments simultaneously, which can reduce the stress experienced by students in the initial period of the study.

To German Universities: Strengthen Preparatory Support Before Students' Arrival

Chinese students in this study were also not familiar with the specific knowledge of the course requirements, group work assignments and assessment, and so on. Thus, the international office of the university should consider extending its services to platforms available to international students before their arrival. By making the most important information provided in the orientation course also available online through social media or other websites, Chinese and international students would be able to prepare better beforehand. In this way, universities can help international students quickly fit into the local educational environment.

The only student who had participated in the preparatory courses benefited immensely from them.

> At the very beginning of the master's program, I had the feeling that I adjusted to the new environment faster than other Chinese students. For example, I was informed of the forms of courses and when I should take down some notes. Although I still encounter some difficulties, without the course, the situation would have been more difficult. (Interviewee 14)

Many Chinese participants did not know these courses were available, and missed out on an important opportunity for assistance. Others lacked patience and wanted to begin immediately with their regular programs in the universities after their arrival, instead of 'wasting time' with courses that were not required.

The international office: the preliminary aid portal for incoming students The first step for German universities to take is to encourage Chinese students to read the available first-hand information. The furious competition for recruiting international students should also prompt universities to reevaluate and improve their services for international students. The international office plays a very important function for students at the university by providing both incoming international students and outgoing home students with important information on the university website. International students can find significant information concerning application and admission (such as language requirements), departure (such as applying for a visa and finding accommodations), and arrival (such as airport pick-up service, welcoming newcomers, and orientation courses).

Unfortunately, most Chinese students participating in interviews had not used any first-hand information provided by universities before departure. One important reason was information asymmetry—Chinese students did not know of the existence of the information provided by the international office. Another reason is information inaccessibility—all information was written in German (albeit, usually with an English option, as well), which frustrated beginners in German language from further reading. Some interviewees complained they had difficulty reading all the information and so did not read it completely.

These results suggest that the international office needs to optimize its services and make information more available and accessible to Chinese and international students. Together with the admission letter, the admissions office can send international students a brochure with all the most important information in a PDF format or link to an external website. The international office also needs to present important information in an efficient way. Considering that many international students are still not fluent in German, the international office should use simpler German language and present the information using pictures or readable figures. In this way, international students can more easily understand the main messages without reading through complicated German language. Furthermore, as there are a large number of English-taught master's and doctoral research programs available, crucial information should also be available in English for non-German-speakers.

Specific academic information Though interviewees received some information from universities concerning daily life in Germany, they expected to be introduced to specific requirements and expectations of German universities as well. One student (Interviewee 5) suggested in the interview, 'It would be nice if we could have received specific information concerning the study in Germany. Except for the letter of admission, we didn't receive any information'. International students, coming from an educational system that was quite different from that of Germany lacked prior knowledge of typical and expected learning methods in Germany (Peroz 2008). Providing information on academic culture is especially important to those students, whose home university culture is different from that of the host country.

Recruiting senior students to respond to inquiries Prospective international students have numerous inquiries concerning programs, facilities, activities, and daily life at German universities. Students in the interviews complained that they had written emails to the international office asking questions concerning application, accommodation, programs, and so on, but very few of them ever received replies. Such a poor response and support system often frustrated Chinese students and pushed them to search for other options to deal with their problems. Considering that international offices typically do not have enough staff to answer every question by all international students, they might want to recruit senior international students as volunteers or student assistants. These co-national students could be assigned as primary contacts to regularly answer questions from students of the same nationality. Senior international students would have encountered many of the same difficulties previously. Thus, they could use their co-national student status to help other international students work through their problems. As they would have encountered similar problems when they first came to Germany, senior students could make useful suggestions based on their own experiences.

In the Initial Phase

To Chinese Students: Be Ready for New Learning Expectations
In retrospect, the initial experience in Germany was the most difficult and helpless period for the majority of students participating in the interviews. During this period, the participants needed to learn German, become familiar with the new learning environment, acquire new academic knowledge, and communicate with lecturers and fellow students at universities. Chinese students' 'hard landing' in German universities, to some extent, is due to a hurried and hasty pre-departure preparation. Thus, German universities should take some initiatives to buffer the challenges caused by this experience.

Take a preparation course Chinese students who feel uncertain about learning in an intercultural milieu should attend a preparation course (in German: *Propädeutikum* or *Vorbereitungskurs*) at German universities before formally starting their studies.

In Germany, there are two kinds of *Studienkollegs*, which are affiliated either with a general university or a university of applied sciences. Graduates of *Studienkollegs* can apply for study at any higher education institutions in Germany (Studienkollegs 2015). *Studienkollegs* offer *Propaedeutikum*. This is a preparatory course of study from technical, mathematical, business, and social fields for the studies at German universities, especially for international students. Some *Propaedeutikums* last for one semester while others last only four weeks. Several German universities offer prospective international students a combined preparation course that includes both German language and basic subject-specific preparation courses, aiming at helping international students improve their German language skills and subject-specific knowledge (such as mathematics for economic students) and familiarize themselves with terminology, so they can have a successful study experience at German universities. At some universities, these courses are free for full-time, registered international students. Although students will spend a lot of time in the short term to take the *Propaedeutikum*, in the long term, they will adjust to the German universities much faster than those who do not attend it.

Focus on academic-oriented information If students fail to prepare well in the pre-departure period, orientation courses are another chance for them to learn about the learning environment. However, interviewees were not fully aware of the importance of orientation courses and missed these additional opportunities to become familiar with the German university system and the expectations of their major discipline. Given this fact, Chinese students are strongly recommended to take part in both the university-wide and department-wide orientation courses.

Continue to learn German Chinese students should always continue to learn German. Inadequate German language skills prevent some Chinese students from further adapting to the learning environment. One of the biggest challenges for Chinese students in the initial phase of academic adjustment was their German language proficiency. They had great difficulty in understanding the lecturers and expressing themselves in class. In spite of the fact that most of them had passed the standardized German test, their language proficiency at the time of enrolment was still far from enough to match the pace of the academic progress in class. Many interviewees strongly regarded German language learning as greatly important and viewed learning in German as a 'protracted war' (持久战 *chijiu zhan*). Though most Chinese students had their own preferred ways of learning German, it is recommended that at the beginning of the academic adjustment process, students first take some professional language courses to improve their skills. In particular, Chinese students majoring in social science and humanities should pay special attention to improving their

German language proficiency, as their academic language use is much more intense in their disciplines.

Hold a positive attitude In the initial phase, Chinese students encountered enormous difficulty. They became unconfident and regarded themselves as a disadvantaged group in Germany. Nevertheless, their feelings of frustration might also 'become a milestone of an individual's life story, marking the moment of greatest crisis and despair but also the turning point of a new start' (Griffiths et al. 2005, p. 277). Facing initial setbacks, Chinese students need to see the process instructively as a learning opportunity rather than a failure. 'Failures, when they are not devastating, […] are often far more informative than successes' (Kim 1988, p. 169). When looking back, the difficulty that once seemed to be a formidable obstacle is often much easier to deal with. For instance, when asked about their learning experience in Germany, interviewees who were close to completion of their study in Germany reported that difficulties were less devastating, compared to those who were still in the initial or developing phases. In the meanwhile, it is important for Chinese students to work past their concerns with 'saving face' and try not to be too sensitive with the critiques and directness presented in the intercultural learning environment.

To German Universities: Offer Additional Preliminary Aid

Optimize orientation courses for international students German universities offer general orientation courses to all students at the beginning of the new semester. Though German freshmen do find much of the information provided in the orientation courses to be new, they still get to know the university system faster than their international counterparts do, having grown up in the German education system. In contrast, international students, coming from culturally and linguistically different education systems like China, often have much more difficulty understanding the new information that is introduced. Within this context, not many international students benefit from the general orientation courses as compared to German students. Considering international students' special needs, in addition to the general orientation courses for all freshmen, universities should customize organization of orientation courses for international students in three aspects.

First, the international office should arrange special orientation courses for international students, according to their different needs from German students. During these courses, organizers should take foreign language proficiency into consideration and provide extra materials for international students as visual aids, such as PowerPoint slides or handouts, as they have more difficulty understanding oral presentations in a foreign language. For students with poorer German language skills who are involved in English-taught master's or doctoral programs, English translations should also be made available.

Second, universities should extend the length of the orientation courses for international students. Given that there is a substantial amount of information to deliver at orientation, universities should work to provide an orientation week instead of an orientation day.

Third, each faculty with large numbers of international students should organize its own orientation courses. As Chinese students reported the biggest challenges for them happened in the initial phase, faculty should introduce the *Modul* and academic resources in detail to help students more efficiently plan their learning. Faculty with small numbers of international students should consider assigning a lecturer or senior students to answer questions raised by international students if they are having difficulty organizing their coursework.

Expand university-level intercultural training Most of the Chinese students interviewed in this study were the first ones in their families who had ever gone abroad, so they did not have much intercultural experience before coming to Germany. Lacking basic intercultural experience caused them to worry about their interactions with others, so they often avoided direct contact with domestic students. Given that scenario, intercultural training, or 'cross-cultural training', is necessary to enhance international students' intercultural knowledge and competence. Thus, universities should consider widening regular intercultural trainings for international students, starting at the beginning of—and continuing throughout—the semester.

In fact, a large number of German universities have already worked to establish intercultural training courses for both international and domestic students. Humboldt-Universität zu Berlin has offered international students an intercultural training course called '*Kultur -und Studienorientierung für internationale Studierende*' (KUSTOS) since 2004, providing training themes such as 'Get Ready for Studying in Germany' and 'Studying and

Living in an International Context'. This kind of intercultural training introduces Chinese students to German 'academic culture', shares professors' expectations and provides suggestions for effective organization of university studies, and promotes good communication with peer students. Universities should consider expanding the scale and frequency of organized intercultural training so that more international students can gain intercultural communication skills earlier, in order to deal with the initial challenges of learning in an intercultural milieu.

Organize effective mentor programs Chinese students were originally looking forward to interacting with German students when first planning to study abroad. However, after arriving, they were too shy to make friends with German students and were later surprised to realize that German counterparts were also hesitant to take the first step in reaching out. The presence of international students on campus does not automatically lead to intercultural contacts (Otten 2003). German universities should encourage friendships between German and international students group by organizing 'buddy programs'. International students who participated in an 'International Peer Program' demonstrated significantly higher social adjustment scores than nonparticipants (Abe et al. 1998). However, these buddy programs only work effectively when both sides have a strong interest in learning the others' culture and/or language. Taking the German students as an example, students who have this motivation will voluntarily invest time to maintain their friendships with international students. German students who major in Sinology, are interested in learning the Chinese language, plan to study or have studied in China, or share similar overseas experiences, and often showed interest in making and maintaining friendships with Chinese and international students.

Furthermore, in order to help international students gain orientation in their discipline, German universities should organize mentor programs for the different disciplines of study. Such discipline-specific program supervision would be between a senior student mentor and an international student. The mentor and the international student should be in the same faculty and meet regularly to help the international student tackle problems in their discipline or other areas. Some of the German universities have already initiated such programs to help their international students work through challenges in their specific disciplines. For instance, *FAMOS Fachmentoren-Programm* at Humboldt-Universität zu Berlin, *Studienstart International* at Universität zu Köln, and *StudentService@School* at Universität Bremen all offer mentor programs for international students.

Improve lecturers' intercultural competence Germany has a relatively short history of holding such a large number of Chinese students on its campuses. Chinese students became the largest international student group only very recently, in the last decade. Thus, German lecturers have relatively little knowledge of Chinese students' previous learning experience, and even less idea regarding how to use appropriate pedagogies to integrate them into class discussions. Some of the lecturers became very confused about the learning styles and habits Chinese students displayed in class, and failed to take their insufficient language skills and poor knowledge of German academic culture into consideration. German lecturers with overseas experience had a better understanding of the actions and intentions of Chinese students.

Therefore, intercultural competence or intercultural sensitivity is not only important for Chinese and international students, but for lecturers in the host country as well. With the increasing number of internationals in class, lecturers need intercultural communication skills as tools to better deal with the conflicts and challenges present in an intercultural class setting. Staff and students should develop their intercultural skills by 'both learning to communicate across cultures and communicating for learning across cultures' (Cortazzi and Jin 1997, p. 76). Furthermore, the attitude of German lecturers toward the presence of Chinese and other international students in class also plays a role in students' academic adjustment. In dealing with this integration, lecturers should 'move from the mind-set of a *deficit* to a *difference* view of Chinese learning and teaching methods' (Holmes 2004, p. 304). Lecturers should also encourage teamwork and cooperation between Chinese and German students, both during and after class.

In the Developing Phase

To Chinese Students: Be Ready to Make a Change

Be creative and experimental Compared with the initial phase, in the developing period, Chinese students successfully learned what was expected or valued academically in German universities. One interviewee (Interviewee 10) reported, 'One lesson I have learned in Germany is to take the initiative'. In spite of that, they still needed the courage to make a change. For example, Chinese students realized the importance of asking questions during consultation hours, but were still hesitant to do so. International students should try to be creative and experimental (Henderson et al. 1993). With the progress they have made in German language, they should have the confidence and capability to try new learning approaches and expose themselves to many types of people and ideas in order to expand their horizons (Henderson et al. 1993).

Find a resource person To deal with the challenges present in this phase, in addition to individuals' efforts, the Chinese need external help in their learning environment. International Chinese students often encountered difficulties in establishing collaborative relationships with peer students in the host country (Chen 2004; Holmes 2005). Chinese students' initial passiveness can be attributed to cultural, educational, and ideological factors, and group work can be used as a way to promote adaptation (Wang 2012). A peer German student or friend could be a 'resource person' to help Chinese students interpret their confusions from a different cultural perspective. For example, he or she could explain why students in the host country are so critical and keep asking lecturers questions in class.

Chinese students are also strongly encouraged to become involved with German students and talk about their experiences. Some of the interviewees complained that they had few chances to connect with German students. But if they did manage to connect with German students outside their circle of co-national friends, then they had many chances to meet locals. By taking courses, attending different activities, living in mixed-national shared apartments, and participating in sports, Chinese students had many opportunities to get to know more people in the host country. When Chinese participants talked about the confusions they encountered at their universities, the 'resource person' could share his or her opinions and explanations on the matter. A good explanation of the situation would help Chinese students rethink their confusions, which in turn would promote Chinese students' understanding of the unspoken rules and conventions in the host learning environment.

The Chinese students' perception that they had no common topics to discuss with German students discouraged intercultural communication.

Given that, it is important for Chinese students and German students, as well as other international students, to create chances for communication instead of passively waiting for common topics to appear. For instance, by participating in intercultural communication, sojourners gradually learn about 'various on-going events, norms, attitudes, beliefs, values and other information about the host culture' (Kim 1988, p. 114).

To German Universities: Provide Courses for Promoting Basic Academic Skills

Help social science majors develop basic academic skills Chinese students in the social sciences lacked some important basic academic skills for writing, reading, and presentations, compared with their German counterparts. Interviewees emphasized that while basic courses in these skills might sound 'simple', 'childish', or even 'absurd' to their German counterparts, it was particularly important for international Chinese students to have them available. In the interviews, they strongly suggested universities organize these courses for Chinese students to train them in basic reading and writing skills. Thus, the language centers of universities should play a more active and important role in organizing specific courses for international students' needs.

Modify pedagogical approaches The intercultural learning experience for Chinese students and the teaching practice for lecturers in the host country should be treated as a reciprocal adaptation (Zhou and Todman 2008). For example, British lecturers who had Chinese students in their classes adapted and became more culturally sensitive over time (Zhao 2007). In order to facilitate an intercultural learning environment, not only should Chinese and international students make efforts to fit into the classroom, but lecturers in the host country should also work to integrate Chinese and international students into the classroom. This kind of change is sometimes very demanding for lecturers, as they have to invest time to modify their pedagogies and find solutions to help Chinese and international students become better involved in their classes. The ability to implement this idea depends on lecturers' 'tolerance to otherness and different styles' (Otten 2003, p. 14), intercultural competence, and pedagogical skills. For example, one lecturer in Study 2 modified the types of questions he asked in the examinations so that Chinese students could make better use of their learning strengths.

> Compared with German students, Chinese students are strong in memorizing the definition, while weak in analyzing the text. In designing the questions of the examination, I can arrange to balance the number of questions of 'definition' and 'text-analysis,' so as to let both German and Chinese have the chance to take advantage of their strength. (Lecturer 1)

In the Final Phase

To Chinese Students

Upon completion of their study programs, Chinese students were busy writing thesis papers or searching for jobs and internships. Based on previous experience writing semester papers, they had succeeded in accumulating basic academic writing skills. However, writing for a thesis is more complicated than writing for standard semester papers. As students write their thesis papers, they should turn to supervisors for help when they face problems regarding difficulties like the topic, structure, and argument.

At the same time, universities organize colloquia to teach students the required research methods and formats for thesis writing. Chinese students majoring in social science or humanities are strongly recommended to participate in these colloquia.

If applicable to their situation, Chinese students must prepare for gradation after finishing their thesis papers. For those who plan to go back to China, they should be prepared psychologically for a readjustment process to their home country. For those who decide to work in Germany, they should prepare for long-term residency in the host country. Transitioning from the role of international student to that of an employee or resident requires much planning and effort.

To German Universities

Compared with the endeavors required in the initial phase, universities do not have a hard job assisting Chinese students in the last period of their academic adjustment. Chinese students encountered some difficulties when writing their thesis papers and hunting for jobs, but these problems were universal. Chinese, international, and domestic students all faced them. Therefore, faculties should hold seminars or colloquia led by experienced staff to help students learn how to navigate these tasks. These would be particularly helpful to Chinese students, who are required to write their thesis papers in a foreign language. Furthermore, compared with domestic students, Chinese students might not be as familiar with the job market in Germany, nor how to navigate it. One interviewee (Interviewee 6) mentioned that she needed help from lecturers and faculty in terms of searching for an internship.

LIMITATIONS AND FUTURE RESEARCH

Limitation

This research achieved the goal set forth in the research design. Nevertheless, there is still much to learn about the Chinese students' academic adjustment in Germany. First, all participants were studying or had studied in general universities (in German: *Universitäten*), while Chinese students studying in universities of applied sciences (in German: *Fachhochschulen*) were not included, even though these institutions also have a large number of Chinese students.[1]

Second, and unfortunately, no German students participated in the research. Although this research intended to interview German students about their views and observations on their Chinese counterparts' learning experiences, no German students in the case study volunteered to participate in the interviews. Considering the important role of domestic students in the academic adjustment process of international students, information about German student experiences with Chinese students is also very valuable. Host students' attitudes toward international students 'has been largely neglected in research on social integration and international education' (Ward et al. 2009, p. 97).

Third, Chinese students who failed to adjust to the intercultural learning environment were not included. The author had tried to contact one Chinese student who withdrew from his program at a German university. Unfortunately, he was not willing to participate in the interviews.

[1] In Germany, higher education institutions are composed of universities, universities of applied science, and art and music colleges. In 2015, there were 110 universities, 223 universities of applied sciences, and 58 art and music colleges. The distribution of international students in universities and universities of applied sciences is 63.8 per cent and 33.0 per cent, respectively. The specific distribution of Chinese students in these two types of higher education institutions is unknown.

Suggestions for Further Research

Regarding research methods and participants in this research, there are some suggestions for further research. One recommendation is with regard to longitudinal research. Given that adjustment is a dynamic process, longitudinal research on adjustment should be given more attention. To follow the development and process of adjustment, future longitudinal research might invest a longer period of time—of over one year. A further recommendation is to include German students' opinions in the participant pool, as well. Future research should invite domestic students with ties to Chinese students to share their knowledge, in order to understand Chinese students' academic adjustment from a peer perspective.

REFERENCES

Abe, J., Talbot, D. M., & Geelhoed, R. J. (1998). Effects of a peer program on international student adjustment. *Journal of College Student Development*, *39*(6), 539–547.

Aich, P. (1963). *Farbige unter Weißen*. Köln: Verlag Kiepenheuer & Witsch.

Anderson, L. E. (1994). A new look at an old construct: Cross-cultural adaptation. *International Journal of Intercultural Relations*, *18*(3), 293–328. doi:10.1016/0147-1767(94)90035-3.

Brown, L., & Holloway, I. (2008). The adjustment journey of international postgraduate students at an English university: An ethnographic study. *Journal of Research in International Education*, *7*(2), 232–249. doi:10.1177/1475240908091306.

Chen, X. (2004). *Lü ju zhe he "wai guo ren": Sojourners and "foreigners": A study on Chinese students' intercultural interpersonal relationships in the United States (in Chinese: 旅居者和"外国人")* (1st ed.). Beijing: Educational Science Publishing House

Cortazzi, M., & Jin, L. (1997). Communication for learning across cultures. In D. McNamara & R. Harris (Eds.), *Overseas students in higher education. Issues in teaching and learning* (pp. 76–90). London: Routledge.

Ehlers, S., & Hemmingsen, L. (2011). Academic schock: The joint move towards a transnational academic culture. *Adult Learning: Teachers as Learners*, *6*, 31–40.

Griffiths, D. S., Winstanley, D., & Gabriel, Y. (2005). Learning shock: The trauma of return to formal learning. *Management Learning*, *36*(3), 275–297. doi:10.1177/1350507605055347.

Henderson, G., Milhouse, V., & Cao, L. (1993). Crossing the gap: An analysis of Chinese students' culture shock in an American university. *College Student Journal*, *27*(3), 380–389.

Holmes, P. (2004). Negotiating differences in learning and intercultural communication: Ethnic Chinese students in a New Zealand university. *Business Communication Quarterly, 67*(3), 294–307. doi:10.1177/10805699042 68141.

Holmes, P. (2005). Ethnic Chinese students' communication with cultural others in a New Zealand university. *Communication Education, 54*(4), 289–311.

Hughes-Wiener, G. (1986). The "learning how to learn" approach to cross-cultural orientation. *International Journal of Intercultural Relations, 10*(4), 485–505. doi:10.1016/0147-1767(86)90047-7.

Kaczmarek, P. G., Matlock, G., Merta, R., Ames, M. H., & Ross, M. (1994). An assessment of international college student adjustment. *International Journal for the Advancement of Counselling, 17*(4), 241–247. doi:10.1007/BF01407740.

Kim, Y. Y. (1988). *Communication and cross-cultural adaptation: An integrative theory* (Intercommunication series, Vol. 2). Clevedon: Multilingual Matters Ltd.

Klein, M. H., Alexander, A. A., Tseng, K.-H., Miller, M. H., Keh, E.-K., Chu, H.-M., & Workneh, F. (1971). The foreign student adaptation program: Social experiences of Asian students in the U. S. *International Educational and Cultural Exchange, 6*(3), 77–90.

Lin, L. (2002, March). *The learning experiences of Chinese graduate students in American social sciences programs.* Annual conference of the comparative and international education society, Orlando, FL, USA. Retrieved from http://www.eric.ed.gov/PDFS/ED474163.pdf

Lin, J.-C. G., & Yi, J. K. (1997). Asian international students' adjustment: Issues and program suggestions. *College Student Journal, 31*(4), 473–479.

Mahr, B., & Peroz, N. (2001). *Studienort Deutschland: Phasen des Studiums ausländischer Studierender. ZiiK-Report Nr. 1: Vol. 1.* Berlin. Retrieved from http://www.eecs.tu-berlin.de/fileadmin/fg53/ZiiK/ZiiK_Reports/ZiiKReport_Nr.1.pdf

Murphy-Lejeune, E. (2003). An experience of interculturality: Student travellers abroad. *Intercultural experience and education,* 101–113.

Otten, M. (2003). Intercultural learning and diversity in higher education. *Journal of Studies in International Education, 7*(1), 12–26. doi:10.1177/10283 15302250177.

Peroz, N. (2008). *Auswertung der Fragebogen für ausländische Studierende an der Fakultät IV.* Retrieved from http://www.flp.tu-berlin.de/fileadmin/fg53/ZiiK/ZiiK_Reports/Report_Nr9.pdf

Smith, P., & Smith, S. N. (1999). Differences between Chinese and Australian students: Some implications for distance educators. *Distance Education, 20*(1), 64–80. doi:10.1080/0158791990200106.

Stier, J. (2003). Internationalisation, ethnic diversity and the acquisition of intercultural competencies. *Intercultural Education, 14*(1), 77–91. doi:10.1080/1 467598032000044674.

Studienkollegs. (2015). Studienkollegs in Germany. Retrieved from http://www.studienkollegs.de/types%20of%20Studienkollegs.html

Wang, Y. (2012). Mainland Chinese students' group work adaptation in a UK business school. *Teaching in Higher Education, 17*(5), 523–535. doi:10.1080/13562517.2012.658562.

Ward, C., Masgoret, A.-M., & Gezentsvey, M. (2009). Investigating attitudes toward international students: Program and policy implications for social integration and international education. *Social Issues and Policy Review, 3*(1), 79–102. doi:10.1111/j.1751-2409.2009.01011.x.

Zhao, T. (2007). *An ethnographic study of the intercultural adaption process between Chinese students and their British lecturers and fellow students in the UK.* Doctoral thesis. University of Southampton, Southampton.

Zhou, Y., & Todman, J. (2008). Chinese postgraduate students in the UK: A two-way reciprocal adaptation. *Journal of International and Intercultural Communication, 1*(3), 221–243. doi:10.1080/17513050802101799.

Appendix 1: Profile of Participants

Study 1: Interviews with Individual Chinese Students

Sixteen Chinese students participated in Study 1, and among them, fifteen were current students and one was a graduate student (Table A.1).

Among the participants, 43.8 per cent ($n=7$) were males and 56.2 per cent ($n=9$) were females. Subjects ranged in age from 24 to 32 with a mean of 25.6 years. Length of residence in Germany varied from 1 month to 87 months ($M=28.9$). Two were exchange students, and the remaining participants (all Chinese students who participated in the interviews were *Bildungsausländer*) were registered with as full-time students (bachelor's, master's, or doctoral) at German universities. Their majors covered natural science, engineering, and social science. The participants' gender, age, and disciplines were considered in order to provide maximum diversity. In addition, two students (one doctoral student and one master's student) received scholarships. Study 1 also included one graduate who had once studied in Germany and was now working in China.

© The Editor(s) (if applicable) and The Author(s) 2016
J. Zhu, *Chinese Overseas Students and Intercultural Learning Environments*, Palgrave Studies on Chinese Education in a Global Perspective, DOI 10.1057/978-1-137-53393-7

APPENDIX 1: PROFILE OF PARTICIPANTS

Table A.1 Demographic profiles of the participants of Study 1

Code	Sex (male/female)	Age	Language of instruction	Discipline	Length of stay in Germany (months)	No. of semesters	Academic degree pursued
Interviewee 1	M	25	English	Natural Science	1	1	Ph.D
Interviewee 2	M	25	English	Natural Science	26	5	Ph.D
Interviewee 3[a]	M	32	German	Social Science	87	6	Ph.D
Interviewee 4[b]	M	24	German	Social Science	1	1	MA
Interviewee 5	F	27	German	Social Science	30	3	MA
Interviewee 6	F	25	German	Social Science	26	3	MA
Interviewee 7	F	26	English	Humanities	19	3	MA
Interviewee 8[c]	F	26	German	Social Science	27	7	MA
Interviewee 9	F	26	English	Natural Science	40	7	MA
Interviewee 10	F	24	German	Social Science	15	3	MA
Interviewee 11	F	25	German	Engineering	26	4	MA
Interviewee 12	F	24	German	Engineering	63	6	MA
Interviewee 13[b]	M	26	German	Engineering	24	4	MA
Interviewee 14	M	26	German	Engineering	28	7	MA
Interviewee 15	F	25	German	Engineering	33	6	MA
Interviewee 16	M	30	German	Engineering	66	/	Diplom[d]

[a]The participant had finished a master's degree previously in Germany and was currently a doctoral student in Germany
[b]Exchange student
[c]The participant started a new major at the bachelor's level, although she had achieved a bachelor's degree in China already
[d]*Diplom* is a traditional academic degree in German speaking countries. Since the implementation of the Bologna Process, the *Diplom* and *Magister* degrees have been substituted with the bachelor's and master's degrees

Table A.2 Demographic profiles of the participants of Study 2

Code	Sex (male/female)	Age	Language of instruction	Discipline	Length of stay in Germany (months)	No. of semesters	Academic degree pursued
Interviewee 17	F	26	German	Humanities	10	2	MA
Interviewee 18	F	25	German	Humanities	22	2	MA
Interviewee 19	F	22	German	Humanities	7	1	MA
Interviewee 20	F	25	German	Humanities	10	2	MA
Interviewee 21[a]	F	21	German	Humanities	10	2	BA

[a]Exchange student

STUDY 2: INTERVIEWS WITH CHINESE STUDENTS AND GERMAN LECTURERS AT THE FACULTY OF GERMAN LANGUAGE AND LITERATURE STUDIES, UNIVERSITY X

Interviews were conducted at the Faculty of German Language and Literature Studies of University X located in the south of Germany and founded in the 1970s. The faculty has a lot of academic exchange with Asian countries, such as Japan, Korea, and China. During the time of conducting the interviews (in July, 2010), over half of the master's students in this faculty are international students (from Ukraine, Morocco, China, etc.), with Chinese students constituting over 50 per cent of that demographic. In contrast, the percentage of domestic German students was small and actually constituted a minority in this faculty.

In terms of intercultural readiness, some professors and lecturers in the faculty had overseas experience in Asia (e.g. China and Korea), North America, and other European countries.

Study 2 is composed of three interviews with students and two interviews with lecturers. Five female Chinese students (four master's and one bachelor's student) in the faculty took part in the interviews (Table A.2). Except for one interview where two interviewees (Interviewee 20 and Interviewee 21) volunteered to participate together, interviews were conducted individually. Among them, one Chinese student had spent one semester as an exchange student before. Chinese students in Study 2 were all self-funded. Unfortunately, no German students volunteered to participate in this research.

Two of the German lecturers in the faculty who participated in the interviews had studied or worked abroad previously. One lecturer had pursued study in the USA and France. The other lecturer had worked in Korea for 5 years and was familiar with its higher education system.

Study 3: Questionnaires: Longitudinal Study

Study 3 is a longitudinal study composed of two rounds of questionnaires. At the beginning of the first semester, fifty-five Chinese students participated in Round 1 of the questionnaire, thirty-one of whom later joined Round 2 (a return rate of 56.4 per cent) at the end of the second semester. Of the original sample, 36.4 per cent ($n=20$) were male and 63.6 per cent ($n=35$) were female. Participants ranged in age from 21 to 26 with a mean of 22.5 years ($SD=2.0$).

The participants were composed of two groups: (1) Group 1: 63.6 per cent of the participants ($n=35$) were studying in Germany benefiting from cross-university cooperation, of whom 60 per cent were majoring in German language and literature studies ($n=21$); and (2) Group 2: 36.4 per cent of the participants were free-movers.

Figure A.1 indicates that 56 per cent of the participants were studying for master's programs in Germany. In addition, 69.1 per cent of the

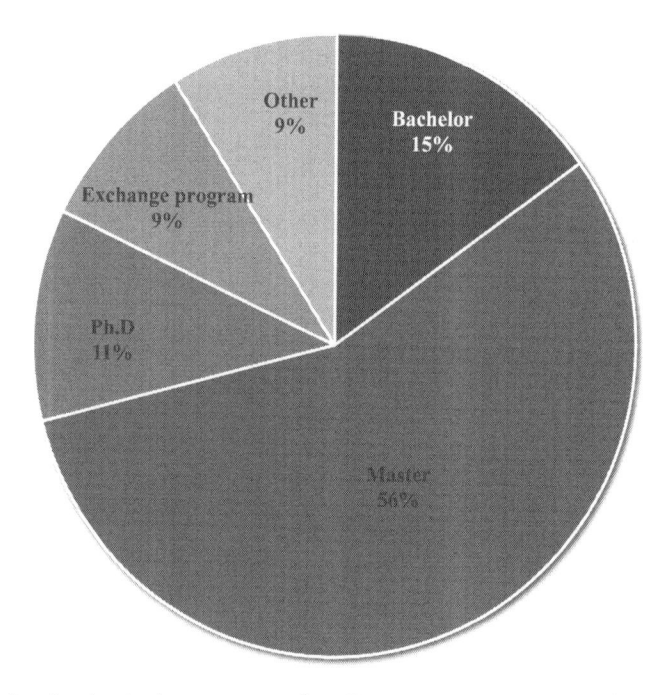

Fig. A.1 Academic degrees pursued at German universities in Study 3 in 2010 (Round 1)

participants were self-funded, while 18.2 per cent had full scholarships and 12.7 per cent were funded by both partial scholarships and their parents.

When answering Round 1 of the questionnaire, all participants ($n=55$) were about to or had just registered at a German university: three respondents were just leaving for Germany (ranging from 1 to 5 days before departure) and the rest were newly arrived (their average length of residence in Germany was 36.5 days). In answering Round 2 of the questionnaire, four out of thirty-one Chinese students had already returned to China (ranging from 2 to 3 months), and the remaining twenty-seven students were still studying in Germany.

Appendix 2: Interview Framework/Outline

Before Arrival

1.1 **Background** (Academic background, language background, and work experience)
1.2 **Motivation for studying in Germany** (Motivation for choosing a major, study abroad in general, and studying in Germany)
1.3 **Applying** (Channels, choosing universities, and difficulty and duration of application)
1.4 **Preparation**
1.5 **Goal/Plan**

Learning Experience at German Universities

2.1 **Types of courses** (Lectures, seminars, exercises, and research)
2.2 **Tasks of academic learning** (Presentation, reading, academic writing, academic tasks for doctoral students, and internship)
2.3 **Assessment of academic performance**

    2.3.1 Exams
    2.3.2 Thesis

2.4 **Special experience**
2.5 **Academic support** (support provider, content, and effect)

2.6 **Social support** (Reasons and current situation)
2.7 **Effort**
2.8 **Comment/Satisfaction with the learning experience**

3.1 **Intercultural communication**

    3.1.1 Circle of friends
    3.1.2 Frequency of intercultural communication

3.2 **Daily life** (TV and radio, hobby/entertainment, and social life)

APPENDIX 3: QUESTIONNAIRE IN STUDY 3

(The following questionnaire was translated from Chinese to English)

QUESTIONNAIRE (ROUND 1)

October 5, 2010

Dear student,

My name is Jiani Zhu. I am a doctoral student at the Humboldt-Universität zu Berlin (http://www2.hu-berlin.de/aks/home_JZ.html), and the topic of my thesis is "Chinese Students' Academic Adjustment at German universities." I would like to ask if you would kindly participate in the questionnaire (for my research study), which is composed of three parts: your academic background, motivation, and personal information. Your answers will be kept confidential. It would take about 10–15 min to finish the questionnaire. Thank you for taking the time to complete this survey. If you have any questions, please feel free to contact me. zhujiani.berlin@gmail.com.

Sincerely,
Jiani Zhu

Academic Background

1. Majors: _____;
2. The consistency between your previous major in China and current major in Germany:
   (1) inconsistent   (2) almost consistent   (3) consistent
3. What university degree have you obtained in China?
   (1) junior college degree   (2) bachelor's   (3) master's   (4) doctoral   (5) junior college degree student   (6) bachelor's student   (7) master's student   (8) doctoral student   (9) other
4. What degree are you pursuing in Germany?
   (1) bachelor's   (2) master's   (3) doctoral   (4) visiting scholar   (5) exchange student   (6) others
5. The language of your program at your German university:
   (1) German   (2) English   (3) German and English

Language

1. According to your current foreign language level, how do you rate your ability to use German at the university?

(Please rate from 1 [Poor] to 5 [Excellent])

		1 2 3 4 5
German	Listening: understanding the lecturers	
	Speaking: participating in the discussion	
	Reading: reading academic books	
	Writing: homework or semester paper	
	Communicating with lecturers/classmates	
English	Listening: understanding the lecturers	
	Speaking: participating in the discussion	
	Reading: reading academic books	
	Writing: homework or semester paper	
	Communicating with lecturers/classmates	

2. According to your current foreign language level, how do you rate your ability to deal with daily situations?

   (Please rate from 1 [Poor] to 5 [Excellent])

	1 2 3 4 5
Expressing yourself in daily communication	
Understanding daily communication	
Reading posts and letters in German	
Reading newspapers/magazines	

3. Have you taken any German language tests?

   (1) Yes, TestDaF: TDN 5   (2) Yes, TestDaF: TDN 4
   (3) Yes, TestDaF: TDN 3   (4) Yes, DSH: DSH-3
   (5) Yes, DSH: DSH-2   (6) Yes, DSH: DSH-1
   (7) Yes, but I haven't passed   (8) No, not yet

Knowledge About Germany and German Universities

1. How much do you know about German universities and German society?

   (Please rate from 1 [Poor] to 5 [Excellent])

		1 2 3 4 5
German universities	Academic resources	
	Academic tasks	
	Examinations	
	Types of courses	
German society	Daily life	
	Society, culture, and customs	
	Political, economic, and historical information	

2. How do you know the above information?

(1) Messages or posts on Internet forums   (2) Consulting Chinese students who have studied/are studying in Germany   (3) Homepage of the German university (4) German courses   (5) German friends   (6) Other   (7) Haven't searched yet

Motivation for Studying in Germany

What is your motivation for studying in Germany?

(please select all that apply)

1. To pursue academic knowledge
2. To improve foreign (German) language skills
3. To obtain an overseas degree
4. Exchange program is available
5. To experience the teaching-learning environment abroad
6. To obtain a better learning environment
7. To gain research experience
8. More courses are available at foreign universities
9. More academic freedom is available
10. Other

Personal Profile

(1) Sex _____;   (2) Age _____;   (3) University _____;
(4) Source of funding (scholarship student or self-funded student) _____;
(5) Is there anyone in your family or circle of friends who has ever studied or worked in Germany?
(6) Have you been to Germany before?
(7) Is the current program you are attending a cooperation program between China and Germany?
(8) How long have you been in Germany?

Thank you for your participation!

Questionnaire (Round 2)

October 25, 2011

Dear students,

Thank you very much for participating in the first round of the questionnaire last year. I would like to kindly request you to participate in the second round (last round), which is composed of several parts: German language skills, knowledge about Germany and German universities, daily communication, and achievements. Your answers will be kept confidential. It would take about 10–15 min to finish the questionnaire. Thank you for taking the time to complete this survey. If you have any questions, please feel free to contact me at zhujiani.berlin@gmail.com.

Sincerely,
Jiani Zhu

Language

According to your current foreign language level, how do you rate your ability to use German at your university?

(Please rate from 1 [Poor] to 5 [Excellent])

		1 2 3 4 5
German	Listening: understanding the lecturers	
	Speaking: participating in the discussion	
	Reading: reading academic books	
	Writing: homework or semester paper	
	Comprehension: communicating with lecturers/classmates	
English	Listening: understanding the lecturers	
	Speaking: participating in the discussion	
	Reading: reading academic books	
	Writing: homework or semester paper	
	Comprehension: Communicating with lecturers/classmates	

4. According to your current foreign language level, how do you evaluate your ability to use German in daily situations?

   (Please rate from 1 [Poor] to 5 [Excellent])

	1 2 3 4 5
Expressing yourself in daily communication	
Understanding daily communication	
Reading posts and letters in German	
Reading newspapers/magazines	

5. How often do you attend German courses?

   (1) Often   (2) Sometimes   (3) Never

Knowledge About Germany and German Universities

How much do you know about German universities and German society?

(Please rate from 1 [Poor] to 5 [Excellent])

		1 2 3 4 5
German universities	Academic resources	
	Academic tasks	
	Examinations	
	Types of courses	
German society	Daily life	
	Society, culture, and customs	
	Political, economic, and historical information	

Daily Communication

1. Your circle of friends in Germany is composed of:
   (1) Mostly Chinese friends   (2) Mostly German friends   (3) Mostly international friends from other countries (excluding China and Germany)   (4) There is no dominant national group   (5) I don't have any friends

2. How often do you communicate with German friends?
   (1) Often   (2) Sometimes   (3) Never
3. How often do you communicate with Chinese friends?
   (1) Often   (2) Sometimes   (3) Never
4. How often do you communicate with friends from other countries (excluding China and Germany)?
   (1) Often   (2) Sometimes   (3) Never
5. How often do you attend local activities
   (1) Often   (2) Sometimes   (3) Never

Achievement

1. How would you evaluate your achievement in the last two semesters?

   (Please rate from 1 [Little Progress] to 5 [Much Progress])

	1 2 3 4 5
Discipline-based knowledge	
German language	
Communication	
Solving problems	
Overall progress	

2. How satisfied are you with your learning experience at your German university?

   (Please rate from 1 [Very Unsatisfied] to 5 [Very Satisfied])

	1 2 3 4 5
In general	
International office	
Institution	
Lecturer	
Resources	
Teaching/research	

Thank you for your participation!

Index

A
academic adjustment
  affective-dimension adjustment, 143–8, 166–7, 177–8
  behavior-dimension adjustment, 148–54, 167–70, 178–81
  cognitive adjustment, 131–42, 160–5, 176–7
academic assessment
  dissertation, 43, 52, 65
  exams, 127, 133, 142, 169, 176, 189, 195
  oral exams, 142, 195
  term papers, 180
  written exams, 127, 142, 195, 222
academic cultures. *See also* learning tradition
  academic freedom, 105, 176, 213
  autonomous learning, 53
  Confucian cultures, 6, 7, 52, 148
  culture-bound norms, 25
  educational beliefs and habits, 215
  learning styles, 52, 76, 137, 215, 227
  pedagogical approaches, 229
  Socratic cultures, 52
  teaching styles, 52, 76, 137, 215, 227, 229
academic degrees, 73, 112, 127, 148, 185, **237,** 238. *See also* levels of study
  bachelor's degrees, 6, 16, 26, 28, 64, 72, 109, 112, 114, 132, 147, 164, 178, 202, 235, 237, 238
  doctoral degrees, 9, 72
  master's degrees, 72, 105, 109, 132
academic disciplines, 28, 66, 67, 142, 191, 208. *See also* academic fields; individual disciplines
  engineering, 5, 28, 72, 75, 106, 107, 111, 134, 135, 138, 149, 197, 201, 218, 235
  humanities, 29, 67, 134, 150, 194
  natural science, 28, 107, 139, 149, 197, 218, 235
  social science, 2, 28, 67, 135, 139, 142, 150, 190, 194, 197, 218, 223, 228, 229, 230, 235, **237**

© The Editor(s) (if applicable) and The Author(s) 2016
J. Zhu, *Chinese Overseas Students and Intercultural Learning Environments*, Palgrave Studies on Chinese Education in a Global Perspective, DOI 10.1057/978-1-137-53393-7

academic experience, 51, 217
  academic challenges, 29, 49, 50,
    111, 125, 160, 211
  academic expectations and
    demands, 2
  academic requirements, 30, 31, 189
academic fields, 72, 189, 203, 213. *See
  also* academic disciplines
academic outcomes, 21. *See also*
  academic performance
academic performance, 1, 15, 42, 43,
  177. *See also* academic outcomes
  classroom participation, 1
academic readiness, 112
academic support, campus-wide, 27,
  32, 62, 69, 83, 191–9, 202, 213.
  See also support
  campus service, 59
  counseling and wellness services, 65
  intercultural training, 124, 125,
    192, 225, 226
  orientation courses, 32, 191–4, 198,
    220, 223, 224, 225
  professional treatment, 65
academic workload, 113, 115, 147.
  See also stress
academic writing, 18, 52–3, 76,
  140–2, 153, 230
  academic writing skills, 140, 178,
    229, 230
accommodation, 49, 70, 121, 125,
  205, 206, 219, 220, 222.
  See also acculturation; adaptation;
  adjustment
acculturation, 20, 39, 79, 80, 88, 96,
  100. *See also* accommodation;
  adaptation; adjustment; Berry,
  John W.
achievement
  academic accomplishment, 24
  academic achievement, 20, 59,
    181, 184
  academic success, 24, 66, 69, 217

adaptation. *See also* accommodation;
  acculturation; adjustment
  academic adaptation, 68, 198
    (*see also* academic adjustment)
  cross-cultural adaptation, 19, 20,
    70, 82
  intercultural adaptation, 19, 195
  sociocultural adaptation, 19, 69
adjustment. *See also* accommodation,
  adaptation, acculturation
  academic adjustment, 19, 38, 39,
    40, 43, 44, 46, 48, 49, 50, 51,
    59, 64, 85, 95, 100, 101, 121,
    144, 185, 186, 193–6,
    205–227, 231–5, 239, 243,
    247, 248
  cross-cultural adjustment, 22, 70, 82
  cultural adjustment, 20, 52, 74
  intercultural adjustment, 19
  psychological adjustment, 62, 68
    (*see also* Ward, Colleen)
  sociocultural adjustment, 19, 62, 77
    (*see also* Ward, Colleen)
adjustment phases
  developing phase, 157, 158, 163,
    165, 170, 175, 213, 224, 227
  final phase, 212, 230
  initial phase, 29, 51, 58, 148, 151,
    202, 212, 222–7, 230
  pre-departure phase, 31
affective, cognitive, and behavioral
  model, 22–3, 211. *See also*
  Anderson, Linda E.
Anderson, Linda E., 19, 20, 22, 23,
  83, 211, 214. *See also* affective,
  cognitive, and behavioral model
anxiety and uncertainty management
  theory, 57. *See also* Gudykunst,
  William B.
application, 96, 124, 127–129, 142,
  156, 160, 183, 201, 229,
  238, 244
APS (*Akademische Prüfstelle*), 110

INDEX

B
background
  academic background, 27, 112, 114
  educational background, 48, 139
Berry, John W., 1, 25, 61, 62, 78.
  See also acculturation
Bochner, Stephen, 20, 47, 55, 56, 57, 58, 59, 67, 68, 103

C
CHC (Confucian Heritage Culture), 6, 17, 18, 26, 42, **82**. *See also* CHC-learners
CHC-learners, 17, **18**. *See also* Chinese learners
China
  economic and technical development, 16
  economic reform, 5
  growing middle-class families, 6
  reform and opening up, 5
Chinese Academy of Engineering, 72, 73
Chinese Academy of Social Sciences, 72, 73
Chinese Educational Mission, 4–5
  Qing Dynasty government, 4
  Wong Foon, 4
  Wong Shing, 4
  Yung Wing, 4
Chinese educational system, 12, 139.
  See also educational system; educational system in China
  preschool education, 8
  primary education, 8
  secondary education, 8
  senior high school education, 9
  senior vocational education, 9
Chinese learners, 14–17, 158. *See also* CHC-learners; paradox learners; rote learners

communication and cross-cultural adaptation, 78. *See also* Kim, Young Yun
cross-cultural friendships, 55. *See also* intercultural communication
cultural comfort zone, 166
cultural distance, 60, 67, 68
  geographic proximity, 85, 86
  (*see also* Galtung, Ingrid Eide)

D
DAAD (Deutscher Akademischer Austauschidenst), 26, 64, 109, 124, 125
decisions, 45, 74, 180, 184
  low-risk decision, 112
  risky decision, 113
development and growth
  academic development, 208
  educational development, 21, 27
  emotional growth, 76
  personal development, 21, 76, 181, 184
  personal growth, 21, 27, 76, 166, 172, 184
  self-confidence, 23, **43**, **177**
  transnational competencies, 68
discussion
  class discussions, 48, 49, 52, 116, 117, 134, 139, 158, 169, 178, 194, 227
  classroom discussions, 213
  group discussions, 76, 78, 135, 137, 168, 170, 172
dream of studying abroad, 104
  dreams of studying overseas, 108
  study abroad fever, 105
dropout, 63
  dropout rate, 27, 63, 64
DZHW (Deutsches Zentrum für Hochschul-und Wissenschaftsforschung), 26, 63, 64

E

educational reforms in China
  Project 211, 11, 105 (*see also* Project 211 universities)
  Project 985, 11, 105 (*see also* Project 985 universities)
educational settings, 51, 166.
  See also milieu, educational milieu
educational system, 27, 67, 84, 232, 235, 237. *See also* Chinese educational system; educational system in China; German university system
educational system in China, 12, 139. *See also* Chinese educational system; educational system
entrance examinations
  entrance exam for graduate school, 8, 104
  junior secondary education exam, 8
  national higher education entrance examination, 113
  senior secondary education entrance examination, 8
  senior secondary education exam, 8
environment. *See also* milieu
  intercultural learning environment, 27, 29, 30, 77, 81, 183, 213, 215, 216, 224, 231
  university environment, 27, 207, 214
ethnic groups, 24
  dialects, 24
  ethnic Chinese minorities, 24
  Han Chinese, 25
'Eureka' moment, 175, 176
experience
  sociocultural and educational experience, 1

F

face
  thick skin, 167
  thin-skin, 160, 167
factors
  pull factors, 74
  push factors, 74
faculties
  administrative staff, 81, 192
  advisors, 196
  professors, 3, 75, 134, 138, 145, 166, 194, 198, 237
  staff, 15, 21, 25, 81, 133, 138, 145, 192, 195, 222, 227, 231
  supervisors, 167
  tutors, 69, 138, 149, 166, 191, 192, 196, 213
filial piety, 148
financial sources
  government-funded students, 5
  self-financed students, 126
  self-funded students, 6, 184
  sources of funding, 28
  state-sponsored exchange programs, 4
foreign language skills. *See also* skills
  foreign language capacity, 56
  foreign language proficiency, 43, 83
foreign universities, 2, 22, 43, 67, 105. *See also* host universities
friendships, 55, 57, 58, 59, 60, 202, 226
  compatriots, 55
  co-national circles, 55, 56
  co-national community, 57
  co-national network, 57, 58
  co-national students, 59, 146, 222
  cross-cultural friendships, 55
  friendship patterns, 43, 53, 57
  'Hi-bye friends,' 54, 202
  relationship development, 56

G

Galtung, Ingrid Eide, 41, 68. *See also* geographic proximity
Gaokao, 9, 10, 11, 110, 184. *See also* national higher education entrance examination
geographic proximity, 85, 86
German first degrees
  Diplom, 48, 178
  Magister, 48, 141
German language. *See also* standardized German language tests
  German language courses, 113, 115, 116, 148, 151, 152–3, 154, 191, 223
  German language learning, 115, 151, 223
  German language training, 115, 125, 152, 199
  language centers, 153, 229
  language partner, 151, 154
German university system. *See also* educational system
  Modul, 132, 133, 149, 153, 191, 195
Gudykunst, William B., 57. *See also* anxiety and uncertainty management theory

H

hard landing, 131–54, 212, 222
hardship
  financial difficulties, 49, 70
  financial problems, 70
  language difficulties, 48, 50, 194
  language problems, 48, 133, 135, 151, 188
hard skills, 83, 111–120
  academic readiness, 112 (*see also* readiness; skills)

heterogeneous individuals, 24
homogeneous groups, 24
host countries, 6, 19, 22, 41, 44, 52, 56, 80, 215. *See also* study destinations
host universities, 1, 21, 41, 77, 113, 215, 216. *See also* foreign universities
HRK (Hochschulrektorenkonferenz), 119, 124

I

IIE (Institute of International Education), 19, 41, 44
intercultural communication. *See also* cross-cultural friendships; intercultural communication skills; intergroup communication
intercultural communication, campus-wide, 21
intercultural interactions, 53
  social interaction, 21, **23**, 48, 55, 60, 62
  social relationships, 68
intercultural communication skills, 32, 226, 227. *See also* intercultural communication; skills; intercultural skills
intergroup communication, 57. *See also* intercultural communication
interpersonal relationships, 20, **23**, 43
student-faculty interaction, 50, 54
student-teacher communication, 54
international education
  exchange programs, 4, 16, 29, 105, 113, 124, 198 (*see also* programs)
  student exchange, 4, 124
international students in Germany, 64, 108, 152

Bildungsausländer, 63, 64, 235
Bildungsinländer, 63, 64, 109

J
job satisfaction, 73. *See also* readjustment; satisfaction

K
Kim, Young Yun, 15, 19, 27, 45, 50, 54, 57, 58, 59, 66, 67, 68, 69, 78, 214, 217, 218, 224, 229
knowledge
discipline-based knowledge, 27, 76, 83, 116, 125, 165, 171, 172, 215
interdisciplinary knowledge, 139, 140, 190
knowledge of foreign language, 51
specialized academic knowledge, 170

L
learning tradition, 61, 162, 167, 178, 215. *See also* academic cultures
levels of study. *See also* academic degrees
bachelor's level, 64, 164, 202
postgraduate, 46, 112
living situation, 64
accommodation, 49, 70, 121, 125, 205, 206, 219, 220, 222
shared apartment, 205, 228

M
MAXQDA, 30
milieu, 21, 27, 41, 46, 81, 215, 222, 226. *See also* environment

educational milieu, 27, 46 (*see also* educational settings)
intercultural learning milieu, 21
learning milieu, 41
Moduls. *See also* German university system
Modul courses, 133
Modul exams, 132
Modul system, 133, 176, 192, 193
MoE (Ministry of Education of People's Republic of China), 10, 71, 73
motivation
career-oriented motivation, 45
extrinsic motivation, 45, 169
general motivation, 104
instrumental motivation, 56
integrative motivation, 56
intrinsic motivation, 45, 169

N
National higher education entrance examination, 113
NBS (the National Bureau of Statistics of China), 12, 24, 107

O
OECD (Organisation for Economic Co-operation and Development), 2, 3, 6, 7, 11

P
paradox learners, 14, 15. *See also* Chinese learners; rote learners
peer students, 13, 54, 83, 165, 199, 202, 203, 204, 213, 226, 228
domestic counterparts, 47, 48
domestic students, 47, 50, 53, 54, 55, 56, 217, 225, 231, 232

local students, 48, 56, 57, 58
native peers, 56, 58, 64
native students, 20, 135
students of the host country, 47, 53
plagiarism, 17, 52, 53, 140, 141. *See also* academic writing
preparation
   pre-departure preparation, 44, 45, 222
   preparation course, 222, 223
   readiness, 43, 83, 103, 111–26, 176, 219, 237 (*see also* academic readiness; psychological readiness)
presentation. *See also* seminars
   group presentation, 136, 137
   solo presentation, 136
pressure. *See also* psychology
   academic pressure, 113, 147
   family pressure, 148
process
   adjustment process, 23, 31, 65, 159, 215, 223, 230, 231
   cyclical and recursive process, 22
   dynamic process, 24, 82, 214
   transition, 47, 62, 65, 112, 135, 164, 214, 230
programs
   academic exchange programs, 29, 113
   bachelor's program, 26, 64, 109, 132
   double-degree programs, 113
   English-taught master's programs, 115, 117, 120, 202, 221, 225
   master's programs, 64, 109, 115, 120, 132, 135, 196, 202, 220
   Ph.D. programs, 117
Project 211, 11, 105. *See also* Project 211 universities
Project 985, 11, 105. *See also* Project 985 universities
Project 211 universities, 11. *See also* Project 211
Project 985 universities, 11. *See also* Project 985
psychological adjustment, 62, 68
psychological readiness, 112, 125, 143–144
psychology. *See also* pressure; stress
   anxiety, 43, 48, 57, 60, 61, 62
   depression, 22, 23, 48, 60, 62, 64, 70, 85, 125
   frustration, 23, 31, 56, 57, 61, 136, 151, 166, 215
   mental health, 64, 65
   psychiatric disorders, 63, 64
   psychological well-being, 60, 69, 80

Q

qualitative methods, 81
   ethnographic approach, 78–9
   ethnographic research, 79
   longitudinal approach, 24–5
   longitudinal manner, 25
   longitudinal research, 25, 79, 80, 232
   mixed methods, 27, 30
   narrative inquiry, 78
   re-interview, 29

R

re-adaptation, 73. *See also* readjustment; reverse culture shock
readiness
   academic readiness, 112
   psychological readiness, 112, 125

reading
  academic reading, 138, 158, 192
  reading skills, 139, 151
  reading techniques, 139
  scanning, 139, 151
  skimming, 151
readjustment, 73, 230. *See also* re-adaptation; reverse culture shock
readjustment and reverse culture shock, 91
reliability, 27, 29, 30
returnees, 23, 43, 71, 72, 73
  brain circulation, 75
  brain drain, 43, 75
  brain gain, 75
  entrepreneurship, 43, 73
  re-adaptation (*see* readjustment and reverse culture shock)
  readjustment (*see* job satisfaction; re-adaptation; reverse culture shock)
  returnee teacher, 91
  return intention, 74
  reverse culture shock (*see* re-adaptation; readjustment)
  transnational human capital, 75
reverse culture shock, 73. *See also* re-adaptation; readjustment
rote learners, 14, 81. *See also* Chinese learners; paradox learners; rote-learning
  compare independent thinkers, 34
  passive learners, 16
  unquestioning learners, 14
rote-learning, 16. *See also* rote learners

S

satisfaction, 1, 19, 23, 43, 44, 59, 60, 74, 75–6, 171, 181, 182, 183, 212. *See also* job satisfaction
schools in China
  colleges, 9, 10, 11
  elementary school, 8
  kindergarten, 8, 9, 143
  middle schools, 9, 13
  primary schools, 9, 12
  universities, 29, 39, 142, 143, 176, 177, 189, 198, 202
seminars, 50, 122, 132, 134, 135–8, 139, 151, 177, 188, 230, 241. *See also* presentation
shock
  academic culture shock, 61
  academic shock, 43, 60–1
  cultural shock, 60
  learning shock, 61
skills. *See also* foreign language skills; hard skills; soft skills
  academic skills, 44, 229
  communication ability, 170, 171
  intercultural skills, 56, 199, 227 (*see also* intercultural communication skills)
  learning skills, 153, 215
  problem-solving ability, 172
  professional skills, 27, 76
  writing skills, 140, 178, 229, 230
social networks, 57
  bi-cultural network, 58
  co-national network, 57, 58
  foreign student-host national mono-cultural networks, 58
  multi-cultural network, 59
  networks, 58
social support, 43, 53, 62. *See also* support
  social companionship, 69
  social support networks, 53
sociocultural adjustment, 19, 62, 77
soft skills, 83, 111, 112, 120–6
  intercultural experience, 28, 31, 42, 44, 45, 46, 65, 79, 112, 124, 140, 157, 184, 194, 197, 198, 225

knowledge about German and German universities, 29, 122, 123, 138, 159, 160, 218
psychological readiness, 143–144 (*see also* readiness; skills)
sojourn
student sojourner, 21
standardized German language tests, 114, 115, 118, 119, 189, 211, 223. *See also* German language
DSD II (Deutsches Sprachdiplom der KMK-Stufe zwei) neu, 118
DSH (Deutsche Sprachprüfung für den Hochschulzugang), 114, 118, 119
Prüfungsteil Deutsch der Feststellungsprüfung an Studienkollegs, 118
TestDaF (Der Test Deutsch als Fremdsprache), 114, 118
Statistical Package for Social Science, 30
STEM (Science, Technology, Engineering, and Mathematics), 67, 176
strategies
learning strategies, 14, 27
secondary literature, 151
stress. *See also* academic workload; psychology
academic stress, 48, 61, 133
acculturative stress, 42, 60, 61, 62, 63, 70
personal psychological stress, 62
study destinations
English-speaking countries, 6, 26, 44, 77, 107, 125
non-English-speaking countries, 26, 77
study plan, 133
course schedule, 143
curriculum, 46, 54, 115
syllabus, 13, 143, 202
timetable, 123, 132

support
academic support, campus-wide, 51
social support, 80, 81, 260

T

teaching and learning in China
exam-oriented methods, 11
learning traditions, 61, 162, 167, 178, 215 (*see also* academic cultures)
teacher authorities, 162
teacher-centeredness, 12
teammate, 165, 216. *See also* teamwork
teamwork, 164, 216, 227. *See also* teammate
group discussions, 76, 78, 135, 137, 168, 170, 172
group projects, 164, 179
group work, 43, 164, 165, 169, 179, 196, 202, 228
peer learning, 164
terminologies, 189
types of courses, 134, 159, 160, 177, 212
excursions, 134, 145
exercise classes, 132, 134, 138
seminars, 153–6
(*see also* presentation)

V

validity, 27, 29, 30
variables
background variables, 66
personality variables, 65
situational variables, 67

W

Ward, Colleen, 19, 21, 22, 68, 69, 78, 80, 231. *See also* psychological adjustment; sociocultural adjustment